THE CALL

by
SAMPSON IRUOHA

Jackie Inee
It is my wish that you draw
strength ~~from~~ through this work on
your path towards spiritual enlightenment and maturity.
Sampson Iruoha.

PublishAmerica
Baltimore

First printing

ISBN: 1-4137-2540-6
PUBLISHED BY PUBLISHAMERICA, LLLP
www.publishamerica.com
Baltimore

Printed in the United States of America

FOREWORD

A new epoch now dawns for mankind when all previously opened cycles have to come to a close and the end be connected with the beginning.

At this time of change when nothing of the old can remain standing the Truth must become known to all who do not wish to be destroyed with what is old.

In order to be able to withstand the effects of the changes in this time man must become convinced about the rightness of his actions. He must strive for conviction. For this he needs to know the truth about everything including the reason for his existence. Only in full knowledge can he make the right decisions, and only the right decisions can prevent him now from being washed away with the old.

To know the Truth one must obey the Will of God, and to know the Will of God one must understand and obey His Laws in Creation.

Fortunately for men a final opportunity to know the Will of God has been provided them in this period of change so that those who wish to remain standing in the new time can avail themselves of the necessary help.

For those who earnestly seek the Truth and wish to know and obey the Will of God I have written this work in order to point them to the Source of this knowledge.

I hope that this work will help them in their efforts to act rightly in this time and in the future.

Sampson Iruoha

Contents

The Call   Page   9

The Great Creation   23

The Incarnation of The Human Spirit On Earth –   37
    The Creation of Man

The Fall of Man   55

Reincarnation   86

The Development of The Human Spirit On Earth   101

Help For The Developing Human Spirits on Earth   130

Some of my Experiences Before Writing This Book   157

The World of Cycles   211

The Final Judgment   226

The Implications of This Time   243

Earthwoman   256

Family   286

Superficiality   301

Mystery and Miracles   318

Narrow-mindedness   329

Responsibility   339

THE CALL

Over millennia there have been questions as to the reason why man was created and why he is on earth. It is widely circulated that God created us, and then cast us out to suffer after we disobeyed Him. There is another popular theory that we evolved from ape-like animals and so do not have to concern ourselves with God.

The latter theory is strengthened by the fact that the human spirit, which is the core of man, has lost contact with its origin and now man cannot make sense of anything that cannot be studied with the use of the earthbound intellect. Man has made this tool (the intellect) his master and so no longer believes or understands issues that have to do with the part of the world that he cannot sense with his physical senses.

The tidings sent down from above, which were brought to man at different times in the past from unimaginable Heights, had to be delivered to man through different individuals in different regions of the globe. These messages were sent down by the Will of the Creator to inform us of the need to change our ways, which were increasingly inclining towards evil, and to point us in the direction that led to the Light.

They became distorted and incoherent because mankind had become too corrupt to understand and interpret them correctly. This led seekers of the Truth to frustration and to a further withdrawal from the Light.

Discrepancies and gaps crept into the teachings of these messages in the different parts of the world, through the narrow-mindedness, ignorance, conceit, spiritual indolence, and in some cases, greed of those who came across the Word from above.

Man could not get the right knowledge out of the tidings from above because of the gaps and discrepancies that crept into them as men tried to understand them using only their intellect, which made a complete picture impossible for him to perceive. The inability of men to reconcile their personal experiences with what the already distorted teachings had to offer caused some people to become dissatisfied with the teachings, and to seek alternative solutions to the burning questions that have never left man in peace.

When science offered a solution to the age-old problem or question of our origin, through the verification of the process of evolution, these people were more apt to accept it because to them it made some sense. However, many of those who accepted the teachings of science decided to forgo the various teachings of the tidings from above, mainly due to their spiritual indolence and the consequent inability for personal investigation and inner reflection with the intuitive faculty. They looked at the situation only from one side, from the gross material side. They had lost the capability to be more objective in their investigations.

Others, who accepted the teachings of the messengers of the Truth, did so only after certain changes or alterations had been made to the teachings, in order to make them more in line with the selfish desires of the adherents of the churches and other groups which spread these distorted teachings, and in so doing to attract more people who could, in the process, increase their economic and political gains.

Even those who accepted the teachings as they were, that is, without evil intentions, but after distortions had already crept into them due to man's heavy reliance on his intellect, which can never take the place of the spirit due to the restriction to the World of Gross Matter of the former, also ran the risk of being misled through the gaps inherent in them.

Interpretations and documentation of some of these teachings many years after the deaths of those who brought them, led to the proliferation of mistakes and gaps in the teachings. The adherents of these teachings of the messages from above, in the different parts of the world in which they were delivered, formed religious groups that proceeded to spread the already distorted teachings to new adherents and to the general public.

Some of the religions formed made further modifications to the already distorted teachings in a bid to hide their ignorance about certain issues that they did not understand. Votes were taken by men to decide what should be hidden and what should be released to the general public. And decisions were often made with those making them being mindful of the potential for the attraction of more adherents into the groups. Groups with large numbers of adherents gave the impression of a successful religion and increased the sphere of power and control of the religions in question.

Man was not able to receive the help intended for him in the form in which it was given. Out of conceit and ignorance, men who thought they new better, or who simply were not open enough to receive the right guidance from above, made additions to, and subtractions from the Word in the teachings. These people were actually committing a serious crime against God because they did not recognize His Magnificence and sought to add and improve upon the Message that He sent through His specially prepared messengers.

They showed their utter ignorance through such acts, because they revealed that they had not tried to live in accordance with the Word which they were trying to teach, and so sought to make changes to It in the areas that raised concerns as to the validity of their own claims. They sought to improve on that which they had grasped only dimly, due to their over-dependence on the intellect and the consequent narrow-mindedness, conceit, and lack of spiritual activity that came with it.

Since only the spirit can understand spiritual work and since the messages from above were spiritual works that were meant for the spirit of man, those who tried to teach them or spread them without first exerting themselves so that they vibrated in the sense of the messages, transmitted them wrongly and misled men by the millions.

They tried to place themselves above Him Who created them by trying to improve on His work. At best they were ignorant and spiritually indolent, which in the end can only lead to their spiritual death. I shall deal with this issue in the course of the following chapters.

I would like to add that the differences in the wordings of the tidings or messages from above, and the fact that the wordings were adapted to the traditions of the recipients and also became distorted through wrong teachings, made them seem different from one another in the different areas where they were delivered.

The envy, jealousy, ignorance, conceit, and narrow-mindedness of mankind in those areas, and on earth as a whole at that time, did not allow for the objective look at the teachings of the messages as they were offered in different parts of the globe. Men rejected the teachings of the tidings that arose from parts of the world that differed from theirs. This led to a multiplicity of beliefs and consequently to a multiplicity of religions and ideas about the Truth and about life outside the gross material (physical) sphere of perception.

The core Message brought by the different messengers was in fact one and the same!

A detailed and objective look at the teachings of the religions that formed around this core Message, as it was delivered in different parts of the world, will reveal that we have been shown how to act in this world time and time again, but have not listened. We have turned the teachings into forms which are convenient for us.

One who is able to absorb the True Message from God with his whole being, by completely adapting his entire life and his every thought, word and deed to the sense of His Word, will be able to spot the distortion that has been introduced by man into the teachings that have come to us in the past, and which have been distorted and spread by men who idolize the intellect.

He will be able to make contact with that power which nourishes the spirit because he would have learned to keep the spirit active and not let it sleep on. He would no longer rely so heavily on his intellect, which has its limit at the boundary of Gross Matter, unimaginable worlds away from and below the Spiritual Realm, the Eternal Kingdom of God, and so cannot receive of anything that is meant for the spirit as a natural consequence of the difference in the species. He would pay more attention to his intuitive perception, through which the spirit expresses itself, and the only medium that is available to the human spirit on earth for the reception of guidance from above.

I wish to direct the attention of the reader or listener, to a Work from the Highest Heights! Here, in this book, I address only earnest seekers of the Truth and no one else; everyone else may keep away from it!

The Work about which I write explains the entire Creation to mankind, how we came to be here, and what it is that is expected of us. It calls our attention to the existence of the spirit as the core and the only living entity within man, through which Power from above streams as It courses through and maintains the entire Creation, and the fact that man has let his spirit become paralyzed through its forced subordination to the intellect.

The intellect, which is the product of the frontal brain, which has no life of its own, and whose sphere of perception extends only up to the highest plane of the World of Gross Matter, and so is subject to disintegration after its period of maturation and ripening, has reached its climax and naturally has to suffer retrogression or disintegration and with this, the total collapse of all that has issued from it which is contrary to the Truth, therefore, which is anti-Truth.

The signs are here with us and can be seen by anyone who cares to look around. However, I sense that I shall still have to do more than just ask the reader or listener to look around.

The spirit has to be awakened for the happenings around us to be put into the right context. Humanity, as it exists today, is destined for certain destruction, which can only be prevented for the individual through his right understanding of the Will of God, and his strict observance of this Will at all times. The Will of the Creator brought about Creation and, in its perfection, manifests in the different spheres that make up Creation in the form of adamantine Laws known as the Laws of Creation. They are also referred to as the Laws of Nature since it is through them that nature and everything else in existence came about.

In their logical and immutable working they maintain Creation with a strictness that is incomprehensible to the human spirit. Since they are the expression of the Divine Will in Creation, it is through the understanding of these Laws that one can hope to understand the Creator, Who remains, and forever will be unapproachable by any creature including the human spirit.

The Work of which I speak has been sent down to man in a form that he can understand and relate to. It helps the earnest seeker to find his way to the Truth in the most complete way and contains no gaps or imperfections. My task here is to act as a signpost or a bridge and direct you to this Work that is in our midst today, but which has not been recognized by many because of the prolonged reign of the intellect, which is the earthbound product of the brain, and which has its activity directed only towards the material and the transient.

I intend to do this in a way that will not add or remove from the Message in this Work, but in a way that will help you become able to start exerting your spirit. The latter point is vital because we are essentially spirits in material or physical cloaks with which we are supposed to function in this world. The brain is a part of this cloak and the intellect is a product of the frontal brain, and so cannot make any sense of a Work intended for the spirit.

The spirit, on the other hand, is not of this world but has been chained down in this world during its period of wandering in the process of maturing, due to the preoccupation of mankind with issues, thoughts, feelings and activities that are only of this world. The attractive force that exists between like-species, as can be seen between birds, animals and even people, keeps human spirits anchored to this world, and prevents mankind from grasping anything from the Light Regions above.

This is because these thoughts, feelings, and activities that are mainly directed towards the material have encapsulated the human spirit and increasingly draw it deeper into the depths of darkness, together with the World of Gross Matter, which contains the earth, and which he was supposed to help ennoble.

The chaining of the human spirits to this earth is the condition referred to as being earthbound. The connections that keep a particular human spirit chained to the earth also keep it from ascending. This is because they cause it to become denser and to sink even more towards the Darkness due to its propensity for that which is of this earth.

While on earth he bears within him cloaks of the same substance as the various planes of the Ethereal Realm, which is a finer species of the World of Matter, through which the departed souls from the earth will still have to journey if they are to return to their origin in the Spiritual Realm. His focus on material things keeps him from gaining access to the spiritual currents that are constantly streaming through Creation, and through these ethereal material planes.

He has cut himself off from these currents because of his volition, which is directed mainly towards base and dark forms. He no longer knows how to disentangle himself from the mesh of dark threads that hold him firmly to this part of the world, in accordance with the Will of the Creator, Which demands that a man must reap what he sows. His every thought is like a seed, which matures to a ripened fruit and returns to him at the time of harvest of that particular fruit.

His volition for only what is material returns to him the fruit of attachment to the World of Matter from which he can escape only when he realizes how the Laws in Creation work and abides by them. In the process he will also realize why he is here in the World of Matter. The more seeds he sows in the absence of this knowledge the more he will entangle himself in this world, and the more likely it becomes that he would not be able to tear himself away from matter before the disintegration of all that is material, which is a natural occurrence that happens with every species of matter, just as it does with plants and the bodies of men and animals.

Men have been concerned primarily with issues of this gross material world and have neglected the nobler and more sublime issues of the spiritual, of which our core is a part. As a result they have effectively bound themselves, over time, to this part of Creation. This has resulted in the accumulation of guilt by this mankind since we have lived for thousands of years without making the right use of the guidance from above. The collective guilt of mankind has dragged the earth and its inhabitants to depths so low that coming to a realization of the Truth on our own is no longer possible.

It is for this reason that I declare to all who care to listen that there will be no way for any individual to avoid the dangers that lie ahead for him, here on earth or after physical death (dropping off of the material cloak used by the spirit during its time on earth), without making the Truth in the Message from above alive within him. Even then man can only minimize the effects of the now due karmic returns.

The machinery of Creation goes on unceasingly irrespective of man's knowledge of it. The machinery operates throughout Creation, the greater part of which most people are completely ignorant about. The activities of man for thousands of years can be described as throwing alien substances into a well-oiled and well-regulated machine, which operates smoothly without a gap, because everything within it works in a cooperative manner.

When the time then comes for the regular check-up of the machine, which, in the case of this world, happens automatically, the alien substances will then have to be destroyed and done away with, together with everything that is still connected with them, including those who threw them in but have not severed their ties with them. Again if you look around you can already see it happening, despite the illogical reasons that friends or books may offer for the occurrences in the world today. The alien substances represent the works of man, his intuitive perceptions, thoughts, words and deeds, which individually have their different cycles which must close at their appointed times as they react back on their originators.

It is to give you a chance to actually realize what life is about, and to take advantage of this knowledge to sever your ties to the alien substances clinging to you (your spirit), through the recognition of the nature of those forms, hence, the nature of their originator, while maintaining a volition for what is good, and thereby have an opportunity to experience a blissful existence while here on earth and afterwards, that I direct you to the Work: In the Light of Truth – The Grail Message.

Appreciation of this Work cannot be achieved without experiencing, because true knowledge only comes through experiencing. Glossing over the Work will not be of any use to you since that would mean reading with your frontal brain, which cannot provide for the spirit that knowledge which it needs to mature.

"Use it or lose it," is a law that many people are familiar with and one that applies here, as well. If you do not exercise the spirit and ask questions about things that do not make sense to you, then you stand to reap the consequences of your ignorance, which latter can be traced back to the laziness or indolence of your spirit. This is because by not exercising your spirit and asking questions of things that do not agree with your sense of right and wrong, you place yourself in danger of being crushed by the machinery of Creation, since you would be ignorant of the ways of this Creation and its machinery.

Having said this, I would like to add that the Message contains all that one needs in order to achieve total and complete knowledge of Creation and how we have to live in it. Because we are a part of it and need to know its Laws in order to return to our origin as conscious and mature human spirits.

One of our greatest mistakes as humans is the feeling that we have to help others whom we perceive to be worse off than ourselves. To begin with, we do not know what is good for us! The intellect is a collection of the thoughts of men on earth, and reliance on it for guidance can never lead one to a sphere that is above the World of Gross Matter, let alone the Spiritual Realm. It will forever remain bound to space and time while the spirit itself is eternal. Judging from this perspective, we know nothing.

We might think we do however, because, having lost touch or contact with any spiritual guidance due to man's over-dependence on the frontal brain, and the resulting over-development of the intellect, we are now left with no solutions to emerging problems but those offered by the limited intellect (a product of the frontal brain).

As a result, we actually consider the solutions offered by the intellect as valid and useful, when in actuality they are the direct opposite. The brain was not provided to us for that reason. The frontal brain is like a transmission center that allows us to receive perceptions from our material environment and then pass this information to the spirit through the hindbrain. Technical issues are also computed using the frontal brain, but the use of anything that results from the frontal brain has to be regulated by the spirit.

This is because one remains connected to all his actions, be they carried out directly by the individual or indirectly through the use of a product of this individual's brain by another individual or group of individuals. Due to this connection, the originator of an evil action will also feel whatever effect his action has, directly or indirectly, on any individual or groups of individuals, when the time comes for reaping the fruit of the action.

He also remains connected to all those whom he may have led astray through his wrong actions, and will stay connected to them until they have been led back to the right path.

This may never happen if the originator of the action never realizes the effects of the action, or that the action was not beneficial to the target or victim of the action.

For this reason I wish to impress upon you the need to know what is good for you, for your spirit that is, since that is what really matters. It is only after you have known exactly what is good for your spiritual development that you can begin to pass on this knowledge to some other individual or groups of individuals. This is because the only thing that benefits man today is that which helps him with his spiritual development, since that is why we are here in the first place. To know the Truth one has to live it. He has to personally experience it.

I have also provided the story of the experiences I had prior to writing this book to illustrate how I had to learn from them using knowledge that I received in the Grail Message. I have done this because there are many misconceptions about what it means to be spiritual. Today it sounds like a term that is out of place with respect to what many see as reality. But in man, the only species that is truly alive is the spirit.

Man is nothing without the spirit. Man is spirit in flesh, albeit he wears cloaks from the other spheres that he passes through on his way down to earth, but it is the spirit that is the living entity in man. He should treat the spiritual then as a subject of paramount importance to which everything else is secondary. Everything else is supposed to aid the spirit of man in his mission here in the World of Matter but not become the primary focus of this mission.

I have written about my experiences to show the serious reader or listener that one can go through this life without ever realizing what this life is supposed to be about, and yet he must come to the realization of the Truth if he is to ever return to his origin as a matured and self-conscious human being, in the completion of the cycle that he began as a spirit seed-germ.

Also, I have tried to show that one does not have to subscribe to one particular way of life or doctrine in order to get to the path which leads *him* to the Light, but he simply needs to maintain a volition for what is good and learn from the circumstances that come his way every moment. They are the results of the closures of the cycles of his past deeds. The cycles have come to a close and are handing him the fruits of his past works.

With guidance from the Light and a steady focus on the maintenance of a good volition, he is then able to recognize the workings of the Laws of Creation in the returning karma with the help of the Word of Truth in the Grail Message that has been delivered to us. This way he would have experienced this act himself and it will be a personal experience that he would be able to take with him into the Ethereal Realm after he has departed this earth, as he continues his journey through the World of Matter to the Spiritual Realm.

Since these Laws never change, but only manifest themselves differently in the different spheres of the World of Matter, he would be able to personally experience their working in the different forms in which they manifest, through his own personal experience. He can then use this knowledge during his journey in the other parts of the World of Matter as a support and a link to the path of truth, which only leads him upwards.

His understanding of these Laws, which govern everything in Creation, will keep him from falling for the traps set by those who seek to adulterate the Truth for the purpose of drawing him into their flock. He would have become independent in his thinking because he would forever have those experiences to call upon whenever he needs to.

I feel that this book will be helpful, if used just as a guide and nothing else, to help seekers of the Truth recognize occurrences in their pasts for what they actually were, in ways that will leave them refreshed and ready for the experiencing of the moment, through which they will get the directions in which they need to travel here on earth and afterwards. This is because we all have different roads to travel, and each and every moment of the day we experience events that are important for the maturity of our spirits, and for finding the right path for ourselves to the Truth.

Maybe a look at my own experiences - which were unique to my case and therefore relevant only to my own spiritual maturity - and how they helped me make sense of my past experiences and my calling, can help readers of this book and true seekers of the Truth make sense of their own experiences, as they read or listen and make the Grail Message become alive within them.

I have made an effort here to word my utterances in a way that may not interfere with your development and maturity. I may not interfere because I have no idea what you need to go through to attain spiritual maturity.

Every person has to find this out for himself, because that is the only way that the spirit can get the exercise and the movement that it needs to wake up and take control of the tool (the brain – the intellect), through which the Darkness has ruled for ages, leaving the real individual to run around like a chicken with its head cut off.

Again, the way to attain the spiritual maturity needed by man today can only be shown to the individual through the Word in the Grail Message. This book is just a guide that might aid you in personally experiencing the Truth, or in understanding it in a way that makes sense to you in accordance with your own experiences.

This necessity of understanding the Truth through personal experiencing, which allows people to develop at their own pace, through their own experiences, is the reason why attempts to colonize a people, or to get a particular ethnic group to adopt the culture of another, have resulted mostly in catastrophe. It is because the proper rules of engagement, so to speak, have not been followed. Any serious observer can see this just by looking around, listening to the news or looking back at historical events.

The rules of engagement that govern everything in Creation, of which we are a part, have been provided to us in the form of the Primordial Laws of Creation or Laws of Nature. They are the Law of Attraction of Homogenous Species, the Law of Gravity, and the Law of Reciprocal Action. These laws and their workings in Creation are explained in the Grail Message in a way that I cannot duplicate! However, I have decided to introduce them here because they are Laws that we are supposed to live our lives by, and so should already know from teachings brought by the Creator's Messengers in the past, and also through the hourly and daily observation of our surroundings.

Moreover, I cannot write anything about the development of the spirit without referring to and stressing the importance of the thorough understanding of these Laws, since they govern every single thing that goes on in Creation, having brought about the entire process of Creation.

They are the expression of the Will of God in Creation!

The Law of Reciprocal Action, which can also be described as the law of sowing and reaping, states that what a person sows that shall he reap. A person cannot sow beans and receive corn. It is impossible. He gets back the fruits of what he has sown and he gets back much more than the seed that he sowed because it goes through a process of maturation, through the attraction of similar species, and brings back to him the final developed fruit. Just like the corn seed brings back a whole cob of corn after the process of its development and growth.

The second law (second only by the way I have arranged them; they actually work hand in hand in all of Creation), the Law of Attraction of Homogenous Species, states that like-species will attract one another. Just like the saying that birds of the same feather flock together. Again, we already know of this. This is observed with what we refer to as nature, which reminds us of the Magnificence of the Creator.

The third law, the Law of Spiritual Gravity, states that one's sins or propensities will act as a burden to one's spirit and simultaneously weigh it down and prevent its ascent from its particular plane of homogeneity. The nature of a species in Creation is described by its consistency and its weight. The denser the consistency of a species is, the heavier it will be, and the lower it will sink in comparison to a lighter, less dense species.

The more material substance the human spirit attracts to itself, the heavier it becomes, because it will no longer have that lightness that is unique to the spirit. It will be dragged down to the level of that substance which clings to it and must remain there until it has severed itself from this substance, or removed the substance from itself and returned to its original lightness.

These three Laws govern everything in Creation. They govern the activities that are in planes higher than we can imagine, and they also govern the activities of the life forms that we find in nature around us here on earth. We human beings are the only ones who do not observe these Laws in our actions. A careful look around you must reveal to you the truth in this. You can get an idea of how much trouble humanity is in when you consider that we exist in a Creation whose machinery is operated, monitored and governed by the Laws of Creation, with which we have made no attempts to familiarize ourselves, but which everything else around us seems to be controlled by.

The time for crushing and tossing out all that has not aligned itself with these Laws is here and that is why I am writing this book. During this time, the same machinery will crush all those who have not sought to remove from themselves those things that are not in line with that which is willed by the Light, since it knows no favors and acts in the most objective sense.

This book is meant only for those who wish to make use of it as a guide to help in understanding, through personal experience, the Truth brought in the Message about which I write. You may put it aside if it does nothing for you.

THE GREAT CREATION

Creation came about through the Divine Will of the Creator, God. It extends from Heights that we cannot imagine, down to this gross material part to which the planet earth belongs. All that we are able to see and discern with our physical eyes, with all the visual aids available, are within the gross material part of Creation.

The World of Gross Matter also has within it the Worlds of Fine Gross Matter and Medium Gross Matter (referred to as Astral by some who have become aware of it) where our thoughts and words take on form. The consistencies of those worlds are different from that of this world, the World of Heaviest or Coarsest Gross Matter, and so they are imperceptible to us while we still use our physical senses.

The Law of Attraction of Homogenous Species allows for only like-species to be able to exist in a way that they can interact or see each other. Therefore, the physical eyes can see only what is of this world, which we use in our daily lives here on earth. A few people, who are able to see images or hear from outside our specific plane in the World of Matter, can do so only when they have been permitted to use the eyes and ears of those planes, which we all carry within us. We carry within us the cloaks of the planes that we had to traverse on our way down to earth, i.e., the worlds that separate this plane from the Spiritual Realm whence we came.

The people mentioned above, however, cannot use their physical eyes or ears at the same time as they use the eyes and ears of such planes that they are able to perceive from. This issue is dealt with in a way that will best benefit the reader, in the Grail Message. I have brought this up because as we stand today, with all the books and the discussions of the

23

metaphysical that have issued from the intellect, the true picture of Creation is yet to be grasped by most of mankind.

The mediums (those who can transmit utterances from people who have passed on, to family members of the departed or to investigators) who can perceive happenings from outside the plane that we reside in, cannot go further in their perceiving, than the level that their spiritual maturity would allow them to. This is due to the Laws of Attraction of Homogenous Species and of Spiritual Gravity. They can only attain to and perceive from that level which corresponds to their spiritual maturity. No serious seeker should then rely on what is received from meetings with mediums as the absolute Truth because it would not be a complete experience. It may at best be the convictions of one who has passed on, whose spiritual nature will correspond to the spiritual nature of the person or persons around the medium at the time.

The one in the beyond, i.e., the human spirit that has passed on from this earth-plane into the Medium or Fine Gross Material Worlds, or even into the higher Ethereal World, can only deliver to those whom he can reach through the medium as much as he himself is able to know by virtue of his particular spiritual maturity at the time. He might not even be able to adequately address the issues of those who still reside on earth, and who have different paths that they have to follow in order to gain recognition, which alone can lead to their liberation from the World of Matter and to the Light.

Also, the experience of being able to receive information from different planes in the World of Matter cannot be shared between the medium and the client, no matter how valid this information or perception is. This is because the client needs to exert his or her own spirit in order to benefit in any way. Only through personal experiencing can one find his way to the knowledge of the Laws of Creation, which alone holds the key to his ascent.

This is because he needs this knowledge in order to journey successfully through the different planes of the World of Matter that lie between this earth-plane and his origin in the Spiritual Realm. Relying on someone else for something that one should be able to develop for, and in oneself is just another way of handicapping the spirit and preventing it from maturing through personal exertion and personal experience.

This is not to say that everyone should be able to develop the abilities of a clairvoyant or a medium, but everyone is equipped with just that which he personally needs in order to experience in this world and in the Ethereal, and in the process mature spiritually. Anything else besides that which leads to the personal experience and maturity of the individual human spirit is a waste of his time and can only now lead to perdition, because he no longer has the time to waste on issues of non-importance to his spiritual maturity. Relying on others for things that may not even be of importance to one's development will only prevent him from developing those abilities which alone can serve him during his journey out of the World of Matter.

He will have to make this journey alone and not with all the people who can be seen around the individual while he is here on earth in his physical body. After departure from this world into the so-called beyond, the human spirit is attracted to the region, outside the physical environs of this earth, which he shares homogeneity with depending on the heaviness of the outer-most cloak which covers his spirit.

Since the densities of the cloaks of the different individual human spirits that reside on the earth-plane differ from one another, it then makes it a necessity that the human spirit spend all his energy and his time in making sure that he will be able to navigate his way alone, through those worlds that will still have to be traversed or lived through, on his way back to the Spiritual Realm. To do this he requires knowledge of the Laws in Creation, which he can only gain through personal experiencing and spiritual exertion. Only through this will he be able to call the gathered knowledge his own. As opposed to something which is learned and which will have to remain with the earthly brain upon his physical death and exit from the earthy-plane.

Today, Radiations pour forth from the Highest of all Heights and stream through the entire Creation. In the beginning, God sent out His Creative Will from the steps of His Throne and there was Light where there was formally nothingness.

At the summit of Creation, the part of Creation closest to the immediate Radiation of God - the Divine Realm, reside those Beings who

25

were able to withstand the pressure of the Light-Radiations close to the boundary of the Divine Realm. Through them these radiations stream down to the rest of Creation.

Those Beings, known as Primordial Spiritual Beings, were conscious of their existence and of themselves, and were able to stay conscious and worship the Creator in that plane where they took on form. This plane in which the Primordial Spiritual Beings reside is still great distances from the immediate Radiation of the Creator. The Primordial Spiritual Beings were able to take on form and be conscious of their existence due to the great distance that exists between their plane and that of the Divine Realm, out of which issues the life-sustaining Power needed for the maintenance of the entire Creation.

They were able to take on form because as the Radiation of the Creator shot out over the boundary of the Divine Realm, there was a cooling off of this Radiation of God from its white-heat nature that forms the Divine Realm, His immediate Radiation. At distances which we cannot imagine, the Primordial Spiritual Beings were able to attain consciousness and form themselves since they were no longer so close to this white-heat, which would have made it impossible for any beings other than those in the Divine Realm to attain consciousness and to exist in definite forms.

The Primordial Spiritual Beings were the first to take on form in Creation and so were the first to be created. They are the ones who were created after the image of God. Because they were able to take on form at a height that allowed them to come closest to the perfection of this image of God, which is the Divine Realm that forms the immediate vicinity of God.

The intensity of the Radiation was able to cool off at greater and greater distances from the Divine Realm. Only at such distances was it possible for species to attain self-consciousness and remain so. Naturally, the further the Radiations went from the Divine Realm, the greater the possibilities for species to take on form or develop slowly to self-consciousness.

All of this was in strict accordance with the Will of the Creator, which then manifested in those planes or spheres that formed, following the cooling off of the Radiation of God, in accordance with the nature of the planes or spheres. The particular ways in which these spheres experienced the working out or manifestations of the Will of the Creator made them appear as Laws. Laws which could never change because they came about through the Will of the Creator, Which is perfect and so not in need of further development, nor will It ever need to be changed or adjusted.

In accordance with the Law of Attraction of Homogenous Species, and the Law of Gravity, the species that could not become conscious on their own could not remain at the plane of the Primordial Spiritual Beings, and as a result they had to move further away from the intensity of the Radiation from the Divine Realm. They repelled further away from the Source of the Radiation. If these beings had been of the same species as the Primordial Beings they would have stayed at the plane of the Primordial Beings due to the same Laws.

The Primordial Spiritual Realm and all the other ones to be mentioned in the portrayal of Creation have divisions within them. These divisions will not be dealt with in this book but might only be mentioned when they can help in clarifying certain issues. The next plane in the process of cooling off or moving further away from the strong Radiation from the Light is the Spiritual Plane, from which the developing human spirits in the World of Matter, of which the earth is a part, descended as spirit seed-germs. This is the lowest part of the entire eternal Spiritual Sphere at the summit of which reside those Primordially Created Beings mentioned above.

So in the Spiritual Sphere there are those Spiritual Beings who came into being or took on form first, and then there were those that took on form further distances away with relation to the Source of all Life. Those who first took on form at the summit of the Spiritual Realm are referred to here as the Primordial Spiritual Beings, and their activities, as they made use of the radiations streaming forth from the Divine Realm, led to the development of the rest of the Spiritual Realm. The process of giving and receiving, which characterizes the Law of Reciprocal Action, led to the passing on of these radiations downwards and the cycling back of spiritual currents from the lower species.

In using the Power that courses from the Divine Realm, through the

Divine Will of God, the Holy Spirit, Who stands at the boundary between the Divine Realm and the Summit of Creation, and through Whose Radiation the Primordial Spiritual Beings and all of Creation came into being, the Primordial Spiritual Beings were able to participate in the development of those beings and those spheres that developed after they took on form and became self-conscious.

In accordance with the Will of the Light, the Power of the Light, that is through the Radiation of the Holy Spirit, Creation developed as more species took on form at their respective levels in the process of cooling off of the Radiation of God.

So after the development of the Primordial Spiritual Beings there were ones that had to slowly develop to consciousness through a gradual process of development with the help of those species that had already attained consciousness. This is the normal occurrence on every plane that developed in accordance with the Will of the Light. And so in the part of the Spiritual Realm, whence the human spirit descended as a seed germ into the World of Matter, there were those who were able to immediately attain self-consciousness at the appropriate distance from the Source of Light, and there were also others who remained unconscious and unable to withstand the pressure of the Light even at such a distance from the Source of this pressure.

As I mentioned earlier, the activities of those who are able to attain consciousness aids in the development of the lower spheres through their activities in the reception of the Light-radiations and the consequent transformation of these radiations through their nature or the nature of their species, acting as transition points and passing on the radiations downward as they receive them from above.

So viewed from on High, there is a gradation in the formation of the different spheres as they form, consequent to the activities of the species just above them in the gradation. This way every species is able to participate in the joyful task of expanding Creation, but always with the power of the Light in Creation, which issues from the Divine Will, the Holy Spirit of God.

Also, as a result of the graded formation of Creation, every species gets just that which it needs for its maturity and development. Just by virtue of the fact that they were able to attain consciousness at a definite level in Creation guarantees that they are not faced with challenges that will become too much for them to handle at such a plane. The faithful observance of the Laws that govern the particular plane or sphere is enough to ensure that the power of the Light is able to flow through them, undimmed, and in a manner that Creation can be furthered in a way that is pleasing to the Light. This requires that the formed species remain active so that they may be able to transmit light to those species that are able to use it in such a transformed nature.

This ensures that there are no gaps in Creation and that every single species that comes into being is able to receive the radiations from the Light and is sustained, as long as it abides by the Laws that govern Creation.

So below the Primordial Spiritual Sphere there is the Spiritual Sphere, which came into being afterwards. In this plane there are beings that were immediately able to become conscious of their existence and so could withstand the pressure from above and take on form at that level, and there were others who had to remain unconscious as spirit seed-germs. These unconscious spirit-germs still could not become conscious at the lower levels of the Spiritual plane. So that within the Spiritual plane there were those who became self-conscious, and were able to consciously serve the Light, and participate in the dynamic process of giving and receiving, and then there were those who remained unconscious.

Again here, the Law of Attraction of Homogenous Species allowed for only those Beings who had become conscious to exist at the plane that they find themselves in the Spiritual Realm, where, due to their maturity, they could consciously use the Power that coursed through them and participate in the expansion of Creation in accordance with the Will of the Light. This Law also made it so that the ones that could not attain consciousness also occupied a particular plane, in the lowest part of the Spiritual Realm, our Paradise.

The urge then arose within some of the unconscious spirit-germs, in the lowest part of the Spiritual Realm, to develop to a state that will allow them to become conscious, and become able to serve the Light in that plane in which they had remained unconscious.

With this urge came a simultaneous expulsion from that plane where they had been unconscious, down through the intermediate worlds to the World of Matter, of which the earth is a part. This expulsion was necessary since they were at a height where they could not attain consciousness due to their closeness to the strong pressure of the Light. The pressure of the Light was still too strong for this species of spirit to attain consciousness and so they had to develop that state of consciousness through a gradual process.

The only part of Creation where development was possible for these spirit seed-germs, which had developed the urge to mature, was in the lowest part of Creation, the World of Matter, where the type of development needed by these spirit seed-germs was still possible due to the distance from the Light of this part of Creation, and the consequent sluggishness due to the density of its species that results in its reduced permeability to Light.

This reduced permeability to Light makes development in this part of Creation slower than is the case in higher, lighter species of Creation. This condition, however, suits the spirit seed-germs, which require a gradual development to maturity, just like the World of Matter is able to offer them.

Being the furthest part from the Light, the World of Matter is not able to feel the Pressure of the Light as much as the Spiritual Spheres. The Spirit seed-germs can therefore be received by that part of the World of Matter that has reached a particular level of maturity where it can no longer develop any further without help from above, through the Spiritual.

Having no inherent warmth, the World of Matter is animated by the animistic beings, which came into being as a result of the activities of the spiritual beings in the lowest part of the Spiritual Realm. The activities of the animistic beings result in the animation and development of the World of Matter, which needs such animation to show any signs of life. So the World of Matter, with its various planes and spheres, form the cloaks for those species that require a field of activity such as it offers for the purpose of their own maturity.

Naturally, in accordance with the Will of the Light, there can be no maturity or Light-willed development without a consequent ennoble-ment of the environment of the species undergoing such development to maturity. Light Itself is Life and the more of Its Radiation is received by any species the more animated that species will become. Animation leads to movement, and movement leads to development and to life.

So it happens that when the urge awakens in the spirit seed-germs in the lowest part of the Spiritual Realm, they descend in the Power of the Light and in response to their urge, to the lowest part of Creation, the World of Matter, where they get the opportunity to mature gradually, by experiencing their surroundings and the manifestations of the Laws of Creation, while at the same time ennobling their environment, which is the World of Matter, as they strive to get back to their origin in Paradise, in the Spiritual Realm, whence they came.

The first spirit-germ thus journeyed down from the Spiritual Plane as a result of its yearning to develop to self-consciousness. Therefore the first spirit-germ and all the other spirit-germs that descended into this part of Creation for their development, incarnated onto this earth as a result of their own wishes. It was our urge to develop that sparked our expulsion from the level in the Spiritual Plane that we call Paradise. It is with the intention of returning as fully matured spirits, to that plane, to Paradise, that we came here to experience and mature.

Our descending into this part of Creation is much like the descent of a ripened apple from a tree. It falls to the ground at a precise point in its maturation. The fallen apple disintegrates and the seeds within it become exposed and get into the ground or become covered with earth, if undisturbed over time. Each of the seeds then undergoes a series of transformations and maturation processes while in the ground (if everything proceeds without any interference).

At the right time of maturity and not a moment sooner, the seedling emerges from beneath the surface of the ground and then strives upwards as it grows into another tree. It grows into another tree because it has undergone a necessary schooling period in the ground. This schooling period is necessary for it to adapt itself to the surrounding environment and draw from it for its maturity and growth.

You can view the life of the human spirit on earth and in the World of Matter as one that is analogous to the period of schooling of an apple seed prior to its germination. Also, our descent into the World of Matter is in accordance with the Law of Reciprocal Action, the law of sowing and reaping. It was because we had the urge to develop into fully conscious spirits that we came down to this part of Creation. We asked for it and we got it. It could not have been any other way. We could not go higher than the plane we resided in as unconscious spirit-germs because we would not have been able to withstand the pressure of the Light there. As far below the Origin of the Light as we were (at the lowest part of the Spiritual Plane), we still could not attain consciousness, making the idea of moving upwards to develop impossible!

We could only have gone farther away from the Source of the powerful Radiation of the Light in order to have any hopes of slowly developing to a level of maturity that will allow us to return to whence we came in full consciousness. Farther away from the Source of Light Radiations, the intensity of the Radiation lessened and forms became less mobile and more rigid and more ponderous.

A simple explanation of this happening can be seen in the science laboratory of today where increased heat and pressure brings about increased mobility of particles, and a decrease in heat and pressure results in relatively less mobile particles. Science is not really at odds with the Truth; it has only been confined in its efforts by the restricted intellect. Science is just the reported observation of the activity of the Laws of Creation. It is because things much higher above the World of Matter are more mobile, hence faster, that the mere urge to develop is all that is needed for the act of expulsion from the Spiritual Realm to become a deed.

In the process of cooling off, substances became denser as they took on form in regions or planes very far from the Source of the Light Radiations. The World of Matter, of which the World of Gross Matter is a part, is much denser in consistency, more rigid and so much less mobile than the lowest part of the Spiritual Realm. Things take much longer to happen here because of its distance from the Light.

It is also because of this fact that man is able to exercise his free will in this part of Creation. The pressure of the Light cannot be felt here on earth in a way that will deter man's use of his free will. This means that man can choose how to channel the Power, which flows throughout the entire Creation, towards good or bad ends, through the nature of his volition. By man here I mean men and women. It is more convenient to use just man since we are all human spirits and have the same mission of experiencing and maturing here on earth in order to eventually return to where we came from. Also, I use the word man here to refer to the species of the Spiritual that is developing here in the World of Matter.

Returning to the issue of free will, man was given free will while journeying here in the World of Matter because it is in making the right choices and making the best use of the Power available to him that his maturity (i.e. spiritual maturity) can be assessed.

Here, again, the Law of Reciprocal Action is in play because it is by making the effort to keep one's volition pure, and through the exertion of oneself to recognize the Will of God and act within this Will, which lies in the Laws of Creation, that spiritual maturity can be attained. The Law of Attraction of homogenous Species causes the person to rise spiritually as he fulfils the Laws. This is because the person who has made the effort to operate within these Laws becomes more and more like the Beings higher above the World of Matter, and so becomes attracted to them. Also the attractive force of those in the Primordial Spiritual Plane pulls the person up spiritually.

Upon departure from the World of Gross Matter following physical death, which is the same as laying aside the gross material physical cloak and passing on to the Ethereal World, that person is then able to be gradually attracted and pulled up to the level of the Spiritual Plane where he descended to earth from, because of his increasing homogeneity with that plane, and as he lays aside the different cloaks of the different planes of the Ethereal World as he passes through them, thus completing an immense cycle that was opened with his expulsion from the Spiritual Realm.

The same Law causes this particular person to be protected from the Darkness (anything that is contrary to the Laws of Creation, therefore anti-Light) as he journeys back home since the Light and the Darkness are of different species. In his childlike nature, the Light will surround him and the Darkness will be simultaneously repelled. His volition for what is good, which is what allows for his ascent, since those Primordial Spiritual Beings above will only attract to themselves that which is good, will exclude the possibility of his attracting evil to himself, thus forming a protective amour around him in the form of the purified cloaks of those planes in the Ethereal World.

The contrary will be the case for the person who decides to ignore the Laws, for whatever reason. He would be dragged further down or held fast to this earth because of the Law of Attraction of Homogenous Species and the Law of Gravitation, and also the Law of Reciprocal Action (sowing and reaping). His volition will be directed to all that is material and so he will be bound to matter accordingly. Like a magnet he will attract to himself those things and those conditions that are like the nature of the outermost, that is, the densest of the ethereal cloaks which he wears within.

When he departs from this Gross Material World, he will sink to that region in the Ethereal World that corresponds to the nature of his volition. He will remain anchored there due to the weight of the burden that he placed on himself in accordance with his particular volition, until a change in this volition allows him to rise higher of sink even lower. He might remain in that region until the time comes when that particular region has to undergo disintegration, making it impossible for him rise any more.

He will go through the painful and long process of disintegration with matter, and be stripped of the personality that he has been able to acquire during his long wandering in the World of Matter, to return to the Spiritual Realm as a spirit seed-germ that was not able to develop to spiritual consciousness, despite the opportunities granted it in the Will of the Creator. He will suffer spiritual death, the worst fate that can befall a human spirit that already attained consciousness of itself.

Those human spirits, who function within the Laws of Creation while going through life on earth, eventually leave the earth after physical death, and after attaining a certain level of spiritual maturity, they are able to go through the worlds between the Spiritual Plane and the World of Gross Matter with their eyes open because they took good advantage of the schooling period while on earth. Thus they are able to find their way back to the level of the Spiritual Plane that they came from. They are provided help during their journeys from those above them in higher planes through the activities of the latter. This time, however, they would be returning as mature and so, conscious spirits.

Those who do not take advantage of the schooling period find themselves lost after laying aside their physical cloaks (physical death) because they never made the effort to understand the Will of the Creator, which lies in the Laws of Creation. They are deaf, blind and crippled in the Ethereal Realm because they did not concern themselves with the possibility of the existence of the human spirit after his departure from the earth-plane, due to their one-sided focus on only what is material. The environment of man on earth and in the World of Matter constitutes the Language of God, since all matter and all of Creation came about as a result of the Will of God, which manifests in Creation as immutable and unchanging Laws.

Understanding the working of the Laws of God in the changing forms of the World of Matter, as the forms go through the process of development, maturity, ripening and decay or harvest, leads to the understanding of His Will. This understanding carries the human spirit through its wanderings through the higher planes in the World of Matter as it rises and eventually departs from this World into the Spiritual Realm. This is possible because he is more able to recognize the Will of the Creator in those realms, having become familiar with their working through his experiencing in the gross material earth-plane.

During this process the activity of the human spirits wandering in the World of Matter for the purpose of their development leads to the development of the World of Matter, which has no intrinsic warmth and which requires such activity of the developing human spirits for its development and ennoblement.

In strict accordance with the Law of Reciprocal Action, the human spirits are able to understand the Laws of God in Creation, through the process of wandering in the World of Matter, while the World of Matter is ennobled and uplifted as a result of the physical and spiritual activities of the human spirits which can only mature by abiding by the Laws of

Creation, thereby transmitting light to the World of Matter.

Man has so far not fulfilled his obligation to the World of Matter, which offers him a dwelling for the period of his schooling and his learning of the Laws of Creation. The present state of the World and the conditions of both men and the environment attests to this. Man has mainly concerned himself with issues that deal with the material alone, and has become cut off from the spiritual currents that he is supposed to use for his development and for the consequent upliftment of this part of Creation.

His focus on only material issues has channeled his volition towards those things that are earthly, and this has caused his progression to be directed downwards, depriving this world of the necessary infusion of light that it needs for its development, and willfully abandoning his mission of spiritual ascent.

His works have led to destruction instead of upliftment and he has increasingly sunken lower into the depths, taking the world along with him.

Now however, when the Light of God permeates this region in a manner like never before experienced in this part of Creation, the fruits of the seeds that man has planted over the thousands of years that he has been allowed to dwell in this part of Creation will be returned to him, so that he may taste of them and be crushed by them if he does not make haste to right his mistakes through the atonement of his guilt, which can only come about through the recognition of the Laws of Creation in the experiences that come his way every single moment.

Issues regarding incarnation into the World of Gross Matter (to which earth belongs), physical death and re-incarnation will be dealt with later on in the course of writing this book.

THE INCARNATION
OF THE HUMAN SPIRIT ON EARTH:
THE CREATION OF MAN

In the process of the cooling off of the Radiation of the Light from the Summit of Creation, which results from the relaxing of the Light-pressure due to the increase in distance from the border of the Divine Realm, worlds, planes, or spheres formed in accordance with the abilities of the corresponding species to take on form, through their ability to participate in the expansion of Creation, through their activities in accordance with the Creative Will of the Light.

The farther away from the Source of Light that the radiations traveled the more ponderous and heavy were the species that formed. The density of the spheres that formed corresponded to their distance from the Source of Life, so that the spheres that formed at the greatest distances from the Summit of Creation were the densest and the least permeable to Light. The spheres that the denser species separated from in order to form themselves, as they descended to further distances from the Light, remained relatively finer in consistency and so were more permeable to Light and more mobile than the ones that separated and sank further downwards as they formed.

The differences in nature of the species that formed as the radiations were passed on downwards, through the Light-willed activities of species that were able to take on form, correspond to the distances of the formed species from the Source of Light.

Automatically the Will of God expressed in His Laws made certain that only those species that could withstand the pressure of the Light at any given level in Creation could be retained there. The rest of the species had to move further downwards and away from the Light in order to be able to take on form, in accordance with the same Laws of Creation that brought about the form or order of Creation.

To take on form here is analogous to being conscious of oneself and of the responsibilities inherent in being allowed to exist at a particular plane in the gradations of Creation.

So only those species that are able to maintain themselves at that particular plane, through constant activity, can be retained at a particular plane. From there they are able to pass on forms of the radiations that they receive from above downwards to those species which were able to take on form below their own sphere. In this way species of beings in Creation are able to participate joyfully in the expansion of Creation. In this way they worship the Creator by making use of His adamantine Laws in Creation for the purpose of co-operating in the spread of light throughout Creation.

To make use of the Laws of Creation is to adapt oneself to their working. To adapt to their working is to show reverence to the Creator since the Laws of Creation are the expression of His Will in Creation. So it is not possible for any species to be in existence in a plane that is not specifically that which is homogenous to its nature by virtue of the level of its spiritual maturity.

All the virtues and radiations, which form the rest of Creation, are absorbed from the Holy Spirit by the Primordially Created Beings at the Summit of Creation. The radiations, which they pass down through their activities, are absorbed by numerous other species below. Each Primordial Being sends out radiations that are used by numerous other species that were able to form below the Primordial Creation.

These species of beings that are able to make use of the radiations passed down from the Primordial Beings are also able to pass radiations downwards to aid in the development of many other species that might vibrate according to the nature of the specific radiations.

So in the process of the formation of the gradations of Creation, the different species that make up Creation are able take on form exactly at that level or position where they are best suited by virtue of their spiritual maturity, hence density, and their abilities or the nature of their activities.

Working in their different positions these individual creatures of Creation are able to channel the power of the Light in ways that can only expand Creation and lead to the formation of even more species as light is spread through joyous activity.

Of the species that were able to take on form there are those that immediately took on form and those which still had to develop to maturity and to consciousness of themselves.

To be conscious of oneself in those spheres above means to be able to consciously use the power of the Creator while co-operating in the expansion of Creation. It means being developed enough to be able to consciously adapt oneself to the working of the Laws of Creation, because that is the only way that a harmonious up-building can be achieved by any species.

So the species that were able to take on form immediately were able to guide the development of the ones who had to go through a more gradual process of development. This sort of development is evident throughout Creation.

In the process of developing, radiations of the Light were passed on downwards and more worlds were formed as the Light-Radiation extended further away from the Source of All Life.

As the lowest part of the Spiritual Realm, which formed below the Primordial Spiritual Realm, at the summit of which stand the Primordially Created Beings, there rested the spirit-germs of the human spirits who would later be allowed to descend into the World of Matter for their own development to maturity.

There, as the very last precipitation of all that is spiritual, they were not yet conscious. They could not withstand the Pressure of the Light as far away from the Source of Light as they were.

The urge to develop, which is the reason the Spiritual was allowed to form itself outside the immediate vicinity of the Creator, the Divine Realm, resides within all that is Spiritual. The spirit-germs at the lowest plane of the Spiritual also bear this urge within them and this urge awakened within some of them. The awakening of the urge to develop self-consciousness is a stage in the natural development of those species in the Spiritual Realm, which remain unconscious until this urge develops.

Below the Spiritual Realm lies the immense World of Matter. The World of Matter is the lowest precipitate of all that is created, and being so far flung from the Summit of Creation, the Source of the Radiations that formed Creation, it is without its own warmth. The Spiritual, however, has its own warmth due to its relative closeness to the Source of Life. Creation was formed through the Radiation of the Holy Spirit, the Spirit of God above the entire Creation.

Through Him the Light-Radiation went forth and the species were formed, all according to His Volition, the Will of God. The Spiritual Realm was formed in the Radiation of the Holy Spirit. The species of the Spiritual bears within it a spark of the volition to develop in accordance with the Will of the Light, through Whose Radiation they came about. The Will of God in Creation is His Spirit, and from this Spirit the first Creation came about, the Primordial Creation. Everything else formed as the Volition of this Spirit spread further into the distance, thus forming worlds and planes in accordance with this Volition, Which is expressed in the Laws of Creation, also known as the Laws of Nature.

The World of Matter which exists as the last precipitate of this Radiation is without warmth, and needs to be animated by the species above it in order for there to be movement and the necessary heat needed for the generation of forms. Here the forms are developed much more slowly and gradually than they are in the higher, more luminous spheres.

This again is in accordance with the Laws of Creation since this part of Creation, the World of Matter, is the furthest from the Source of Light and so is the densest and least permeable to Light. It is because of these characteristics of the species of matter that it could only develop at such a distance from the Summit of Creation. It could not have developed at a higher level in Creation because it would not have been able to withstand the Pressure of the Light at that level.

Between the sphere of the Spiritual where the human spirits developing on earth have their origin, that is, the lowest part of the Spiritual Realm, and the highest part of the World of Matter, there exists a species of Creation known as Animistic Substantiality.

The species of this Realm form a ring around the World of Matter and animate it through their activities. Just like the higher species of the Spiritual have their activities directed towards those species that developed further downwards below their spheres, including the Animistic Species, these Animistic beings have their activities directed towards the development of the World of Matter.

They are the ones who animate the substances of the World of Matter, which results in the generation of heat through movement. This movement, through the generation of friction, leads to the generation of heat and the consequent development of forms. It is they who are responsible for the development of the forms, through the formation of unions in the World of Matter. It is through their activity that the World of Matter is able to be animated and to have the appearance of being alive. The World of Matter is their sphere of influence and they develop it as they themselves develop.

In the Sphere of Animistic Substantiality, that is, the sphere of the Animistic Species, there are also species that were able to attain consciousness right away and others that had to develop to consciousness. But this consciousness, which they develop towards, is limited to their origin and so differs from that which is attainable by the Spiritual.

So the World of Matter, which does not have its own warmth, as I have mentioned above, acts as a covering for various Animistic species, which have this plane as their field of activity. In the provision of this cloak the World of Matter is lent to this species for its own development. At the same time the development of the World of Matter is ensured as the Animistic beings carry out their Light-willed activities.

This leads to the further spreading of light throughout Creation and a further expansion of Creation, since the animation of the World of Matter through the Light-willed activity of the Animistic beings allows for the possibility of light to be absorbed by the substance of matter. It prepares the soil for the reception of light by this part of Creation, which is the furthest from the Source of all Life.

Absorption of light through the Light-willed activity of the Animistic beings allows for a closer connection between the World of Matter and the part of Creation that is able to more readily receive and make use of the Light-radiations from above.

This closeness ensures that the World of Matter, which itself is a part of Creation, is not lost through becoming too cold and rigid due to its distance from the Source of all Life. The Love of the Creator, Which is inseparable from His Will, shows Itself in this extension of help to this part of Creation which has formed as the last precipitate of Creation!

So through the activities of the Animistic beings, that is, through their use of and passage of the Light-radiations, which they receive from the higher Spiritual Sphere, the World of Matter was able to develop. At the same time the species of the Animistic were also able to mature within their species and participate in the development of Creation.

The World of Matter comprises of the Finer and Coarser parts. The Finer Part is referred to as the Ethereal Realm while the Coarser Part is referred to as the Gross Material Part. Within these parts are also other divisions.

The gross material part, also known as the World of Gross Matter, is a precipitate from out of the Ethereal Realm. This means that the Ethereal was able to form first before the coarser and denser species of the gross material.

Therefore standing closer to the Animistic Realm is the ethereal part, which is of a distinct species from the gross material part, even though they both make up the World of Matter. The difference in their species is the reason for the designation finer and coarser. The ethereal substance of the Ethereal World of is of a finer consistency than that of the World of Gross Matter.

The denser of the two is naturally the one that had to develop further downwards as it sank due to its density or the nature of its species. In this the precise nature of the working of the Laws of Creation shows itself.

But despite the difference in species, both parts of the World of Matter remain connected as one, for there are no gaps in the entire Creation. Only the species are different by virtue of their degree of lightness and ability to absorb light.

The Laws work uniformly in the entire Creation but they manifest in forms that are adapted to the nature of the individual species. Each species is therefore able to work with the same Laws in the ways that are familiar to them depending on their nature. It is like this throughout the entire Creation.

In the process of developing the World of Matter, there came a point beyond which the Animistic could not go further.

Following several millions of years of development a point was reached where the work of the Animistic Species, to which belong also the soul of the animals on earth, had reached its zenith on gross material earth, and needed assistance from the species above its origin, as a natural process of development, if the point of development already attained was not to be followed by standstill and retrogression. This was around the middle of the cycle of development of matter.

This was the point when noble animals had developed, who could already show limited signs of intelligence displayed through the ways that they acquired their nourishment and defended themselves. These were the animals commonly referred to as Primeval Man.

At this point in the process of the development of the species on earth, the Animistic could not do any more without the help of the Spiritual, which is the next higher species in the order of Creation.

During the process that led to the development of these nobler animals, the spirit-germs, within whom the urge to develop to maturity had awakened, were already descending downwards into and through the planes of the World of Matter.

They were expelled from the Spiritual Realm downwards into the World of Matter following the awakening of the urge to develop. They could not develop to consciousness of themselves at that plane where they were in the Spiritual Realm, neither could they go upwards towards the Light. And so they had to descend from that plane to a region that was not as close to the Source of Light above as their origin is. Only such a descent could have given them the opportunity to mature, since they would be able to withstand the Light-pressure at a further distance from the Source of Light and from their origin.

In the process of wandering through the denser and coarser World of Matter they were to develop those abilities which lay dormant within them and which needed to be developed to full activity. This required maturity of this spirit spark through experiencing of the various ways in which the Will of God is expressed in the World of Matter. He would be forced to use his inherent abilities to deal with the obstacles that come his way. To defend and to nourish himself while adhering to the Will of the Light, and in the process, develop these abilities as he gains knowledge of the Laws of Creation.

While the Animistic beings were developing the World of Gross Matter to the point where the first spirit-germ could incarnate, the awakened spirit-germ, which at the moment was only just aware of its existence, was journeying through the World of Ethereal Matter.

During his descent he made decisions as to the types of vibrations he wished to taste more of. These vibrations were emanating from the coarser regions of the World of Matter and reaching right up to the finer parts. The vibrations were the results of the activities of the process of development that was already going on here in the World of Matter. The process of development includes the stages of sowing, development and forming, blossoming and flowering, ripening and harvest or decay.

It is the same process that can be viewed by anyone who cares to look around. It is absolutely necessary for everything developing in this World of Matter, for it to follow the path of development that leads from sowing to ripening and harvest or decay. It is a cyclic process that keeps the World of Matter fresh and ensures its vitality and the development of those to whom it is made over as a home for the period of their development.

In the course of disintegration or decay, the forms of the World of Matter, which have reached the end of the development process, return to their basic units so that they can reform in more beautiful ways. This keeps the World of Matter fresh and lively, and prevents rigidity and stagnation, which bring about a coldness that will push it even further away from the Light. Since only movement generates heat and warmth is needed for the maintenance of the right kind of movement, stagnation is prevented through the perpetual change in the forms of matter.

The process that brings about the change in the forms of matter is one that follows strictly the Laws of Creation. Through these changing forms, which can be experienced in all the spheres of matter, one is able to understand the Language of God, since His Will brings about the forms and their development to maturity.

The awakened spirit sparks which were descending through the planes of the World of Matter towards the World of Gross Matter, were attracted to those vibrations from the World of Gross Matter that they were inclined towards. In the Ethereal Realm, every urge turns immediately into deed because it instantly takes on form. The urge to taste of a particular kind of vibration, or to experience more of a particular kind of happening is what eventually attracted the spirit sparks to the earth. These vibrations, which they perceived and which attracted them downwards, were the products of the activities of the Animistic species in the World of Gross Matter.

In order that the development of the species of the gross material sphere would not be halted, with the risk of an inevitable deterioration following the stagnation, the descending spirit sparks were incarnated in bodies that were provided to them by the species of the World of Matter, through the activities of the Animistic beings.

The first spirit-germ was incarnated into the growing body of the baby in the womb of a pregnant female so-called Primeval Man.

The incoming soul, during an incarnation, enters into the womb of the mother-to-be around the middle of pregnancy. This happens in every earthly birth. It is around this time that the mother-to-be feels the first twitching of the baby, and it is around this time that the incoming soul fully takes over the body of the baby as it goes through the further stages of development in the womb of the pregnant mother-to-be.

This first incarnation was the actual creation of earthman. The coming together of the incarnating soul, of which the spirit is the core, and the cloak made of gross material substance, with which the soul forms a union for the purpose of interacting with the species of this gross material earth and to survive in it.

In the case of the first incarnation of man on earth, the incoming soul, which had already traversed the different planes of the World of Matter that precede the earth when looked at from above, entered into the developing body of the baby in the womb of the female so-called Primeval Man. This pregnant animal, however, had an animal soul, but only served as a bridge towards the further development of the World of Gross Matter, by providing a cloak for the spirit-germ, without itself becoming human in the process.

Neither does this mean that man himself is descendant from an animal. The only thing that is shared between the animal and the human being is the fact that they share the physical substances of this earth including the physical cloak. But even in this there are differences. The body of the human being of today is very different from that of the so-called Primeval Man, who long since became extinct since it no longer had any need to be around.

So the animal has a soul as its core, while man's core is spirit. The spirit is the animating factor in man, while the soul animates the Animal. The soul of the animal, however, is different from the soul of man. The soul of the animal comes from the animistic realm, while the soul of man is the spirit core from the Spiritual Realm with the material coverings or cloaks which he had to put on during his journey through the spheres of finer material species.

The ability of man to bear within him the finer cloaks within his physical cloak is because of the relative density of species of the substance of the physical cloak, compared to that of the other lighter species. This relative density makes the lighter ones able to permeate the denser one, in accordance with the order of Creation.

So the spirit with the different cloaks of the other lighter species of the World of Matter is the soul. It is in the form of a soul that the first awakened spirit-germ incarnated onto earth, into physical flesh, to start its development.

The preparation of the cloak that would be used by man for his work on earth, which is to connect this part of Creation with the stream of light that courses through Creation, so that development of Creation can continue in this furthest part of it, was faithfully carried out by the Animistic beings. After the incarnation of the first spirit-germs into earth there was no longer any need for the existence of that animal which had served as a bridge in the development of the cloak that would be used by man to co-operate in the further development of the World of Matter. It became extinct in the course of time.

During the course of his development man was able to transform this cloak into one that conformed more to the upright form that it has today. The form of the body of man is given to it by the spirit, which imparts this form to its cloaks as a natural consequence of its very nature, and as it becomes conscious. This form, in a much more beautiful state, is the form of the spiritual in the spheres above, right up to the Primordial Spiritual. So in becoming conscious the developing spirit assumes the human form.

It is because of this reason that those elemental or nature beings, from the Animistic Sphere, which take care of the plants, the water bodies, fire, rocks, and so forth, also have human forms. They take on human form in the process of becoming conscious, in the process of developing in the World of Matter, as they animate the substance of Matter.

The nature of man on earth is dependent on the nature of his soul, i.e., the state of the cloaks which he wears inside the physical body, and to which are connected those threads that link him with the consequences of his decisions.

He needed to have the different cloaks of the different planes covering his spirit core because he could not have interacted with the species of the corresponding planes in any other way but through that means which alone is familiar to them, and which alone is possible.

Like species can only interact with those of a like nature. This can be noticed everywhere and amongst the creatures of this gross material earth.

It is only by covering himself with the same substance as the surroundings that one can interact with the species of the surroundings. If he is to work in an environment he must adapt himself to the nature of things in that environment or he will not be able to do anything. There would not be an effective interaction and he would not be able to achieve anything. Between him and those with whom he may wish to interact there will remain a gap, which can only be bridged by abiding by the Laws of Creation.

For this reason and because there is no other way open to it, but that which is expressed in the Will of the Creator through His Laws, the spirit-germ had to be cloaked repeatedly as it descended down through the different planes of the World of Matter. This was also a period of awakening from unconsciousness for the spirit-germ, because it was then in a coarser environment and could feel the heaviness of this environment through the pressures that made impressions on it, as the Laws of Creation worked themselves out in the various spheres.

His every urge was a decision that immediately connected him through a thread that was woven by the Animistic Beings responsible for it, to that path which would bring him closer to the fulfillment of his urge.

In this way he was drawn closer and closer to the World of Gross Matter, until he was incarnated on earth. During this period of tasting of this or that vibration, he was awakened to consciousness of his existence, which is still different from the consciousness that comes with maturity of the spirit.

Also, during this period he was already becoming entangled in many a thread of fate, which inevitably brought to him the developed fruit of the seed sown with his every decision. His every wish was a decision, and his every decision was an expression of his volition, which initiated the development of a form of the same nature in a corresponding plane in Creation.

So he was sowing the seeds of wanting to experience of various vibrations and he received the results of such wishes in the form of the conditions that he found himself in. In this way he was to choose which of the paths open to him he was willing to continue to follow, and which he wanted to depart from.

Every thought, word, or deed takes on form in the different planes of the World of Gross Matter. These forms remain attached to the originator of the form by a thread. The connections are made instantly through the workings of the Animistic beings, which work tirelessly and always in accordance with the Will of the Light.

They are responsible for the development of anything that has been placed into Creation through the exercise of the volition of the spirit. They work towards the inevitable development of everything, whether good or bad, so that in returning the fruits of the seeds sown, they hand back to the originator exactly the kind of form that he placed in Creation. But they hand it back to him fully developed, because in the course of the development, these forms attract other similar forms, or are attracted by other similar forms.

So just like when a person plants a grain of corn he not only gets a grain of corn back, but he also gets many grains of corn back in return, it is exactly the same with the volition of man. When he expresses this volition in his intuitive perceptions, his thoughts, words, or deeds, they develop and return to him.

If he sows seeds of evil he reaps evil, and if the seeds are of good he reaps good, many times over.

So the arrival of the awakened spirit to earth was preceded by decisions, which he had made at various points during his wandering through the planes of the World of Matter as he descended downwards.

The threads that link him to the different forms which had been developed according to the nature of his volition, were attached to the corresponding cloaks which he wore inside his physical body and which he had to put on, so to speak, on his way down.

Every cycle opened in the process of the expression of a spiritual volition in the World of Matter strives towards the closure of the cycle. This follows a Law in Creation that demands that everything in completing the cycle of its development must return to its origin. So the cycle opened when one makes a decision eventually comes to a close, delivering to its originator the finished product of the process of development. In this way he is able to determine whether or not he wants to continue to plant the seeds that bring about such fruit.

He also learns of the working of the Laws of Creation. He is able to see the strictness of and the justice behind the Law of Reciprocal Action because he will know that he receives in accordance with the type of seeds he plants.

On earth, man has the opportunity to fully awaken and shake off the entire burden that he has placed on himself through the expression of his volition. He is able to experience the effects of the radiations from the different parts of the World of Matter and so has ample opportunity to learn and differentiate between right and wrong, beneficial or destructive.

Here on earth he experiences the final effects of all the happenings in the higher spheres of Creation, and so is surrounded by a wealth of information waiting to be tapped at the will of the human spirit. He only needs to consciously experience the working out of the Laws of Creation in order to mature through adapting his activities to them. With a focus on doing good he will be led through those paths that let him see and experience the Will of God in Creation.

He is able to make the right decisions when the opportunity arises because he is in a position to survey the different spheres of the World of Matter at the same time. He is able to access the higher spheres of the World of Matter in his intuitive perceptions, which are the expressions of the Spirit, the inner voice.

He is also able to see, hear, and feel the physical effects here on earth of the working of the Laws of Creation. He is in a position to draw light to this part of Creation because he remains connected to the Spiritual Realm. And this connection grows stronger and becomes more perceptible to him when he continues to make those decisions that are in line with the Laws of Creation, because they cause him to mature through the experiencing of the perfection of these Laws, and thereby also the experiencing of the perfection of the Creator.

As he develops in his maturity he will make those decisions that will uplift the World of Matter because the developed fruits which will be the result of the expression of his volition, made manifest through his every decision, will only lead to a harmonious and peaceful development of his surroundings in the World of Matter.

Simultaneously he would mature as he helps in the development of the World of Matter. Originating from the Sphere of the Spiritual as he does, he is the only creature in the World of Matter that can, in his activities, span the entire World of Matter while also remaining in connection with the Spiritual Realm. He is supposed to bring undimmed light into the World of Matter so that the development in this part of Creation can be one that can serve to keep it more firmly connected to the higher spheres of Creation.

In the World of Matter he is given the right of free will. The right to decide which direction he wishes to channel the neutral power of God, which courses through Creation and through him. He develops himself and his surroundings exactly according to the way he uses this power. To return back to the Spiritual Realm as a matured human spirit will mean to use this power for the good, so that he can mature and be attracted upwards towards the Light and towards his origin in the Spiritual Realm.

The incarnation into a physical body on earth of the soul of the developing spirit was necessary for his development, and for the development of the World of Matter. This, however, is not the beginning of the process nor does it end with his departure again from the physical World of Gross Matter, for man still has to go through the process of development in stages. One lifetime on earth is just one of those stages.

During the process of wandering through the planes of the World of Matter in his descent downwards, the first spirit-germ used mainly its coarser intuitive faculty. He did not make much use of the finer intuitive part, which then became completely severed from him, according to the Law in the Ethereal World that demands that every expression of volition must instantly take on form.

The awakened spirit spark's use of mainly the coarser intuitive senses was due to its preoccupation with fending for itself and engaging in coarser activity, and which led to the limited use of the finer intuitive faculty.

This developed as an expression of volition and, since there was no exertion of this finer part, it became severed from the coarser part and remained behind as the severed heavier part separated by sinking further downwards. The spirit-germs leaving the Spiritual Realm and descending downward towards all that is material, and which were inclined towards masculine and more positive activities or vibrations, incarnated into the form generated by the coarser intuitive perception. Those spirit-germs, which upon leaving the Spiritual Realm inclined towards the more delicate, finer and thus more passive and more negative activities, incarnated into the female forms which were generated by the finer intuitive perception.

The activity of the woman is more of a receiving kind. Her sensitive nature allows her to perceive the very fine vibrations and radiations, from within and out of the World of Matter, which are able to permeate the coarser part- species, the man. In this way she is able to radiate light from above into the sphere of Gross Matter.

She forms the gateway for all the radiations that come into the sphere of Gross Matter. Correspondingly womanhood in the higher, lighter spheres above also serve in forming the bridge between the sphere of the species and the next one higher up. It is the same down here on earth. Womanhood should serve as a bridge between the sphere of Gross Matter and the world beyond the physical gross material world. Also, right up to the Spiritual Realm.

For this reason the physical bodies of men and women on earth show marked differences that indicate the differences in the types of activities that the bearers should be engaged in. The manifestation in the Ethereal made itself visible in gross matter in the form of the different physical bodies of men and women.

But that is just the outward manifestation, the physical manifestation of these differences. The spiritual manifestation of these differences is in the activities of the spiritual part-species, man and woman.

Man cannot survive here in the World of Gross Matter without a link to the Spiritual Realm for the mediation of spiritual currents to this part of Creation. He needs the guidance from the Spiritual Realm in order to develop to maturity, since he is spiritual and can only get spiritual nourishment from the Spiritual Realm.

For this he needs his intuition. It is in his intuition that his spirit expresses itself. It is also in his intuition that he receives guidance from above. The severance of the finer part of his intuitive faculty before his incarnation into earth did not mean that he would not need this part, but just indicates the necessity for the spiritual to work in two parts here on earth, the positive and the negative.

The negative-acting part is the finer receiving and preserving part, while the positive-acting part is the coarser executing part. Working side-by-side these two parts of the species are to ennoble their surroundings as they individually strive to develop their abilities.

Neither the coarser activity of the man nor the finer, more delicate activity of the woman can be neglected without harmful consequences to the species. Both are equally necessary for the maturity of the spirit and the harmonious development of the World of Matter.

The woman's ability to receive of the radiations from the Light through her increased sensitivity cannot be matched by any man.

Consequently, a community or a nation is as good as lost if its women are not focused only on drawing Light-radiations down from above for the development of their surroundings. The woman cannot engage herself in the coarse activity of men and preserve this ability to purely perceive, and she lacks the coarseness of the man to be proficient enough in the masculine activities.

If she strives for coarseness through the kind of activities she engages in, or in the nature of her volition, then she neglects her responsibilities as a woman and her womanly abilities shrink in the process.

She would not be able to draw Light-radiations into the World of Gross Matter, and a gap in the flow of these spiritual currents is experienced in the form of an increase in the hold of the Darkness around the Sphere of Gross Matter, and the entire World of Matter as a matter of course.

So when the Bible narratives describe the woman as one who was made from a part of the man, so that she may act as his helper, this must be understood in the spiritual sense, as must every other narrative in the Bible, if the investigator is to benefit from it.

The woman possesses the finer intuitive qualities that are unique to her nature and which cannot be possessed by a man. For this reason she is the mediator of Light-radiations from above and can perform this duty to the benefit of all mankind if she strives to keep herself pure, and therefore, keep her intuitive perceptions light.

In this way she is the transmitter of light for mankind. The man is responsible for the coarser activities that need a closer association with matter and which do not require as fine an intuitive perception as that which is possessed by the woman.

In this way, in accordance with the one-time resolution made by the spirit-germs which were leaving the Spiritual Realm for their development, those spirit-germs which inclined towards the finer, more delicate, preserving and negative activities, incarnated in female bodies. Those who decided to partake in coarser activities were incarnated in masculine bodies.

With both parts working at their positions in the course of the development of the World of Matter in accordance with the Laws of

Creation, and as they develop to maturity, the split-species were to draw from the Primordial Spirits above those rays that can only ennoble the World of Matter.

Today man faces the consequences of all that he has placed in Creation as a result of his activities. They come back to him because he has to answer for what he has done with the power given to him through his ability to decide and to steer the neutral power of God one way or another, towards good or towards evil.

Because of this power that is available to him he has the responsibility to use it wisely, which means to use it in accordance with the Will of the Light, because only then can he hope to succeed.

He has not succeeded, and the time to assess for a final time what man has done with his abilities and gifts is here. He is to give account for all that has developed through the expression of his volition, good or bad, for only through recognition of his guilt can the possibility of salvation be allowed him.

Strictly, and in accordance with the Will of the Light expressed in the Laws of Creation, the reciprocal actions of all the works of men are returning to them. Man can feel the pressure of this time but does not yet understand why it is so.

Man must pay strict attention now to the Laws of Creation and their observance if he is to be helped at this last hour, because only through understanding and abiding by them can he find his way out of the mesh of dark threads with which he has entangled himself over millennia.

THE FALL OF MAN

Man is supposed to be the mediator of Light-radiations between the Gross Material World and the higher lighter regions of Creation. He alone on earth has the ability to perform this duty. It is to carry out this duty of transmitting light to this part of Creation that he was allowed to descend to earth for the purpose of maturing to consciousness of himself through his experiences. These experiences were to lead him to the right understanding of the Laws of Creation.

Man could only gradually come to the right understanding of the Laws of Creation through experiencing, and the World of Matter was the only place where he could achieve this. In return he was to transform this knowledge into deed here in the World of Matter. He was to do this through his activities while living here and enjoying all that this part of Creation has to offer. He was given everything that he needed for this purpose here on earth. All he had to do was to observe the working of the Laws of Creation and adjust his every thought, word, and action to these Laws.

In doing so man would have brought about such works as would only be in line with the Will of God, since the Laws of Creation are the Living expression of the Will of God in Creation. Abiding himself to these Laws would have been the same as achieving his goal of transmitting light to this World of Gross Matter.

At the same time he would also have become familiar with the ways that these Laws work in their various manifestations. Through this he would have attained the maturity necessary to ascend to the Luminous Heights above, because he would have become able to pass through those

55

planes which he traversed on his way down to earth, as a matured human spirit who is able to make his way back by consciously abiding by the Laws of Creation, the Will of God, following his exit from earth and from his physical body.

Since the spirit is eternal and has only put on the cloaks of the material spheres that it traversed on its way down to earth, it does not die or stop existing with the death of the physical body. The physical body is a necessary cloak or covering that the spirit needs for it to be understood here on earth, because he can only deal with and interact with the species of this earth in a similar body as the material of this earth.

But when his time on this earth is over, due to the necessary process of development which ends in the disintegration of matter at the stage of over-ripeness, or due to its bad treatment by the spirit leading to a premature departure, the spirit leaves the body and continues its development in other planes of the World of Matter to which his outermost cloak or covering at the time is homogenous.

The spirit is only able to fare well in the other planes of the World of Matter, which it has to go through after earthly death, when it has taken the time to know the Laws of Creation through his experiences on earth and matured in the process.

His goal is to return to the Spiritual Realm, from where he descended as a spirit-germ in order to mature here in the World of Matter, as a mature spirit who, having gone through the different planes of the World of Matter between the Spiritual Realm and this earth, has become quite familiar with the Laws of Creation as they manifest in all the different planes.

It is only when he has been able to gain this much knowledge that he can help those developing in the World of Matter below, because he would have become thoroughly familiar with life in the World of Matter and will be able to assist from the Spiritual Realm those who may, like him, need to come down for the purpose of maturing in the World of Matter.

Since he wears the cloaks of the different planes of the World of Matter beneath his earthly cloak, he is able to draw radiations from those planes that he remains connected to. He is also, because of the same connections, able to transmit light to all those regions as he matures spiritually and experiences the fulfillment of the Will of God in the manifestations of His Laws in Creation.

Standing as he is in the World of Matter, as the only one who is able to draw radiations directly from the Spiritual Realm, together with his connections to the different planes of the World of Matter, he has within his abilities the power to attract favorable, i.e., light radiations, or dark radiations to himself and to his surroundings.

The shaping of the World of Matter is done through the expression of his volition. The world develops wrongly or in darkness if he attracts mainly those radiations that are base and dark, and it will develop beautifully and harmoniously if he draws radiations from above by making those decisions that are in accordance with the Laws of Creation.

He is able to make these decisions in his intuitive perception, which is the expression of his spirit. The spirit alone is able to make contact with the neutral power of God which courses throughout Creation and through man himself. There is nothing that is not permeated by this power. But man has the ability to direct it one way or another through the expression of his volition. He alone in the World of Matter has this ability because he alone is spiritual.

In accordance with the Law of Attraction of Homogenous Species, a member of a species can only make contact with another member of the same species. This can be noticed everywhere. A person is able to rest on the ground because his body is of the same species as the hard substance beneath his feet. If this substance were to give way, then the space formally occupied by the hard substance will be instantly filled with air, which is of a different species and which will no longer be able to support him, and which he would no longer feel in the same way as he did the ground. He will fall through the air if nothing in the form of a viable substitute is put in the place of the hard substance on which he formerly stood.

In the same way as the air beneath his feet was not able to support his body, because of the difference in species between the air and the hard substance of the ground, only the spirit can make contact with what is spiritual. Similarly only animistic substance can make contact with what is animistic, only ethereal substance can make contact with what is ethereal, and only material substance can make contact with material substance. There is no deviation from this.

So the key to the release of the power of God in Creation is the intuitive perception of man. His intuitive volition directs this neutral power upwards or downwards because the intuitive perception of man takes on form in accordance with the nature of his volition, base, or light, and this form is able to radiate its energy to similar species throughout the World of Matter.

During its journey downwards through the planes of the World of Matter, i.e., during its first incarnation, the spirit-germ becomes attached to many forms which are generated through the expression of its volition. Its decision to taste of certain vibrations which emanate from the earth and from the various parts of the World of Matter, leads to the attachment of forms which correspond in density to the kinds of vibrations that it is inclined towards.

He becomes connected to these forms by threads woven by the animistic beings responsible for the task. The density of the forms to which he becomes connected draws him closer to those regions where he can taste more of the vibrations to which they remained connected.

Following this urge to taste of the different vibrations, which then develops into the desire to actively participate in them, the spirit-germ incarnates on earth. So he incarnates on earth already connected to different forms through very fine threads, which are invisible to the physical eye because of their finer nature, which characterizes their species.

Here on earth the awakened and developing spirit-germ has the opportunity to shake off all karma, through the experiencing of the effects of all that he attracted to himself through his decision-making, as he traversed the planes of the World of Matter downwards.

In experiencing the effects of his decisions, he was given the opportunity to recognize the working of the Laws of Creation. He then had the chance to make his further choices based on this newly acquired knowledge, and develop his trust and confidence in the strictness and perfection of these Laws. Since on earth he is able to experience the radiations from the other parts of the World of Matter, he stood the best chance of ridding himself of all bad karma, i.e., the effects of all the forms that he attracted to himself through making the wrong decisions, by countering the evil volition that led to the generation of the forms with good ones.

At the same time he was given the opportunity to develop spiritually through his right understanding of these Laws. Thus the earth is a major turning point in the course of the development of the human spirits that have to mature in this part of the World of Matter. Here on earth they come into contact with all kinds of radiations from the different spheres of the World of Matter, and are also able to influence the happenings in those planes as they recognize the Will of God in the Laws of Creation and abide by these Laws in their activities.

He was not meant to remain bound to this part of Creation. Man has not been able to rise to the Spiritual Realm where he descended from because he has not yet been able to disentangle himself from his ties to the World of Matter. He remains bound through the base forms that he has continually nourished for millennia.

He has failed to carry out his mission and instead of striving to recognize the Laws of Creation, which speak to him of the Wishes and the Will of God, he has directed the neutral power, which is available to all in Creation, towards the generation and maintenance of base forms which, as they go through their individual cycles of development and disintegration, have taken him through times of suffering and despair.

In his reaction to his self-willed condition, he has even fallen deeper into the depths of darkness because, in his ignorance, he has never really understood the reasons for his state of despondency and has naturally acted blindly and without spiritual guidance, with the resultant effect of a further sliding downwards into the realm of darkness.

It was not always like this with man. In the beginning stages of his development on earth he acted more naturally than he does now, and was more in touch with his inner spiritual core. His relationship with his surroundings was more harmonious than it has been for a very long time now. Back then, a very long time ago, he was able to follow the guidance that he received from above in his intuition, and also through the animistic helpers, which he was still light enough to see.

His reliance on his inner voice allowed him to develop more naturally, since the inner voice is the channel through which man on earth receives guidance from higher spheres.

This inner voice, which is also known as the intuitive perception, is the expression of the spirit. It is through the intuitive perception that man is able to make an impression on his surroundings. Conversely man senses of the guidance from above through this capacity to intuitively perceive. In his activities, and as he reacts to the pressure that he meets from his surroundings, he forms his volition. This is then expressed in his intuitive perception, which is able to take on form in the plane of the World of Matter that it belongs to with respect to its weight, or even in the Spiritual Realm.

The kind of intuitive perceptions a man has determines the weight or density of the form that is generated in response to this intuitive volition. The weight or density of this form then determines how high the intuitive perception will rise, or how low it will sink.

He is drawn up higher towards the lighter spheres above when the forms of his intuitive perceptions are light, and so, of a species which is close in nature to the species of the spheres of Light above. Alternately, he is dragged downwards towards the Darkness when the forms of his intuitive perceptions are dark or clouded in dark forms, because they are attracted downwards by the dark centers which exist in the regions of darkness below. The more dark forms he attracts to himself through his decision-making, the darker the cloaks that he wears inside become. In the Ethereal World, the forms take on the nature of the soul. If the soul indulges in dark activities and harbors dark thoughts and base propensities, then his inner cloaks will indicate this through their corresponding darkness and density.

If on the other hand the nature of the spirit is one that is light, this will also be reflected in the state of his inner cloaks. It is only here on earth that a man can hide his true nature, i.e., the nature of his soul, which is the spirit with all the material coverings of the other material spheres traversed by the descending spirit spark.

So in the beginning man's inner nature was not as dark as it is today.

It has only become so dark because of man's one-sided preoccupation with only those issues that concern matter. He has directed the neutral power of God towards the development of the intellect, a product of the frontal brain, to the detriment of his spirit, which alone makes him human, and which is supposed to take the leading position over the intellect.

The intellect was supposed to be used by the spirit as a tool here on earth for his interaction with the physical world around him. It was supposed to form a bridge between the spirit and its gross material surroundings. Just like the physical body and all the other material coverings of the spirit, the intellect is perishable, and so, transient.

It is without life and only exists through the animation of the body by the spirit. Consequently it cannot be placed above the spirit, which is eternal, without dire consequences to both spirit and body. Its activities are directed mainly towards gross matter, and so it cannot make sense of anything meant for the spirit because of the difference in the species involved.

The intellect is composed of the forms that represent the thoughts of man. These forms are generated when the frontal brain is used to think. The brain, as is the physical body of man, is of material substance and as such is equally perishable. The same goes for all that it is able to produce. So the forms of the intellect are also perishable and transient, even though the intellect is of a species that is finer in nature than that of the physical body, since it is formed in the Realm of Fine Gross Matter.

However, it is still limited to the World of Gross Matter in its perception, which is the coarsest and densest species of Creation.

The frontal brain, which produces the intellect, absorbs impressions from the physical environment and passes this on to the spirit through the hindbrain. The delicate nature of the hindbrain makes it possible for it to pass on the impressions from the frontal brain in a form that is perceptible by the spirit. So the impressions from the frontal brain get passed on to the hindbrain, which passes it on to the spirit, which is connected to the body in the solar plexus. The impressions passed on to the spirit cause it to generate intuitive perceptions, which then take on form in accordance with the nature of the spirit and the intensity of the impression or experience.

The lighter the spirit is the lighter the intuitive perceptions it produces in response to external pressure. Also, the nature of this pressure, together with the nature of the spirit in question, determines the amount of the neutral power the intuitive perception is able to absorb, and hence, the strength of the intuitive perception.

The impressions from the spirit reach the surroundings of man in the reverse way. The impressions are passed from the spirit to the hindbrain through the solar plexus. These impressions, which are usually in picture form, are then transformed by the hindbrain and passed on to the frontal brain. From the frontal brain signals then pass on to the different parts of the body which may be implicated in the kind of response required for the particular impression passed on by the spirit. Such responses may include the formation of words and sentences, writing, or the movement of parts of the body to achieve a specific aim under the direction of the spirit.

This also causes the generation of thoughts in the brain and influences the blood composition of the body. The thoughts generated in response to the spiritual impression then aid in the execution of the will of the spirit on earth. The thoughts generated are also responsible for the arousal of feeling and imagination, which are not the same as the intuitive perception, because they are preceded by it. This intuitive perception is often referred to as the first impression and it never errs.

So with alternating currents of impressions the spirit and the intellect are supposed to cooperate in the development of the surroundings of man. The impressions which he receives from his surroundings with his frontal brain help focus the kind of help that he seeks from above, and when this makes an impression on the spirit, it is able to draw help in the form of an idea or a plan as to how to best take care of the problem. This impression is then passed on to the frontal brain at the completion of its development. The frontal brain is then able to transform this plan or idea into something that is possible on earth using the intellect. This all happens so fast that it is easy not to realize the process involved, and to think that the intellect alone was utilized to arrive at the solution.

The purer the intuitive perception the better his decision-making will be and the longer his works will last, because they will not be as perishable as the works of one whose inspiration is from a lower region. The higher one is able to perceive from the purer his intuitive perception will be, and the more far reaching the effects of his works. This is because the higher one goes the more he is able to oversee, and so the broader his perceptive horizon, and hence the more he is able to take into consideration in his decision-making.

And since the higher spheres are able to receive more light than the lower ones, the one who is able to receive from higher planes is also able to mature faster through his ability to recognize the working of the Laws in a broader sense than would be the case in lower spheres, or on the earthly plane. Also, the higher he is able to perceive from the faster he is able to come up with viable solutions to the obstacles that he comes across. The increased permeability to light allows for a faster development of the forms of the intuitive perception of his spirit, because the lighter species of those higher spheres allow for a higher mobility of the substance of the species, which leads to the faster generation of heat for the generation of forms.

This was supposed to be the natural way that man experienced his environment and developed on earth. He was supposed to mature in the process of striving for purity of thought.

To help man develop in the World of Matter, in Subsequent Creation, Lucifer was sent down from the Divine Realm. He was an Archangel of God.

He was supposed to guide man and help him in the recognition of the Laws of Creation, so that in his decision-making he would bear this in mind and grow stronger in his knowledge of these Laws, through being led to further recognitions in his further experiences.

However, along the way Lucifer deviated from the strict obedience of the Laws of Creation, the Will of God. In the Divine Realm, in the immediate vicinity of the Creator, there is no free will. It is not possible to have free will where the intensity of the Radiation of God is as it is in His immediate vicinity. Only His Will prevails there. But Lucifer, in his activities, had to descend to the level of the World of Matter, while remaining outside the World of Matter, and so was no longer in the immediate vicinity of the Creator.

Yet having his origin in the Divine, he was well equipped to carry out his duties without falling. But he fell. He introduced the principle of temptation, which is devoid of Divine Love. True Love! Not the kind that man imagines when the word "love" is mentioned, but the real love that only knows of the well being of the other and strives to protect him from harm, and to help him rise higher towards the Light and back to his origin in the Spiritual Realm.

To be able to practice this love one has to know the Laws of Creation, because he would have to know what is good for his fellow man in order to advise him rightly or to help him. Most of what man does today in the name of love is not love at all and is often motivated by wrong desires and opinions, which in the end serve to drag the "loved one" further downwards instead of helping him.

So Lucifer introduced the principle of temptation partly because of his impatience with man who had to slowly develop to the point of spiritual maturity. He himself was no longer in the Divine Realm and was at a level where he automatically had free will. He could fall through making the wrong decisions. He became the strongest spirit in the region through this and, as a result, he was able to exert his influence on all the other spirits, which were not as strong and still were developing in the World of Matter.

His principle of temptation, instead of a principle of love, led to man thinking that he could solve his problems using his intellect. He set a trap for man so that those who succumbed to his temptations would be eliminated and only the strong ones will prevail. But he only got more irritated when those who were weak fell for his trap and this made him rage even more.

Naturally with his deviation from the Will of the Light he cast himself out of the Divine Realm because he was no longer homogenous to his origin in the Divine Realm. His expulsion was self-willed and automatic.

But the wrong principle that he instituted had taken on form and lay as a trap for all those developing human spirits who were not strong enough to resist the temptations. The temptation to do that which is not in accordance with the Will of the Light. He lured man to place the intellect above the spirit, instead of the other way around.

Yet man did not have to fall or succumb to the temptations. He stands more firmly in the World of Matter than Lucifer does because he is in the World of Matter, and is able to survey the happenings in his surroundings in the World of Matter, and to experience the working of the Laws of Creation for himself, while Lucifer is outside of the World of Matter and can only send forth his influences but cannot force anyone to do anything.

He can only use the services of those who have succumbed to his wrong principle and who then actively try to enforce the outgrowths of this principle here on earth.

It is man's fault for yielding to these vibrations instead of listening to his inner voice and maintaining a firm connection with the guidance from above. He alone it was who, upon succumbing to the temptations and willfully accepting the fruit of death offered him, transformed the radiations to the dark forms which are in existence in the World of Matter today.

Man perceived the radiations sent out by Lucifer and turned them into the forms of conceit, envy, greed, sordid sensuality, hatred, fear, spiritual ignorance and spiritual arrogance, narrow-mindedness, and all the other forms that make up the host of attributes of the Darkness, which seeks to drag this humanity deep down into the depths of darkness, and towards disintegration.

In order to achieve his aim, Lucifer attacked the bridge that connects man with the spiritual currents coming from above, earthwoman.

Womanhood in all of Creation is the bridge between the sphere occupied by a species and the next higher one. Thus it is through her that the favorable radiations from the Light are to reach the different spheres of Creation. Because of her higher sensitive and intuitive nature, she stands in the position to determine the nature of the radiations that reach the species, because she it is who first senses of the radiations which get passed on to the rest of the species.

The woman is charged with drawing radiations from On High for the benefit of the species, while the man executes the Will of the Light through the coarser activities of the species.

As mentioned previously it is also like that here on earth as it is all the other spheres of Creation. The activities of the woman and that of the man are supposed to complement each other and lead to the perfection of the species. It is only in the Divine Realm that the positive and the negative acting parts exist within each Being in complete harmony. In the rest of Creation these activities are split between the split-species of each species, i.e., the positive and the negative acting part-species, because the white heat of the Radiation of God in the Divine realm does not exist in Creation. Outside of the Divine Realm there is a further increase in the separation within species and between species as they take on form.

Together, while performing their individual activities as willed by the Light, the split-species strive upwards for the perfection of the species.

Also, in the process, members of the split-species are able to contribute to the development of the other complementing part by awakening the abilities which have remained dormant in the process of focusing on one kind of activity, thus making it possible for the individual spirits to wholly develop their abilities, negative and positive, and rise higher in the process.

As the more intuitive part of the split-species, the earth woman is charged with being the Guardian of the Flame of Holy Longing For the Light. She is supposed to keep this flame alight through her constant focus on drawing only those radiations which are pure, therefore, those which are willed by the Light. With her being active in her position man would have no choice but to follow her lead in the execution of the Will of the Light here on earth.

Everyone should be able to see how women are able to affect men here on earth. Men can sense something about the woman, which makes them regard her differently and with a certain kind of respect. He often tries to act rightly in her presence as if he does not want to do anything that will embarrass him in her view.

Today this feeling of respect has given way, in many cases, to more impure instincts, but the root of the issue is nevertheless the same. The woman, by virtue of her higher sensitivity and intuitive perceptiveness, stands a bit higher than man in their basic species. She stands closer to the next higher species in Creation. As a result she is able to influence man as is possible for every higher species with respect to the lower ones. She is able to penetrate to him because of the delicacy of her intuitive perception. The role of the man requires that he work more closely with gross matter and so he is coarser in nature, in accordance with the Laws of Attraction of Homogenous Species and of Gravity.

This leaves the woman to her task of attracting the uplifting Light-radiations to her species. This she is quite capable of doing due to her more delicate nature, which is also indicated in her physical form, as the coarse nature of man is indicated in his rougher physical form.

Being able to perceive the finer radiations from out of the sphere of gross matter she is also able to attract to herself impure or dark radiations, and is the first to sense of these. In this she is not matched by any man. The type of radiations she attracts to herself depends on the nature of her soul. If it is dark then according to the Law of Attraction of Homogenous Species she will attract what is dark.

She will then be able to pass this on to her surroundings in the form of intuitive-forms or thought-forms. These can then act to influence those who may not be strong enough to resist them, and cause them to succumb to such currents as emanate from the base forms, and to produce similar forms themselves, thus adding to the impetus to act in the sense of the volition at the core of such forms.

Through this a people could be dragged down to the depths, especially if this base radiation is maintained, and the forms of it nourished to the point that no more pure radiations are able to make it through to the species.

If the radiations are of a light nature then they can serve to uplift the people by stimulating and encouraging others to think and act in the manner that accords with the nature of the light radiation. Communities and nations can be uplifted in such a manner. It only requires that the woman strive for purity in all that she does. This includes of course what she thinks and says.

It was this knowledge, the knowledge of the role of the woman that Lucifer had and which he made use of in his assault against the Light.

He enticed the woman to deviate from the reception of pure radiations and to taste of the base radiations, which led her to recognize the effects of her charms on man and to exploit this knowledge.

In response to this man sought to please her in order to keep her to himself. He then started to concentrate his efforts on the acquisition of wealth and a life of comfort and ease to please the woman. This then led to the numerous other outgrowths of the failure to receive purely the Will of the Light.

Through this envy, vanity, distrust, avarice, fear, hatred, spiritual indolence, arrogance and a host of other dark attributes were developed and nourished.

In the process of indulging in the base activities that resulted from these dark forms, man fell from his position of being the mediator of Light in the World of Gross Matter. He became a nuisance in the World of Matter because the works he produced were no longer inspired by his love for the Light but by the urgings of the earthbound intellect, which was already in the service of the Darkness. He over-developed the intellect in the process of indulging in such schemes as would allow him to acquire as much power and wealth for himself here on earth as was possible.

The power that courses through Creation was diverted to the wishes of the intellect, which is incapable of recognizing the Will of the Light. So man was cut off from such recognitions, and for many ages rummaged in darkness.

The spirit was stifled in the process because of man's dependence on the intellect. Soon man forgot about the spirit and about the need to listen to the inner voice and obey it. Since his works, that is, his thoughts, his words and his deeds, were directed by the intellect, which is incapable of making contact with the spiritual currents from above, and so could not possibly know the Will of the Light, man darkened the World of Matter with his every act of will!

He effectively made the intellect the master of the spirit through his over-dependence on it. Consequently, everything that he put into Creation was distorted, upside-down, the other way around, and in complete opposition to the Will of God. He became one-sided in his actions and in his thinking, because he no longer had access to other spheres in the World of Matter or in Creation, being so bound to the realm beyond which the intellect cannot rise.

He effectively made himself earthbound, without the ability of a clear vision as to the causes of the happenings which he was able to experience in his earthly surroundings. Since he was not able to perceive beyond the realm of gross matter, he could not see the causes, the starting points of the radiations whose final ramifications alone he could experience, and under which he often suffered.

This caused him to be able to see only part of the whole in every issue, and consequently to sink further into darkness as he made more decisions based on the limited information that he had.

His conceit was boundless, and his ignorance pitiable. He thought himself to be the center of Creation, so that all should bow to his wishes. He could no longer see himself as a part of Creation, as a creature in Creation who has to abide by the strict Laws of Creation or suffer the consequences of disobedience towards them.

His ignorance of the happenings beyond the boundary of the gross material world led him to live frivolously and carelessly. When he had to suffer the consequences of his past actions he either cursed the Name of the Creator or denied His existence. However when he met with favorable conditions, he attributed them to his own efforts alone. He could not see how man is forever in control of his fate. He could not see this because he had not taken the time to understand the working of the Laws of Creation, because his perceptive scope no longer could rise above the gross material limits. He could not understand the Creation of which he remains a part, and he could not understand his Creator or His Will.

Every thought that is generated by man takes on form in the World of Fine Gross Matter, while his intuitive perception, which generates intuitive forms, takes on form in the higher Ethereal World of Matter and also in the Spiritual Realm.

The intuitive perception alone can make contact with the neutral power, which courses through Creation because it is of the spirit. It is the expression of the spirit. The frontal brain or the cerebrum however, generates the thought forms. The thought-forms generated by the frontal brain are not able to make contact with the neutral power in Creation and so are gradations of the more powerful intuitive perception.

The amount of power that is absorbed by the intuitive perception, with which it subsequently is able to attract similar substance in the Ethereal World and form itself, depends on the strength of the intuitive perception. Through the generation of these forms man shapes his surroundings and the entire World of Matter.

As soon as the intuitive perception is formed, as a result of an impression made on the spirit, it takes on form. This form, which is connected to the spirit, is able to make contact, through threads woven by animistic beings, to centers, planes or regions of a homogenous nature. From there reinforcements are drawn and return to the originator of the form through the form.

The form remains attached to its originator by a cord, like a baby in the womb of an expectant mother remains connected to its mother, and receives nourishment from her until it is ready for the separation that comes with earthly birth. In the same way the form remains connected to the originator who continues to nourish this form as long as he continues to maintain the kind of volition that generated the form in the first place.

The form goes through a cycle of development, as does everything else in the World of Matter, and attracts to itself similar forms produced by other people who are inclined towards the same kind of volition. The form can also be attracted to other forms if those forms are stronger, i.e., are able to absorb more power than the one that is attracted.

During the course of its development, all those who contribute to the development of this form of intuitive volition, let us call it one of envy, through the attraction of homogenous species, as they themselves indulge in similar intuitive thoughts, also contribute to the growth of the centers of homogeneity for envy, which exist only because of the volition of men and their inclination towards envy. Thus men form these centers using the neutral power of God in Creation.

The contributors also receive radiations of envy from the centers as reinforcements. This prompts them to continue in the nourishment of those forms of envy to which they remain connected, and which cannot be severed from them without their genuine inward change for only what is good, and without also reaping the consequences of the harm done through the existence of the forms which they put into Creation using the neutral power of God in Creation. This reaping is done in the form of the returning effects of their acts in accordance with the Law of Reciprocal Action.

So at the completion of the cycle of development of this form of envy, the developed form, which would have been modified in the process of attracting other forms or being attracted by them, returns to the originator who remains attached to it.

He is then able to experience a much worse version of the form, which he placed in Creation, if in the meantime he has not changed for the good in order that the returning effects of his previous base volition will not hit with full force, but may be substantially reduced to a symbolic experiencing.

A voluntary move on the part of the originator of the form is needed in order for him to lighten the impact of the returning karma. It is this voluntary effort that will help in satisfying the requirements for his redemption from that particular guilt. Because he is supposed to learn of the nature of his guilt, and make a genuine change for what is good and noble when the impact of the effects of the Law of Returns hits him, and the returning effects must come without fail in any case.

He is given the opportunity to reflect on the reason for the experiencing of the returning effects, and resolve not to repeat the act which led to the activation of such effects.

In this he will find Divine Love as well as Divine Justice, because in the carrying out of Divine Justice he is also given the opportunity to see how the Laws of Creation work and to adjust himself to them, so that his activities, visible or not visible, can be such that bring blessings and not suffering to his surroundings and to himself.

All those who contributed to the development of the form of envy will also receive their fair share of the returning effects of this form, depending on their contributions and the nature of their souls at the time that the effects of the karma have to hit them.

The originator's redemption from his guilt is also dependent on whether or not he harmed someone else through the form that he placed in Creation. If so then he becomes attached to that person by a thread, and must remain attached to him until that person is no longer under the influence of the form, or other forms which may have arisen through such an influence from the original envy form. Naturally the conditions of the release from the forms, which he places in Creation, also apply to that person who is so influenced. So that person will also have to go through his own period of recognition of the baseness of this guilt, and atone for it through a necessary reciprocal action and a genuine change towards what is good. Only then can his tie to that person be severed.

This may take a very long time, and if this does not happen while he is here on earth, then the originator of the envy form will have to follow his victim to the level which he has to go to in the beyond after his departure from earth following physical death.

He must remain bound to him until the necessary conditions are met, and not a moment sooner. Only then can he continue with his own ascent if there are no other souls which may have also been affected by this particular form.

So through his inner activity man shapes the World of Matter. The effects of the forms of his intuitive volition are able to reach all parts of the World of Matter, and even right up to the Spiritual Realm, and so he holds the key to blessings or destruction in his hands and only has to adjust his attitude one way or the other in order to shape the world in a dark or luminous way.

The process as explained above also takes place when the form of a man's volition is a benevolent one. It immediately attaches to those centers which are homogenous to it, and contributes to the growth of such centers through the activities of the man who remains connected to the form and receives reinforcements through it.

He is uplifted by the returning effects of the reciprocal action and is able to help many others by strengthening their resolve to do only what is good. In this way the World of Matter is brightened and made more luminous because light is able to penetrate the World of Matter through such centers as are formed in the process. The individual human spirits are able to mature and return to their origin because they would not be tied down to the World of Matter as would those who, because of their ties to base centers, are dragged down towards the Darkness, in accordance with the Law of Attraction of Homogenous Species, the Law of Gravity and the Law of Reciprocal Action.

The thought-forms, which are produced by the intellect, act in a similar way, only with reduced power. They are dependent on their originators and cannot absorb from the neutral power in Creation.

They however cause a lot of damage through the concentrated power of many people of a homogenous nature. This concentrated power is able to influence the growth of the centers to which they are connected to, and from these centers threads reach down into the realm or darkness. If the thoughts are light in nature then they can penetrate into the higher regions of the World of Matter by way of light threads.

These thoughts are generated by the frontal brain and form the intellect, and so they affect the way that man is able to form his environment here on earth. They also serve as channels through which the returning effects of the volition of men reach them. So the environment of man is ugly and full of suffering if he has indulged in mainly base thoughts and has incurred corresponding karma. This is different from where he has accepted in advance such conditions, which may be necessary for his preparation for a spiritual mission here on earth. In such a case the experiencing of such conditions might arm him for something that he may have to deal with in the course of his mission. But it will still be in line with the Laws of Creation because it will come to him in accordance with his volition.

His intuitive and thought volition affect his speech and his visible deeds. This means that all of man's actions are wrong if his volition is wrong. But man can only know what is right, and so channel his power of volition towards what is good, when he has recognized the working of the Laws of Creation and adjusted himself to them.

This he has failed to do because he has since cut himself off from the spiritual currents from above, which alone can guide him to such recognitions!

He has since placed his intellect, the tool, over his spirit through over-cultivation of the intellect. And in the process he has over-developed his frontal brain, which produces the intellect, because of the exertion he had to put it through in the process of over-cultivating his intellect.

The resultant effect and the reciprocal action of this deed is that the bridge between his frontal brain and his spirit, the hindbrain or the cerebellum, which is also called the small brain, has become stunted over millennia.

He is no longer able to receive clearly if at all from his spirit. Neither is he able to transmit impressions to it for the formation of pure intuitive perceptions, which alone can make contact with the neutral power in Creation and draw strength from those spheres which lie above the Sphere of Gross Matter.

The cutting off of radiations from and to the spirit has caused the spirit to remain feeble due to lack of exertion or exercise. Just like would happen to any limb of the physical body which is not adequately exercised.

As a result of this condition of his man has relied only on his intellect for the assessment of the impressions that come his way in the course of his experiences. Being blinded from the actual causes of events he cannot interpret accurately the happenings in his surroundings. He cannot rightly see the relationship between his attitude and the way things turn out for him and so he relies even more on the intellect in a bid to out-think his fellow man in the race of survival on earth.

In his dark world he has attached the wrong conceptions to words, events, and circumstances, the right interpretations of which alone can open his eyes to the working of the Laws in Creation.

Without the knowledge of why he exists on earth, man has proceeded to aspire for those things which he thinks will bring him earthly influence. His interpretation of success has also suffered due to his spiritual ignorance as he seeks after worldly acclaim at the expense of his soul.

In the process of attaining these worldly goals he further exaggerates the cultivation of his intellect, which then results in the further development of his frontal brain. His further enlarged brain provides the basis for more of those instincts which have only to do with the physical body, such as the sexual instinct and the instinct of motherhood.

As man kept himself busy with thoughts of sordid sensuality, greed, envy, love of ease and comfort, and also the unnatural and hindering emphasis on following rigid traditions and dogmas, he lost all connections to the Light and to paths leading to his salvation and liberation from the ties which he continually made with base forms.

He lost the clear view to the meaning of life. All that was left in him was the burning urge to make something of himself. But being blinded by his gross vanity, he only reached for those goals which flattered his intellect and which prompted him to think even more one-sidedly with his frontal brain.

Whenever he sensed that things were after all not quite right with the way that he lived his life, fear and doubt rose from his intellect, and together with lack of confidence and spiritual ignorance, they forced him to ignore his inner voice.

"Use it or lose it" is a Law in nature and also applies in the case of man with regards to his intuitive perception. Because he did not listen to it and obey its urgings, it became more and more difficult for him to hear it. His intuitive perception, or inner voice, became greatly drowned out by the numerous thoughts from his frontal brain, which, following the attraction of similar thoughts became so strong that they controlled his every action. Thus man became a slave to his intellect.

Man's conceit and his need to feel important and appear so in the view of his fellow men led him to become more competitive with his neighbours and he became more distrustful, fearing that someone else would take that place which he lusts after.

He saw everyone through the lens of his darkened soul, and suspected him of the same things that he bore within himself, often to a far greater extent. He blamed everyone else for his shortcomings without ever looking within himself to find the faults which he constantly criticized others for. His goals became directed solely towards the gross material since that is the natural direction of the activity of the earthbound intellect.

So when he heard of anything about the Light he brushed it aside because it did not coincide with his idea of reality. He could not fathom the likes of that which is entailed in Light-activity. He did not know why he exists in the World of Matter. Being cut off from everything else, or better said, having cut himself off from the higher spheres, he only saw the activities willed and understood by the intellect as worth dealing with. As worth his time!

His vanity was such that he expected that the Creator should bless him with all the fineries of life just in the manner that he pictured it to himself, in the manner that pleased him, and then maybe he would indulge Him and do what His messengers say! He wanted to know what he would get out of doing the Will of the Light before embarking on it. He no longer had any way of knowing that it was his urge to develop to self-consciousness that automatically expelled him from the Spiritual Realm, the Paradise of the human spirits developing on earth, into the World of Matter for the purpose of fulfilling this urge.

Now he demands that he be rewarded with good fortune for his complete failure! For his deep-seated ignorance! He demands that the Creator bend his strict Laws of Creation so that he could be accommodated, with all his base desires and wishes!

He thought himself great when he discovered the working of the Laws of Creation in the process of doing his earthly work. He was able to recognize the physical manifestations of the Law of Cycles, the Law of Gravity, the Law of Attraction of Homogenous Species, but rather than also apply these Laws to himself and abide by them, he gave his "discoveries" names and described them in complex ways just so that he would appear great in the eyes of men. With his inventions, which are mere discoveries of what already exist in Creation, he sought to make himself wealthy and to elevate himself in the eyes of men.

In his attempt to elevate himself, through using high-sounding language to describe his work and his findings, man made the different fields of activity on earth unintelligible to one another. The simple truths, which they all discovered in their activities, for instance, in the fields of science and so forth, were enveloped in complex language and were not correlated for the understanding of the greater mankind, and for application to the spiritual development of man. They were not integrated because man wanted to preserve his position in society and on earth. He did not realize that his discoveries were just the final and coarsest manifestations of the working of the Laws of Creation, which eternally work throughout Creation, and indeed, support the entire Creation.

His self-centeredness prevented him from recognizing the truth in the messages brought by prophets and Called ones who did not hail from his part of the world. If he was really sent from the Creator he must then come from his own community or from within his own religion, since his was the absolute right one! Such is the way man thought and still thinks today. He has only fallen deeper since the time when the prophets and Called ones came to try and direct man back to the simple way of the Light.

At that time when they came, they individually incarnated amongst those people to whom they were to bring help. Naturally they also had to live amongst them and participate in their traditional activities until they received the Call to spread the Word of God to men. Each of them had been prepared to carry out his task, which he had vowed to fulfill before his incarnation on earth.

Fulfillment however could only come through the recognition, by the called one or prophet, of the Darkness and the way that it had held down those to whom he was to teach about their God and His Creation. At the right time he awakened to his Call and he set out to fulfill.

His utterances and his mode of teaching had to be adapted to the nature of the people he was trying to help. Since men on earth are naturally diverse in their traditions and customs, which in reality should represent the different forms in which the Laws of Creation manifest in the different parts of the world, this meant that the modes of spreading light had to differ from place to place, and had to agree with the conditions prevailing on the ground with the people to be taught.

This alone is the reason for the apparent differences in the teachings of those who have been sent in the past to help mankind escape from the Darkness. Among these were the Forerunners of the Light, Krishna, Zoroaster, Lao-Tse, Buddha, and Mohammed. The messages they brought were one and the same, but they had to take into consideration the maturity and the nature of the people to whom they were delivered.

But in his narrow-mindedness and morbid conceit man rejected all that he did not already think to be true and all that required that he exert himself a little bit.

Those who chose to accept the teachings of the prophets and called ones inadvertently added mistakes to their interpretations due to their already existing narrow-mindedness and the one-sided development of their brains, at the time when the messengers came.

The messages became dilute and more incoherent with time, following more translations, and as they were passed on from one person to another. Added to this is the fact that most of these messengers did not write anything down, and so those who later heard their teachings only heard the already distorted versions, which could no longer stand for the truth. There was no way to preserve the messages in the sense in which they were given by the personalities who brought them.

It is not possible for two people to hear, see or experience an event in exactly the same way, and so the differences inherent in the way that each person perceives the experience makes itself felt also in the way that he transmits this experience to others. It can never be transmitted in exactly the same way as another person who experienced the same event at the same time.

This is because no two individuals are identical, or have traveled identical paths in the weaving of the threads to which they are connected at any given time, and which affects the way they view their surroundings. There will always be differences in this and so their transmissions must also be affected by these differences. So distortions were able to creep into the wise teachings of the past.

This further alienated men who tried to understand them but could not quite bring certain aspects of the distorted teachings to agree with their intuitive perceptions of the truth, i.e., what they really felt inside of themselves as sensible and logical.

So, not long after the deaths of these Truth-Bringers, religions and cults were formed around what often well-meaning adherents could remember of the actual teachings of the messengers. In many cases these cults and organizations were formed around the person of the Truth-Bringer himself, diverting all attention to this person instead of his actual message.

Naturally, due to man's narrow-mindedness and conceit, which still existed because he had not taken the trouble to change inwardly by adjusting himself to the Will of the Light, the different groups which formed after the deaths of the Truth-Bringers became polarized and, in many cases, further encouraged the narrow-mindedness of men.

Man was definitely heading for the abyss because the reciprocal action which was due to hit him, as a result of the neglect of his duties as a human spirit, was certain to result in him falling even deeper into the realm of darkness, because he would not be able to respond to it in the right manner. Being as ignorant of his mission on earth as he was, man was not in a position to consciously balance his past wrong deeds with good ones. He could only do this with knowledge of the working of the Laws of Creation.

As an Emergency Act of Love, the Creator severed a part of Himself, the Love part of Himself, and incarnated It on earth, in flesh and blood, by a process of radiation, so that He may bring help to those who still yearned for it, and help them turn around from the impending doom in time, before the inevitable destruction of all that is dark together with all those who remain attached to it, during the period of the Final Judgement which has already begun.

So Jesus Christ, the Son of God, was incarnated on earth a man among men, but with a core of Divinity, Which is much higher than the spiritual core of the human spirits, since He descended from God Himself for the sole purpose of bringing Light to those who still wished for it, and who were being threatened by the Darkness which had encircled the World of Gross Matter and held it in its grip.

Only such power could cleave through the thickness of the Darkness, which encased the soul of man, in order to penetrate to him and lead him out from the grasp of the dark tentacles.

He came to show the way to the Light to those who still yearned for it for He is the personification of Divine Love and would not let those who deserve help to suffer disintegration with those that are evil. Man was then to follow this path, which was shown to him by the Son of God, to his salvation. He was not relieved of the responsibility of receiving the effects of all that he put into Creation through the expression of his volition, because this will be a violation of the Will of God expressed in the Law of Reciprocal Action.

It was impossible for the Son of God to do that! For He came to uphold and fulfill the Law, not to overthrow it! He came to show man the way to live in simplicity and all naturalness so that he may, in the process, recognize the working of the Laws of Creation, which alone can help him make the right decisions which would not fetter him but liberate him. He came from the Law and so knew the Law, and with this knowledge he tried to guide mankind.

All those who are able to live in strict accordance with the Teachings of Christ, Who came from the Divine Unsubstantiate Itself (God) for the sole purpose of teaching and living this Message, no matter in which part of the world they might hail from, will be redeemed from their sins, because they would make the best use of the moment and experience consciously the working of the Laws of Creation as the closing cycles of their past deeds bring to them the fruits of their past labor, in accordance with the Law of Reciprocal Action.

But this did not sit well with those who at the time thought that they had the right knowledge. The worst of them came from the temples and the learned circles. They felt threatened by the Word of Truth, which was brought by the Son of God, because it exposed the emptiness, rigidity and lack of life of their doctrines and practices, with which they exerted influence over their servile flock.

They saw that they would be exposed for the ignorant men that they were and so they attacked the Bringer of Truth with all kinds of accusations, just like was done with the other messengers sent by the Light before Jesus Christ. They sought to besmirch His reputation in the face of the public so that He would have no credibility, instead of admitting that what He had to say bore the Truth. They could not admit that, not while at the same time they were spreading false and rigid doctrines in the thinking that their lack of real knowledge of the Will of God will remain hidden.

They clearly were not expecting Jesus Christ the Son of God because they had the wrong perceptions of what the Truth really is. With the right perception, however, they would have gladly welcomed Him and protected Him as One Who was much higher than they were, and Who alone could lift them out of their woeful ignorance and guide them onto the path to the Light with His Teachings and His way of living.

But they were high and mighty and were afraid of a hard fall! They were full of fear, envy, conceit, lack of confidence, lack of spiritual knowledge, and suffered from indolence of the spirit. For the one-sided cultivation of the intellect and its adverse effects affected all of mankind, and it was the accumulation of the base forms in the nether regions of this World of Matter, as a result of the enslavement of man to the intellect, which led to the evil acts of those who allowed themselves to be used by the Darkness to attack the Bringer of Truth, Who, in the person of Jesus Christ, was a representative of the Light here on earth.

So those who felt themselves threatened the most by Him plotted against Him and finally found a way to eliminate Him. He however maintained His stance as He had to, because He knew Who He was and exactly why He was being attacked. It was His Origin, with God Himself, that made it possible for Him to rise above the gross material happening of the time at Golgotha, and, while experiencing the events in full consciousness, pray to God for the forgiveness of those who were killing Him, because He knew they did not realize the magnitude of their dastardly crime.

He knew that He had to maintain His stance until the end because anything else would have put in doubt the validity of all that He had said. Men would have started to say that in the face of death He no longer claimed to be the Son of God! The knowledge of His Origin and the seriousness of His Mission, which was to bring salvation to mankind in His Word, i.e., through His teachings, gave Him the strength to endure all that was done to Him.

His Great Sacrifice was to bring mankind help in a world that was already under the rule of the Darkness, and with the knowledge that He might even have to suffer death at the hands of the servants of this Darkness in the process of carrying out His actual Mission.

His mission was not to come down to earth to die for man so that his guilt, which he incurred all by himself, would be automatically taken away from him while he persists in ignorance and sin. Nothing of that sort is possible with God, Who is Perfection Itself, and so His Laws must also be perfect and do not need to be altered, nor will they ever need to be! They will eternally remain the same!

It is only the conceit of man that allows for such a conception to arise in his imagination! He sees himself as one who is so needed by his Creator that He would trouble Himself so much as to change His own perfect

Laws just to please him.

He does not want to believe that it was actually the worst of crimes that the human spirit could commit against his God, because it barred him from the connection with the Divine which the Son of God was able to establish by His presence here on earth, and through which undimmed Power could flow to man for his own salvation as he recognized the Laws of God that rest in Creation, in the clarity of the Truth, Which only a Part of God Himself was able to bring.

To believe that the crucifixion of Jesus Christ, the Son of God, a Part of God incarnated in flesh and blood so that He could lead mankind out of danger, through His Teachings and by His examples, was an outright murder, would mean for man that he would have to exert himself spiritually as was demanded by Jesus Christ Himself in order to attain salvation. It would mean that he would have to do the work of disentangling himself from the self-willed fetters that hold him down, by adhering strictly to the Teachings brought by the Son of God, the actual reason He came down to this dense and coarse part of Creation.

His death on the cross was a separate act which stands on its own and testifies to the degree to which man had become enslaved to his base desires before the coming of the Son of God. His actual Mission lay in His bringing of enlightenment to mankind and He fulfilled in this Mission to the end.

It was then left for mankind to take up the Cross, that is to take up the Truth and enforce It. Because the Cross of Equal Arms is a sign of the Living Truth Which Jesus Christ bore within Him and Which could be seen radiating behind Him by one so blessed. Man was to follow in His footsteps and enforce the Truth, which He brought in His Teachings and His Person.

Mankind failed to realize the importance of the Mission of the Son of God and so did not take up the Cross.

In addition to the fact that He was murdered, thus He and the Truth that He brought were rejected, mankind never truly recognized the value of the Teachings, and so they never lived in strict accordance with them. The reciprocal action of this is the deeper plunging of the entire mankind into the Realm of Darkness following His death. It is because of this further failure on the part of man that the world is darker than ever before today.

Those who try to understand the mission of Christ are misled by the teaching that He came just to die so that mankind could be rid of the sins they committed. To say that it was necessary to kill Him for the Work of salvation to be completed is to call the Creator imperfect and is to diminish the radiance of the great sacrifice of Love made by the Son of God in His coming to this dark world to help mankind despite His knowledge of the potential dangers.

When this is done, that is, when the crucifixion is presented as being necessary, then the actual Teachings of Christ are forced to the background, because all one would have to do is to believe that the sacrifice of the Son of God has taken away his sins. There will be no motivation left in the human spirit to strive for the recognition of the Laws of Creation through the purification of his soul, which can only happen when he pays attention to the lessons of the moment, brought to him in the completion of the cycles of his past deeds.

To maintain this belief is tantamount to driving more nails into the hands of Jesus Christ, because you will be taking away from His actual Message. You will be diverting people, through your volition, from the recognition of the actual Mission of Christ. Which is what those who hung him to die on the cross hoped to do by their act. Therefore, you will be preventing the possibility of the fulfillment of the Laws of Creation, which obedience to the actual Teachings of the Son of God helps one achieve. You would be declaring warfare against the Holy Spirit through Whose Radiation the entire Creation came about, including all the Laws therein.

You will be affirming for yourself certain spiritual death because you will remain chained to the World of Matter and to all those who succumb to your false teachings, until the disintegration of matter occurs, which will bring about the destruction of all that have not been able to rise to the Spiritual Realm by that time in a quite natural process.

Today the evidence of the inability for man to understand the Will of God is quite clear. The one-sided development of the intellect has resulted in his one-sided view of himself and everything else that has developed in Creation. He has not been able to read the Language of God through the expression of His Will in the Laws that bring about the fulfillment of every single happening, no matter how small it might seem to this conceited mankind.

Following the death of Christ on the cross He returned to His origin Which is with God and united with Him, while remaining personal as the King of the Divine Realm. This was the only course open to Him because He came from God as a Part of Him.

Mankind however did not strive to benefit from the sacrifice of Love which was the Mission of the coming of the Son of God into a hostile environment so that He could show man how to disentangle himself from his self-willed bondage in the World of Matter. They repaid this Love with enmity and gross disregard. They dragged it down to the level that their lowly intellect could turn it into something which only served their base desires.

So mankind fell even further into the realm of darkness. They entangled themselves even more with more base forms which have kept them in despair and in a state of suffering and gross misunderstanding since. They further distorted all concepts since they could not see clearly through their darkened souls. In this state they have sown more dark seeds since there is no pause in the activity of the Divine Laws in Creation, which demand constant movement from all creatures in Creation; whether upwards or downwards is up to the particular creature. As it wills, so will it be rewarded!

Therefore, man, wake up now to the truth as it really is and not as you will like it to be! Today we stand in the promised Judgement, brought about through the activities of the Son of Man, Who was promised to mankind by the Son of God Jesus Christ before His death. This period was also talked about by some of the other messengers whose mission was to prepare man for this time. This is the time of the mandatory separation of the old from the new, the diseased from the healthy and strong, through a process of purification before the disintegration of all matter.

In this period of the Judgement, which is intensifying in its activities, all that has remained slumbering in the soul of man will be awakened and brought to Judgement. This means that all that man has put into Creation and everything that he still has attached to him, be it good or bad, shall become more animated and be forced to develop to fruition, like hothouse plants, delivering to its originator the developed fruit. This way all will be judged accurately and minutely in strict accordance with the Will of the Light, and in accordance with the volition of the individual human spirits concerned.

The increased Light-pressure now being witnessed here on earth quickens the development process for both good and evil forms. See to it, man, that you strive for what is good and noble.

Strive for the recognition of the Laws of Creation and abide by them in all that you do so that you may rise instead of fall deeper at the completion of the cycles of your past deeds.

REINCARNATION

Man was supposed to develop to spiritual maturity in the World of Matter, while at the same time passing on the rays of Light, which he is able to absorb in the course of his activities, to his environment for its ennoblement and maintenance.

The earth was supposed to be the turning point of this cycle of development which begun in the Spiritual Realm with the awakening of the urge to develop to self-consciousness, and which must end in the Spiritual Realm, either yielding matured Spiritual Beings or spiritual seed-germs, which follows an arduous and painful period of separation of spirit from matter, during which the human spirits concerned had to undergo the torment of spiritual death, whereby they lost all their developed spiritual personality and reverted to primordial seed.

Like every other cycle in the World of Matter, the development of man had to occur in stages. Through his experiences in the World of Matter he was supposed to develop to the point where he could consciously recognize the activity of the Will of the Creator and thereby recognize the Creator. For man can never actually see the Creator nor even be in His vicinity. The separation between the species is too great. Man is of the spirit, which issued from the radiation of the Holy Spirit, While the Creator is above all that exists, including the Divine Realm, to which man can never attain in his most perfect form!

The recognition of the Laws of Creation is the only way that the creatures of Creation can appreciate the Magnitude of their God, because these Laws express His Will in Creation. God presents Himself to His Creation in His Will, which, as immutable and adamantine Laws, runs through everything that exists, and drives all happenings. To know the Will of God then is to know the Laws of Creation. This can only be done by observing the working of these Laws in Creation and abiding by them in our activities. There is no other way open to man for this! He must personally experience this and make it a part of himself, a part of his consciousness!

In order for the other creatures in Creation to survive and remain active in their respective fields, they have to abide by these Laws, which govern everything. Man can notice this when he looks around his own gross material surroundings, in what we know as nature, which is actually the result of the activity of a certain species of the animistic beings. Their works and their development will be furthered because they would be able to receive the help for this through the natural and logical working of these Laws. However these same Laws will crush anything that proves to be unable to vibrate in their rhythm. It will be discarded as useless and as a hindrance in Creation.

Man is no different in this, because he is a creature in Creation, a concept that he has not yet understood, or has refused to accept due to his immense vanity.

To develop, man had to descend down to the World of Matter, where he had the only chance of developing together with the Sphere of Matter, which itself needed to be animated and ennobled in order to bring it closer to the more luminous regions above, so that it may not be lost and may act as the field of activity of the animistic beings, and also of those creatures which still could not attain consciousness at the lowest part of the Spiritual Realm.

And coming from this lowest part of the Spiritual Realm where it remained unconscious, the spirit-germ descended into the World of Matter to gradually develop with this world into a fully conscious form. The only way that he could do this was by observing the process of development of the world around him and the experiences within him, and by recognizing the working of the Laws of Creation in the process.

As the highest species in the World of Matter, man was given the ability to cooperate in the development of the World of Matter, because implanted in him by the Creator, as a quality of his spirit, is the striving for self-consciousness, which, as a motivating factor, causes him to will and to express his volition. If in the process of expressing his volition he wills what is good, he will receive what is good in the reciprocal effect of his volition, and this will also affect his surroundings in a beneficial way.

As he gets attracted upwards in this effort of willing what is good, the World of Matter will simultaneously be uplifted. To do this he will have to observe his surroundings and, through his experiencing, make those decisions which are in line with the Will of the Light. As I have explained already, the Will of the Light is expressed in the Laws of Creation, which man is able to observe from his surroundings and also from the effects of the decisions he makes.

Like everything else that has to develop here in the World of Matter, man's ability to recognize had to correspond to his maturity at any given time. The more mature he became the more he was able to recognize. This was supposed to continue in an upward direction which would have resulted in the maturity of the human spirit who is able to return to the Spiritual Realm, and who also has become thoroughly familiar with the Laws in the World of Matter, having observed and abided by their working in the different spheres of matter, where he had to live through the different consequences of the decisions he made during his wanderings.

To do this he was given free will. He could make his own decisions, which immediately connected him with the sphere of the species that will allow him to experience that which he wished for in the process of making his decision.

He is free to make the decision but he is subject to the consequences of the decision. He is handed the developed fruits of the seeds planted with his every decision, when their cycles of development have been completed. This way he is able to recognize the simple working of the Laws of Creation.

His first incarnation on earth was a result of such a decision-making process. His wish to taste of the different vibrations, which emanated from the gross material sphere to which the earth belongs, connected him to those threads that attracted him downwards and led him to incarnate on earth. In the process of descending downwards to earth he made several of such decisions through the expression of his volition. His life on earth was then the consequence of those decisions. He received the fruits of his works, the fruits of the expression of his will.

Here on earth he then had the opportunity to enjoy more fully that which he could only slightly taste of on his way down to earth in the form of vibrations. He also had the opportunity to discriminate between what was good and what was bad through the experiencing of the results of his decisions. And as an added Grace from the Almighty, he was able to sever his ties to those forms which he had attracted to himself as he made his decisions, and which he no longer wanted to nourish through his thoughts and deeds.

Being still connected to all the spheres that he had to traverse on his way down to earth, while in the physical body of the earth, he had the advantage on earth of being able to sever those ties which linked him with base forms in the different planes of the World of Matter which corresponded in species with the cloaks he wore inside his physical body. Thus the earth is a unique place in the sense that one is able to receive radiations from all those spheres that he remains connected to through his decisions, and through the cloaks that he had to put on as he passed through those planes on his way to earth.

Here on earth he is able also to coexist with others who may differ from him spiritually, and who may also assist in his experiencing by providing him with the opportunity to see the lighter side of things. This is opposed to the conditions in the Ethereal World, where one is strictly bound to those spheres which correspond to the density of the densest cloak that a human spirit wears around it as part of its soul, and where coexistence with another of a different spiritual maturity is not possible. There the effects of the working of he Laws are more intensely and sharply felt by the human spirit.

Due to its density, the physical body worn by man on earth provides him with some level of insulation from the radiations from the Ethereal World so they do not impact him as strongly as they would in those spheres from which they emanate. This affords him the chance to gradually sever ties to base forms, which may weigh him down after he has left the physical body following physical death. He is also able to live in close proximity to others of different views and insights and from whom he could learn as he matures.

Through the process of reciprocal action and by recognizing the wrong in his decisions, a man is given the opportunity on earth to counter his past wrong deeds with good ones. So not only is he able to contribute to the development of those spheres to which he remains connected through fine threads, because of the cloaks that he wears beneath his physical body, but he is also able to bring enlightenment to his fellow men who might not have realized something which his experiences might have led him to acquire.

Through this mutual exchange of fruits, in their intuitive perceptions, thoughts and actions, men are able to ennoble their surroundings as they develop to spiritual maturity themselves.

Since every intuitive and thought volition takes on form in the spheres beyond earth, and since these forms remain attached to the individuals responsible for them, as has been explained in previous chapters, the human spirit developing on earth is able to form his surroundings in the world beyond the earth-plane, which is further divided into numerous planes, in accordance with the nature of his volition, while he is on earth. So he forms for himself that environment which according to his volition he aspires towards. These surroundings are luminous if his volition is good, and they are dark and gloomy if his volition is dark and base, and correspondingly they react back upon his life here on earth when their fruits are mature enough.

At the moment when he no longer is able to maintain the necessary union with his physical body, i.e., when the radiations of his soul are no longer able to maintain a connection with those of his physical body, due to physical ailment, old age, or maltreatment of this body, then his soul will separate from this body and be attracted to that region beyond the earth-plane which is densest amongst all the ones to which he may be connected to.

He will always descend first to that place which is densest because the density of the form, which as a species of this plane is homogenous to it, will not allow him to ascend any higher. This is strictly in accordance with the Law of Gravity, which man is already able to experience here on earth.

He will have to live through that particular guilt-form to the end before he is able to ascend higher. This is however a good thing for him because he gets the opportunity to sever his ties to that form and be free of it for his ascent. This can only happen when he has genuinely changed his attitude towards that particular guilt form, and has expressed his need for help from above.

It may take decades or even centuries for him to arrive at this recognition. This is because there, one is only able to interact with other souls which are just like his, being of a homogenous nature to his, which is the criteria for being allowed to exist together in that plane where the effects of the Law of Attraction of Homogenous Species are more acutely felt by the departed soul, which no longer has the dense physical body to shield it.

Everything in its surroundings will be the result of the kind of activity that predominates in that sphere. If it is a sphere where those descend whose volition was mainly that of envy while they were on earth, then an environment that is shaped and nourished by envy will surround the soul. There he will be able to exercise this base volition to his fill without being able to harm anyone, because those on the receiving end of such treatments will also be of the same kind as he and will be fully deserving of such treatments. Only through fully experiencing this environment, which they helped create, can they grow to become disgusted by their activities and yearn for a change and an opportunity to leave that environment.

The willingness of one in such a plane to draw another's attention to the wrong in his activities, which is an expression of love, might for instance eventually develop into a prayer and afford him the opportunity to receive help from above that particular environment, through the Law of Reciprocal Action and the Law of Attraction of Homogenous Species.

But while he is in that sphere, his perceptive scope is even more narrowed than it was when he had access to other points of view here on earth. His conceit, therefore, is greatly increased and so he could live in that condition for years without knowing any better.

He has to go through this process for every single form which he has placed in Creation through the expression of his volition, and which he takes over with him after death. During this process he might develop the urge to ascend, and this might take on the form of his return to earth to redeem the karma that might have become ripe for harvest on earth. In accordance with the Law of Cycles, every form that is placed in Creation returns back to its point of origin, i.e., to its originator and to the sphere of origin. So those actions that originated on earth would have to be redeemed by their originators on earth when they have matured and borne fruit.

The ones which originated in the finer spheres of matter and which form the environment of their originators in those spheres, forming their paths upwards or downwards in the Ethereal World, must be redeemed by their originators after they have left their physical bodies following physical death.

The soul, which has been able to rise from the dark planes to which it had to sink due to its weight, can then be drawn closer to the process of reincarnation onto earth. However, the conditions that he will be drawn to will be those that correspond to the natures of the forms which he has still to sever from himself, and which, in developing to ripeness, draw him in for a closer connection with, and a closer experiencing of what he had formerly willed.

Necessary for this is a pregnant woman, or one in whom procreation has just taken place, who is homogenous in nature to the soul which is returning to earth to continue its development. Someone else who is often in the vicinity of the pregnant woman might also be the determining factor, through his inner nature, in deciding the kind of soul that is attracted. For this reason women are advised to be careful whom they allow around them when they are pregnant. It is often observed that some couples attract to themselves a child who is different in nature from both parents, either in a good way or in a bad way. It is because of the above explanation.

At about the middle of pregnancy the incoming soul is able to take full control of the body in the womb, through the strengthened radiations between the latter and the former. At this point the developing body would have fulfilled all the requirements for incarnation of the particular soul in question. It is also because of this that its mother feels the first movements of the growing baby's body around this time, in the middle of pregnancy.

The Law of Attraction of Homogenous Species plays a key role in the attraction of the soul to the pregnant woman. The Law of Reciprocal Action also plays a role where the attracting radiations emanate from threads which were knotted strongly in a previous lifetime between the souls involved, and which receive the opportunity for fulfillment with the incarnation of the incoming soul.

It is also because of the homogeneity that often exists between the incoming soul and its future parents that accounts for the apparent inherited abilities or weaknesses, which leads both parents and offspring to similar directions with respect to their chosen professions or habits, or which causes them to succumb to the same faults like drunkenness and gambling.

But the inheritance of such abilities and tendencies are only apparent and are actually never so. There can never be any spiritual inheritance, but only an attraction between already formed souls of a similar nature. Only those things which concern the physical body can be inherited, such as temperament and susceptibility to certain diseases. But the incoming soul is always attracted to those parents that will provide it with the environment that will allow it to develop through experiencing the fruits of his past deeds.

The soul is attracted to those conditions which correspond to the kind of volition that predominates within it. By living in this condition he is presented with those treatments which vibrate with his volition, that is, those treatments which he meted out to others, in his thoughts or his actions, and which produced threads that have woven for him the environment to which he is attracted at the time of his re-incarnation onto earth. Even his name is no accident and always corresponds with the nature of the soul, and what it has woven for itself for the lifetime that it is about to begin with his incarnation into earth.

Here it does not matter how arbitrary the name-picking process by its earthly parents appears, the radiations which shape the surroundings into which the soul incarnates always play a part in such a way that there can be no mistake or arbitrariness as to the name that is finally given to it when it comes into the gross material world of the earth as a child. The surname or last name, which is usually also borne by the parents, also has to agree with the nature of the soul if he is to be attracted to that particular family. In this there is no issue of a mistake or arbitrariness! Man is exactly what his name says! The soul gets exactly what it deserves for the purpose of carrying out its mission in its new life on earth!

He is then in the best position to experience first hand the fruits of his volition, and if it is dark, this may lay the foundation for the urge to change his nature and turn to what is good. He always receives exactly what he has woven for himself through the expression of his volition, even if the fruits of the seeds he sows do not materialize until another lifetime.

This should settle the issue for those people who, in amazement, watch or hear of someone whom they were certain carried out many heinous acts, and who, despite his deeds, lives out the rest of his earth life in relative bliss and apparent peace. No one escapes the working of the Laws of Creation! It is only ignorance of the order of Creation, which is maintained by these Laws, that allows for such thoughts to trouble a person so! There is no crime committed against these Laws that will not have to return to its perpetrator sooner or later in the form of a reciprocal action, in the present lifetime or in the a following one! It all depends on when the fruits of the seeds sown by the human spirit have ripened so that they can be presented to him for reaping. And reap them he must, because there is no postponement of the working of the Laws of Creation!

It only appears as though one gets away with a crime because, firstly, man has become so narrow-minded that he has bound himself to the gross material sphere through his base volition, and consequently, he has narrowed his perceptive scope. Also, man's conceit allows him to expect and demand things of the Light, because, in his view, things should work out in a certain way which is understandable to his earthbound and limited intellect, which he has crowned master over his spirit.

He does not know that the greater part of the experiencing of man occurs in the Ethereal, and that his life on earth is but a short span compared to the total length of time he has to spend in the World of Matter. The life on earth is a short but extremely important span in the time of man's development. Here he has the opportunity to experience

94

the radiations from all the different parts of the World of Matter, while in the beyond he is restricted to only that part to which he belongs with respect to the nature of his outermost and densest cloak.

His ability to experience the radiations from the various spheres in the World of Matter to which he may be connected gives man the opportunity to sever his ties to the base forms that he may be connected to in those spheres, so that when he leaves the earth-plane he will not have to be held down by such forms for however long it might take him to come to recognition at such depths as he could be dragged to. So his life on earth is a very vital one in the process of his development to maturity. He stands the chance of hastening his ascent when he takes his every earthly moment seriously.

But whatever a person wills in his intuitive perception, and whatever he says and does, remain bound to him by unbreakable threads of fate which are faithfully woven for him by animistic beings responsible for the task, and develop to maturity to return to him in the present life, in the spheres beyond the physical earth-plane, or in another earth life if he is so fortunate.

The need to see earthly punishment meted out and the misconceptions about true justice, have led to the various assumptions that people do get away with crime. If these crimes are not detected or punished by man, they still will have to go through the process of development, maturation, ripening, and harvest, just like everything else in the World of Matter. Every human spirit must reap the fruits of every single seed that he has planted in Creation through his thoughts, his words, and his actions. So not only will he receive the just compensation for his physically visible actions, but he will also be repaid for his intuitive and thought volition, as well as his spoken words. There is nothing that can escape the working of the Laws of Creation!

It is also because of this lack of understanding that some people wonder why there seems to be an apparent injustice in the way that conditions of men on earth are shaped. Again, here it is man's ignorance of the Laws of Creation that allows him to think like this. If there is an absolute trust in the working of the Laws of God in Creation, then the mere fact that people exist under different conditions must mean that they deserve to live in those conditions, because to think otherwise will be to accuse the Creator of being unjust and of acting arbitrarily, giving this person this, and the other person that.

It does not work that way! The Creator Himself is Perfection! His Will is Perfect! The Laws of Creation, which express His Will, are perfect! If the Creator is perfect then it follows that everything that issues from Him must be perfect! Therefore His Laws, which work throughout the entire Creation, must also be perfect! This means that they can never change because it is only that which is imperfect that needs to be developed and so can change or be changed! But from eternity to eternity, the Laws of God remain perfect!

It is the human spirit who is not perfect and who can never reach the perfection of the Creator. All he can hope for is to reach the perfection of his species, and to do that he must remain active in his recognition of the Laws of Creation, which never change in their working.

The moment he relaxes in this effort he reaches stagnation and is swept downwards by the constantly moving effects of the activity of the Laws of Creation. If man does not understand the working of the Laws of Creation, it is his fault, and he must not hesitate in attaining this recognition because his entire existence depends on it!

When the spirit-germs left the spiritual Realm they bore within them the same gifts, which they were able to develop during their wanderings through the planes of the World of Matter. This Jesus Christ already brought to man's attention in one of His parables.

They were also given the freedom to decide how to use their abilities in the shaping of the World of Matter with the power of the Creator, which runs through Creation as a neutral Creative power.

Each human spirit is able to direct this power one way or another, upwards or downwards, for the development upward or the destruction of matter and himself.

The only way that man can learn of the Will of the Creator is by observing the working of the Laws of Creation, and adjusting himself to them in his thoughts and his deeds. This was only possible in one place, the developing World of Matter. As an unconscious spirit-germ, the other spheres in Creation were already above its level of maturity in accordance with the Law of Attraction of Homogenous Species and the Law of Gravity, so the spirit-germ could only descend downwards for its development and maturation, and could not go any higher than where it was when the urge to develop awakened within it.

Man's development on earth has taken millions of years up to this point, and during that time he has been given the opportunity to express his volition in a varied number of ways and has had several lifetimes to do so. So stage-by-stage he has been given the chance to do this, to use the different radiations prevailing on earth and in the World of Matter at different times during all this time for the purpose of strengthening his knowledge of and trust in the working of the Laws of Creation.

However, man failed to fulfill his mission in the World of Matter, and he decided to focus his attention only on material things, and only on those things which he could understand with his earthbound intellect. He stifled his spirit in the process, and consequently made the wrong decisions most of the time, due to the self-willed gap in the flow of spiritual currents, which were supposed to play a leading role in the development of his thoughts.

So his thoughts became base and dense, and the conceptions that he formed in the course of his experiencing became distorted. He could no longer see clearly.

His dependence on his intellect caused an over-exertion of his frontal brain, which became disproportionately enlarged, further weakening his ability to perceive intuitively and pass on spiritual impressions through the stunted hindbrain. He developed his brain wrongly and it became diseased. He passed this diseased brain on to his descendants, who, upon attaining physical maturity, became predisposed to over-cultivate their intellects through excessive use of their brains, thereby maintaining the distortion, a one-sidedness in every thing that was formed by man.

In accordance with the Law of Attraction of Homogenous Species, dark souls were attracted from the spheres beyond the gross material earth-plane, through the correspondingly darkened earthwoman, who for a long time now has fallen from her high role as the bridge for the admission of Light radiations. So darker souls have been able to incarnate into earth before they were mature enough to do so, because man stretched out his hands to them through the expression of his base volition. These souls were able to further poison the environment of the earth, further increasing the impetus to make the wrong decisions.

During this process, every developing human spirit made his own decisions and became entangled in his own special web of threads. These threads weave a carpet of fate for each individual and no two are alike. So each person in atoning for his past guilt must walk a different path from that of the next man. Only in so doing can he balance his past guilt, which is detailed in the formation of his own specially woven carpet of fate, with good works. He thereby receives the motivation to do this through his condition, because previously he refused to do so voluntarily. He must live through the fruits of his labor.

It is in the balancing of his past guilt with the right decisions that he will recognize the Laws of Creation. This means that when men return to earth at different times, following periods of experiencing in the spheres beyond the earth-plane, they face various conditions which are always the fruits of their volition waiting to be harvested.

This however is love, for in no other way can man ascend but through the strict observance of the Laws of Creation, which includes the recognition of these Laws as they are fulfilled in the returning of the fruits of the seeds sown by men, to their originators in accordance with the Law of Reciprocal Action.

Since man weaves a special carpet of fate for himself, and since no two carpets of fate are alike, that is, no two people would have made exactly the same decisions in the past thousands of years, then the fruits that mature for the individual human spirits at any given time must also be different. And not only must they differ from one another but they must also be in strict accordance with what the particular souls need in order to ascend. It is only when the conditions of man are looked at from the perspective of the lowly intellect that it appears as though there is injustice in the working of the Laws of the Creator.

Whatever happens, it is just, for it can never be an arbitrary act on the part of the Creator and His Laws! It only points to the fact that man has sown the wrong seeds for a very long time. The returning effects have to be commensurate with the kind of seeds sown.

If man will only take the time to focus his attention on himself and the experiencing of the moment in order to discover the lessons held for him in that moment, he will have a lot revealed to him. The conceit of today's mankind makes man incapable of concentrating on himself in a critical and objective manner. He looks around for someone to blame for every misfortune, and falls even deeper in his attempts to run away from himself and from his responsibilities.

We live in the midst of the returning effects of our past deeds. Every moment holds the possibility for the redemption of a past wrong deed. It is in the entanglements of the threads of these past wrong decisions that man has buried his free will. So now he allows himself to be controlled like a puppet by the Darkness through base and ugly forms, which remain attached to him, and which weigh him down and do not leave him in peace. He must sever his connections to these forms, and thus to those base spheres to which they are connected, if he is to once again regain his freedom.

This does not mean, however, that man has no control over his life because he has bound his free will in the entanglement of his threads of fate, but he must strive constantly for the Light through the recognition and strict observance of the Laws of Creation in order to settle all his debt and become able to ascend. He still has his free will, but now he must choose between the way of the Light and the way to further entanglements in these threads, which only drag him down towards disintegration. Currently the entanglements of the threads hamper his freedom of movement, i.e., the movement of his spirit, which is encased within.

It is high time that man realizes the opportunities inherent in being able to return to this earth for the purpose of continuing his development. Here he can do more than he is able to do in any other part of the World of Matter, with respect to freeing himself from fetters that hold him down. If he does not allow himself to be distracted by the detractors around him, and if he focuses on maintaining a good volition, then he will receive help from the Light because he would have met the condition required for a connection with help from the Light in accordance with the Law of Attraction of Homogenous Species.

He will be able to sever all those ties which link him to base forms and to dark centers in the beyond, because he would no longer see them as worth his time. He will also put an end to the need for atonement because he will no longer be sowing those seeds which will need to be redeemed through the process of reciprocal action.

Man must become simple in his thinking. The Laws of Creation are simple and require a simple mind to understand them. Today men pride themselves with being intellectuals, not realizing what it actually means, not knowing what they imply by such utterances, and by the harboring of the volition to want to be intellectual.

It is the worship of the intellect that has made it impossible for man hitherto to simply observe the Laws of Creation, which also express themselves as the Laws of Nature. As a creature of Creation man must make the observance of these Laws a part of his whole being if he wishes to form that environment for himself which is pleasing to the Light, and which will lift him upwards for the completion of his mission here in the World of Matter.

Already man has wasted many an important earth life in the pursuit of mere trifles. It is high time that he focuses on his actual mission on earth while he still has time. Awake!

THE DEVELOPMENT OF THE HUMAN SPIRIT ON EARTH

The development of the human spirit in the World of Matter is meant to follow the course of development that all the other creatures which have to develop in the World of Matter must follow. It must go through the sowing stage, then the forming and the developing stage, the maturation stage, the stages of blossoming, fruiting, ripening and harvest or decay.

The sowing stage involved the descent of the spirit seed into the World of Matter from the Spiritual Realm where it was still unconscious and in an undeveloped form. The descent of the spirit-germ into matter was in accordance with the Laws of Creation, which also govern the development of all species since they govern everything in Creation, having brought about the development of Creation and express the Will of the Creator in it. So in accordance with this Will those spirit-germs, which had developed the urge to develop self-consciousness, were expelled from the Spiritual Realm so that this volition of theirs could be fulfilled.

This is a process that occurs continually, and which results in the implantation of spirit seeds into the parts of the World of Matter which have become mature enough to receive them. For there are seven Universes in the World of Matter and the earth is only a part of one of them. The mutual attainment of the right points in the maturity of the spirit seeds seeking the opportunity to develop and the particular corresponding part of the World of Matter, brings about the prospect of such a happening, which must then proceed in accordance with the Will

101

of the Light regarding all development in Creation.

Just like when a ripened fruit falls from a tree at the point in its maturation when it is able to proceed towards further development into a mature tree, through the proper development of its seed, so is it with the spirit-germ which has developed the urge to mature to consciousness, and which consequently is expelled downwards towards the World of Matter, towards the region where it receives the opportunity for further development in accordance with its volition.

In this chapter, however, I shall only talk about the spirit-germs which incarnated into the part of the World of Matter in which our earth serves as the turning-point in the process of their wanderings through matter. So this chapter deals with the development of the mankind of this earth. Man was created when the first spirit-germ incarnated into the body of flesh on earth. Through the experiences of man on earth the human spirit within him, his living core, was to develop and become stronger in the knowledge of the Will of God.

During the ensuing millions of years after the initial incarnations on earth, the human spirit was supposed to develop, mature, and in receiving the fruits of his labor at the time of their ripening, be judged. Then follows the harvest of the purified human spirit from the World of Matter, which is akin to his resurrection from matter into the Spiritual Realm, which was talked about by the Son of God as the goal of the developing human spirit in the World of Matter.

This resurrection can only happen if he is successful in developing to self-consciousness through the recognition of the Laws in Creation, and through his assimilation of these Laws into his being, or else decay must follow in the process of disintegration due to his inability to make proper use of the time allotted to him for his maturation and leave the World of Matter in time.

Each of the stages of man's development on earth is further divided into sub-stages, which individually also contain the different stages of development common to all material forms as mentioned above, including the stages of sowing, of development and maturing, and of ripening and harvest.

And during each of the stages and sub-stages of his

development(stages within the stages), different radiations are predominant in the World of Matter, which affect man and his development according to their particular natures, and in all the different spheres and conditions that he has to live through.

The human spirit experiences a vital period in its development in the World of Matter here on earth in the World of Gross Matter. During the periods that make up their time so far on earth, which cover millions of years, mankind have gone through different degrees of development.

Following the first incarnation of the spirit germ into earth it was able to further develop its physical body, which it had incarnated into and which had been prepared for it by the animistic beings through their activities. This body was ennobled through the activities of the newly incarnated spirit, which had become aware of its existence and was on its way to maturity and to attainment of self-consciousness.

The radiation of the spirit was able to bring about a transformation of the physical body to a form that was not possible for the preceding animal soul, which had reached the height of its achievement when it developed the body to the state prior to the spirit's incarnation. Those animals that formed the bridge to the form that was taken over by the awakened spirit-germs became extinct because they no longer served any purpose in Creation.

The radiation of the spirit was able to give the present human form to the body as it developed to self-consciousness, as it also did with the cloaks that formed around the descending awakened spirit-germ. This earthly human form is the coarse replica of the more beautiful and original form of the Primordial Beings in Primordial Creation, who were created after the image of God. The developing human spirits can only develop in their form to the point of being a rougher copy of this original form of the Primordial Spiritual Beings, even at their highest point of development in Paradise. Hence man was made after the image of those who were created after the image of God!

In his further activities, as he subsisted and wandered the earth for his survival, he experienced the effects of his actions and his decisions and slowly developed his physical body, which he had to bear during his period of experiencing on earth, and which had to serve him as a tool while he lived on earth. He started to become more conversant with the happenings in his surroundings, and, with the guidance that he was able to receive from above through his spirit, he developed more and more.

In response to the constant movements all around him, in the working of the Laws of Creation, which demand constant movement, and whose effects bring about constant movement, the developing human beings on earth spread out into races of different kinds and populated different parts of the world, all in accordance with their volition.

In the different parts of the world the developing man could experience the different manifestations of the Laws of Creation, and, in trying to survive, had to adapt to the different conditions that prevailed in the areas where he found himself in any particular lifetime. He slowly matured spiritually in the process.

The nature of his environment in a particular lifetime was always a consequence of the decisions he made previously, and with each lifetime he was given the opportunity to develop through the experiencing of these conditions, while at the same time, through the Grace of God, severing ties to base forms which he no longer wanted to nourish through his thoughts and his actions. He could only learn by experiencing, and being spiritual, he attracted to himself all that he willed in his intuitive perceptions, his thoughts and his actions in the course of his experiences.

This way he was to gain knowledge of what would benefit him and what would not.

During this early period of development he was able to see and communicate more easily with the animistic beings to which he was still very closely associated in accordance with the state of his spiritual maturity. Due to this fact the little animistic beings, for instance the elves, the gnomes and water sprites, which tend to plants, the earth and water bodies, were the highest in the realm of all that is beyond the physically visible that he could see and experience.

They guided him and warned him of coming changes in the forms of nature, which man regards as disasters. This they were able to do because they are involved through their activities in the development of such forms, which, when they reach certain stages, have to undergo disintegration or transformation into new forms, all in accordance with the Law of Development in the World of Matter. Man listened to them and revered them, because he thought them to be the causes of the events in his environment, which seemed to have very dramatic effects, and which he could not readily explain.

He treated them like Divine Beings out of ignorance, because he often received guidance through them. This caused him to even pray to them for his safety and for protection.

These beings were the highest in the order of Creation that he could see, because he was not yet mature enough to see any higher. He had to carefully go through the steps or stages of development, starting from the lowest steps.

Some men in some parts of the earth have also at some point or another paid the same kind of attention to thought-forms generated by men, thinking that these were entities to be worshiped. These thought-forms, however, are different from the elemental beings, which work in the Will of the Creator and in accordance with His Laws.

The thought-forms generated by men, and which could be seen by some men who ignorantly revered them, could be dark or light, depending on the nature of the volition that brought them about. As I have already mentioned, these thought-forms are also formed for men by certain species of animistic beings, because they carry out the Will of God and help develop the works of man for him to harvest. In their working they often appeared to men of the past as beings with power to bring about all kinds of happenings, and that is why they were often revered and worshiped.

The clairvoyants, clairaudients and mediums amongst the different peoples of that time were able to see and hear these beings who influenced man through his intuitive perception. He was still in the beginning stages of his necessary process of development in the World of Matter. Through the Law of Attraction of Homogenous Species one is only able to see up to or sense from that level which is homogenous with his inner nature, i.e., with the maturity of his spirit.

Meanwhile, the world around man was also developing and, in response to the different radiations which permeate the World of Matter from out of the cosmos, different forms and conditions were arising in the different parts of the earth. Men at this point had become dispersed all around the earth for various reasons, which had to do with their volition in response to the changes around them. The exertion of his spirit in response to the obstacles that came his way, or which he attracted to himself in the course of the expression of his volition, in the course of his everyday life, caused him to develop and to experience things differently from how he did previously.

The more he matured the more he was able to perceive from the environment that he lived in. He was also in a position to learn of the Laws of Creation through their expression in the Laws of Nature. His adaptation to these Laws helped him in his ability to fend for himself. He formed a relationship with his environment and through experiencing, learned how to take from it what he needed for his subsistence.

When he returned to earth, through the process of reincarnation, he did not always return to that place where he spent his life in the previous lifetime, but he incarnated in the place where, in accordance with his weaving, he could reap the consequences of the seeds that he sowed previously, which had matured for him and which offered him the opportunity to develop further. This way he was able to live at different times in different earthly bodies, strictly in accordance with what he attracted to himself, or what he was attracted to in accordance with the Law of Attraction of Homogenous Species.

When he left the earth-plane he was drawn to that region that was homogenous to the nature of his soul as previously explained, and there he had to live through the consequences of the forms which he caused to develop due to his volition while he was on earth. He could not return to earth until he had purified himself enough, to the point where, through the attraction of homogenous species, he was able to be attracted back to earth through bonds formed between similar radiations.

So man developed gradually through his different experiences. Each lifetime offered him the opportunity to shake off all that he had attached to himself through the expression of his volition, and this opportunity came for him at the attainment of physical maturity. He could then be fully impacted by the forms which he had placed in Creation through his past deeds, and also could influence his surroundings more effectively through the current expression of his volition.

At this point in the life of man, in every lifetime on earth, when he has attained physical maturity, his spirit is able to make contact with the spheres of the material world around him and all the radiations therein. They can affect him in the reciprocal effects of the forms he places in them, just as well as he is able to influence them through his own volition. He attains the generative age, when he is able to use all the experiences that he has been able to acquire on earth in the course of his wanderings up to that time to affect his environment, in a good or bad way.

The attainment of the generative age, together with generative power, which is around the period of puberty or when the person becomes a young man or woman, allows for the unfolding of his or her spirit. It is at this time in the life of man that his spirit is able to make contact with the neural creative power coursing through Creation, and is able to create intuitive forms, which he must then answer for at the end of the development cycle of said form. It is the time of the setting in of responsibility, when he must then be careful as to how he uses this power that he now has access to.

It is also at this time that the effects of all that he bears within him in the form of karma from previous lifetimes can be shaken off with the most ease, through the countering of previous wrong decisions with good ones, as the reciprocal actions of his past deeds bring to him the fruits of his past works. Prior to this time he is shielded from the effects of his karma in his physical body, which would not have developed to the point of letting the spirit unfold to make contact with his material surroundings.

Again, one is able to see the vital nature of an earth-life, since it is only here that the human spirit is given such a chance to lay aside all the forms of his guilt through the opportunity to atone for them. This generative power helps him ascend quickly upwards if he takes advantage of its spurring effect, which can be noticed in the nature of an unspoiled male or female youth of today.

The unspoiled youth of today who has just come to this point in his or her life is usually filled with the urge or longing for something better, or to achieve great things for humanity, or to alleviate its pain and misery, because it is at this point that the animistic nature of the child, which had been predominant during the imitative period of his childhood, gives way for the spirit which, as it unfolds, is able to feel the pressure of the darkness in the world.

This often causes the young adults, especially the young girls or women, to feel depressed and no longer want to participate in certain activities which they had previously taken part in. It is the time of the setting in of responsibility for the human spirit, when it becomes responsible for its actions and when their reciprocal effects hit him more fully.

Unfortunately today many of these youths are sedated with drugs because the real cause of their anxiety and depression is not known and often is not even sought. They are denied the opportunity to rightly unfold their powers here on earth through wrong education and advice from parents and others who know nothing about the Laws of Creation.

Now back to the early stages of man's development. He was able to sever his ties to base forms, to which he had become attached in previous lifetimes, in every subsequent lifetime. In the process he could recognize more of the working of the Laws of Creation, because he would have to live through the conditions resulting from the radiations of such forms and be exposed to their effects. This could then affect the way that he made his decisions in the future.

The opportunity to experience life on earth in different bodies and at different times gives man the opportunity to develop a sense of broad-mindedness. It gives him the chance to see how life is in a different part of the earth, even if he does not remember what his past life was like. The important thing is the experience that is acquired during each moment of each lifetime, which he can take over with him into the beyond. It is only the experiences of the spirit that one is able to take with him after physical death, to help him in his experiencing in the spheres beyond the earth-plane, and also for his support in his next earth-life if he should be allowed to return. The things that are learned with the brain alone remain behind when man has to pass on into the beyond, because they belong to the gross material, having never made any impressions on the spirit which lives on.

Also, at any given time on earth, the intuitive experiences of the different peoples of the earth are able to help in creating the kind of variety of experiences which alone can lead to a harmonious development of the earthly humanity.

Just like a flowerbed is able to please its admirer because of the variety of colors displayed by the different types of flowers on it, so is it with the variety amongst the peoples of the earth, who are always at different levels of development. Perfection can only be achieved through this variety, and because of what each of the different peoples of the earth are able to give to the whole species as they develop themselves in the recognitions of the different ways in which the Laws of Creation manifest.

This variety makes for a wholesome development because to get to perfection, the different parts have to be in full cooperation, since the different parts all came from one perfect Source. So man has gained tremendously from being able to return to earth in different bodies and amongst different kinds of people.

Since everything came from out of the Radiation of God, Who is perfect, it will take the expression of all the differences inherent in the various ways that His Laws manifest in all the species resulting from the splittings-off of His Radiation, which make up the entire Creation, in order to approach this Perfection. The same applies here on earth, where the species of the developing human spirits are cloaked in physical bodies of various shades and colors, where they have to live through different circumstances and conditions.

It is in the manifestations of the Laws of Creation within the different races and peoples, as they carry out their various lawful activities in response to the different radiations from the stars, their spirits, and from their environments, that a harmonious development can arise from the collective humanity on earth.

Without this variety there would be a fusing together of all the different parts into one, resulting in the suppression of all that could have developed had the normal course of development been allowed to proceed. There would be a lack of exchange of necessary radiations between the different groups and this would lead to stagnation or a standstill in development.

Also, the one form which would be adopted, if there were to be a

SAMPSON IRUOHA

fusing together of all the different parts or races into one, would have to
be deficient because it would suffer from a one-sidedness that could have
been balanced out by the qualities that were not allowed to develop due
to the fusing. It would have to result in the propagation of one-sidedness
in all of man's activities, and this, being an attribute of the Darkness, must
lead to destruction and decay. It would lack all necessary vitality for the
uplifting of the human spirit to Luminous Heights. It would lack any
sense of balance, which is needed in any Light-willed development.

Such a fusing would disrupt the necessary stages of development of
the individual groups, just like the treatment of children and adults in
exactly the same manner must lead to a greatly hampered development of
all concerned.

This is of course supposing that this fusing is possible, for in Creation
there are many checks which are built in, in the perfection of the Laws of
God, to prevent such aberrations from being maintained, or from taking
on form at all. I shall mention just one of such checks which can be
witnessed by anyone who cares to see, for there are so many of such
checks that it will not be possible to describe them all.

One of these checks is the rejection of foreign customs which are
forced on a people by some other group simply because the latter, in its
narrow-mindedness, thinks its way is the only right way to live, without
considering the necessary indigenous development of the former. This
narrow-mindedness always causes the neglect of so much that is
necessary for a peaceful and harmonious development that it inevitably
leads to chaos and collapse. Because the stages of development
prescribed by the Laws of Creation, which take into consideration all the
radiations that affect each of the peoples of this earth in their particular
parts of the earth, are not adhered to.

Whatever does not develop in accordance with the Law of
Development in the World of Matter, which stems from the Laws of
Creation, must collapse at the time when it is supposed to bear fruit. The
bitterness of this fruit then serves as an indication of the faultiness or the
diseased nature of the planted seed. For this reason a people must be
allowed to develop in their own way because it is not by accident that they
find themselves in that particular part of the earth in which they live. It is

only selfishness, narrow-mindedness, greed, conceit, ignorance, fear, and many other dark factors, that cause man to ignore the signs that point to the false way of thinking amongst men.

The result of forced assimilations will always lead to chaos and disaster because the natural process is ignored. The Laws of Nature come from the Laws of Creation and cannot be transgressed without corresponding punishment. But this punishment or reciprocal action is itself a natural occurrence, mandated by the Laws of Creation, which have brought about the entire Creation and so must govern every single happening in Creation, be it small or great.

In this one can also learn of the Will of the Creator and make future decisions accordingly. So, in this apparent punishment, the Love of God also shows Itself as justice is delivered. This is because those who have to suffer in the reciprocal action of this transgression of the Laws of Creation are able to learn of them through experiencing the pain that comes from the resulting chaos.

So, over time, mankind on earth developed in their various parts of the world, at different rates and in different conditions. Following the explanations given above, one can see that the developing human spirits in gross matter have alternately lived in the different parts of the earth, and as members of the different groups that make up the variety of the peoples of the earth. They have contributed to the growths as well as the detriment of the different peoples of the world. So some of the people in Africa today could have lived in Europe or in Asia previously, and only live in Africa currently because they have been attracted to that zone because of experiences which they cannot escape due to their nature at the time of their reincarnation into earth from the ethereal.

The human spirit must remain active in his ascent or he must suffer retrogression due to inactivity. He is not immune from the Laws of Creation, which demand constant movement from all the creatures in Creation. His particular level of maturity and the nature of his soul due to his weaving determine the conditions that he must live under, because they must correspond to the nature of his volition. The nature of his volition determines what he must yet experience if he is to ascend. Only these experiences can offer him the possibilities for further development, and opportunities to atone for his past guilt and learn of the Laws of Creation in the process. Only knowledge of the Laws of Creation can enable man attain spiritual maturity and rise upwards to the Luminous Heights of this Creation.

Just like no two individuals are the same in their spiritual maturity, no two nations or peoples are the same in their development. But this development of the nations must not be confused with spiritual development, because one who is born and raised in a nation that is considered less developed than another would not necessarily be less spiritually mature that one who is indigenous in the more developed nation. Here the issue is that of physical development.

A person in a "more developed" nation could be very dark inside or spiritually lukewarm, for different reasons, while another in a "less developed" nation or part of the earth might be more spiritually active and alert than the former, often because of the conditions under which he might have to live. The attraction to the specific zone of indigenousness during the time of incarnation is strictly in accordance with what the incoming human spirit needs in order to develop further, through severing old ties and atoning for past wrongs deeds. He is also given the opportunity to develop the area into which he incarnates in the best way possible, using his knowledge of the Laws of Creation, which he gains only through such experiencing.

The different nations and regions of the earth are in different stages of physical development, much like a human being goes through the different stages of his physical development in every lifetime here on earth. Each lifetime, the human being on earth has to go through the period of childhood, adolescence or early manhood or womanhood, then through the period when he is able to fully make use of his abilities and further develop them, and finally the period of old age when he is mostly reflective of his life and begins to ready himself for the transition into the next step in his development, beyond the earth-plane.

Before we proceed it is important to mention the development of the human body from childhood to old age and how this affects the development of the human spirit.

The human spirit works through the radiation of the blood. Through this it is able to make an impression on his surrounding gross material world. There needs to be a transition, as in all happenings in Creation, in the transmitting of impressions from the spirit to the gross material environment. Without this transition the spirit would not be able to work in the much denser environment of Gross Matter because of the vast gap between the species.

The radiation of the blood serves as the bridge or transition medium for the impressions that come from the spirit, and also from all the cloaks which man wears under his physical body and which are set aglow and animated by the spirit core, to the gross material world, and also for those radiations that impact the spirit from the gross material world.

Earlier, I described the transmission of spiritual impressions from the spirit to the frontal brain through the hindbrain. The impressions made on the brain affect the composition of the blood, through the secretions from several glands in the body, following the stimulation of certain nerves in the process. Also, depending on the nature of the spirit within man, he is guided to that type of food or activity which best suits the purpose of developing rightly, both spiritually and physically, at any given point in time.

The types of food and exercise, and also the maturity of his physical body, help determine the composition of the blood. The composition, i.e., the make up of the blood, directly influences the radiation of the blood. The change in the blood composition causes a corresponding change in the blood radiation, through which the human spirit involved is then able to affect his material environment.

The blood composition at any given time determines the temperament of the human being, because the temperament is determined by the particular radiation which results from the particular blood composition. The kind of radiation that the human being is able to attract to himself depends on the kind of radiation he produces himself.

Through the radiation of the blood the spirit of man is able to work on earth, in the World of Gross Matter. He is able to make connections with radiations of various kinds and through this he is able to influence his surroundings just like he can be influence by them. The more he is able to draw Light-radiations to himself by channeling his thoughts and volition

113

towards the Light, the more he will attract to himself those radiations which are favorable and uplifting in nature. He will be guided to those activities and the kind of nourishment that will lay the foundations for the production of the blood radiation which will be just right for the attraction of the beneficial radiations from his environment every moment.

The combination of emanations or radiations from the physical body of man, through which his soul works on earth, contribute to what is called his aura. This surrounds him in a manner that can afford him protection from darker radiations, or form a bridge to the surrounding darkness, in accordance with the nature of his volition.

Also, through this formation around him, one who is so gifted can notice points of weakness in man's radiation, due to some ailment or disturbance in a corresponding organ or region of his physical body. The radiation of energy in that area of weakness in the aura is usually seen to be lower than that of the other parts which correspond to healthier parts of the physical body.

As mentioned above, the composition of the blood influences the temperament of the human being. The changes in temperament help him experience different radiations from his environment, and this helps and furthers the maturity of his spirit core.

His ability to fully experience his surroundings in a way that benefits his spiritual development depends on how well he experiences each period, each moment, when one type of radiation or one temperament is prevalent. The more fully he experiences each period of time the more he will get out of the next one, because each stage or period acts as a foundation for the next one. The next necessary step in his necessary development does not materialize until he has fully experienced the preceding one.

He is not able to ascend until he has fully and correctly experienced the different individual stages. If he strays from the right path he will have to return to the point in his experiencing up until which he was still in accord with the Will of the Light. From there he can then gradually work his way up.

This is a Grace from Almighty God which ensures that man is always

114

capable of rightly dealing with any situation which he is presented with or which he might find himself in, provided, that is, that he makes his decisions in accordance with the Laws of Creation. For only in this way can he bring to bear all the talents which lie within him and which were given to him by his Creator for the purpose of fulfilling in Creation.

He will always find himself in that situation for which he has been duly armed in the course of his development. He will never be placed arbitrarily in a situation which he has not attracted to himself due to his volition and his capability to prevail. Where he fails, or where he finds the condition too overwhelming, he has not yet summoned all his strength and explored all avenues open to him. Only when he has fully experienced, absorbed and recognized the Laws of Creation is he able to ascend to a higher stage in his development.

As he experiences these individual periods or stages, while striving to make his decisions vibrate in the sense of the Will of the Light, he will affect his environment in the most beneficial way, because he will not sow any seeds which will bring disharmony to it or cause harm to anyone. He will exist in harmony with his surroundings and spread light with his every deed. In the process he will also become more familiar with the working of the Laws of Creation. His knowledge of the Laws will grow because by adapting himself to them he will see the effects of their working in the moments, hours and days of his life.

His trust and confidence in the strictness and perfection of their working will become more visible to him because he will be involved in the constant experiencing of the multifarious ways in which they manifest, while still working in the same way. He will see the strict logic behind their activity because they will never deviate from such strictness. His trust in the Creator and His Laws will grow and with this growth will come conviction, which he cannot do without in this time if he is to make it through the storm of the ongoing purification.

So the more he strives for purity of thought the better he will form his blood for the production of the most beneficial blood radiation. His thoughts will align better with his intuitive perception, which will take the lead in the upward striving of the human spirit. He will grow strong in the process because he will experience the diverse conditions brought about through his interaction with the different radiations that emanate from his gross material environment, as the composition of his blood changes in response to his activities and the maturation of his physical body.

The right experiencing of one's environment during the time when a particular temperament predominates in a human being is paramount for the right use of the temperament. With the temperament under the right guidance of the spirit, man is able to impact his environment in a harmonious way, because he would not place himself under the control of the temperament but will guide it with his intuitive perceptions and use it for his work of experiencing and interacting with his surroundings.

He will then experience every moment in the best way possible, that is, in accordance with God's Will, so that nothing but good will result from his actions. He will also be able to interpret his experiences with more objectivity and with the right understanding, because the guidance for this will come from the spirit, which is able to perceive from the highest planes in the World of Matter, and even from the Spiritual Realm.

If the human being is not focused on doing the Will of the Light in the course of his activities, and is not striving for purity of thought, then he will fall for the trap of acting on his feeling, instead of his intuitive perception.

The body produces instincts, which, guided by the intellect, form the feeling, in response to the gross material environment. Feeling is able to cooperate with the intellect to produce imagination, which reacts back on the feeling and reinforces it.

If the human spirit does not strive for purity of thought, and has lost his ability to hear his intuitive perception in the process, then his thoughts will not be in line with the pure intuitive perceptions of his spirit. Consequently, his instincts will be guided wrongly by the intellect to produce the wrong kinds of feeling which will negatively influence the way he views his surroundings and the way he makes his moment-by-moment decisions. This will lead to the formation of wrong concepts and assumptions. He will sow more dark seeds in this condition because he will act in ignorance of the truth.

He will also form his blood accordingly because he will not be able to make those decisions which will lead him to the right kind of nutrition and activity. He will not be able to benefit from the right use of the temperaments that will prevail during the times of differing blood compositions, for instance, as his body matures from one stage to another. And since the spirit works through the radiation of the blood, and the blood composition plays a major part in this radiation, the spirit will not be able to work effectively therein, either in its absorption of impressions from its material environment or in the transmission of spiritual power to its environment. There will be a lack of clarity in his experiencing and perception.

The intellect will act as a hindrance to the purer currents from the intuitive perception of the spirit, yielding a development of the blood radiation that will exert a negative influence on the surroundings of the human being in question. In the reciprocal action of this he will receive the wrong kind of development of his blood, his physical and spiritual being.

For this reason it is important for man to strive to actively exert his spirit, and to strive for purity of thought, because when his light thoughts coincide with the light intuitive perceptions of his spirit, then the corresponding blood radiation will also be one that impacts his environment in a harmonious way. The feeling that is generated in the process will also harmonize with his intuitive perception in order to provide man with the best help in his earthly activities.

For some time now man has neglected his intuitive perception and has put all his trust in the intellect. This has led to the generation of misleading feelings and the formation of wrong assumptions and conceptions. He has confused the intuitive perception of the spirit with the feeling that is connected with the physical body and with gross matter. This has led him to gross misunderstandings of his surroundings and the working of the Laws of Creation.

Consequently, man has abused his physical body which was lent to him for the purpose of his experiencing while here on earth, through the wrong choice of foods and activities, which all express the one-sidedness of the volition of the current mankind. He has never as yet realized the great significance of the need to maintain the right balance in everything because he has neglected to listen to his intuitive perceptions, his inner voice, which is the expression of his spirit. He has neglected his spirit.

During the different stages in the life of man on earth his blood composition varies. It is the predominance of certain blood compositions, at specific periods in the development of his physical body during his earth-life, which brings about the different major stages of his development. So that within one of such stages, for instance the period of childhood, a predominant blood composition may prevail, yielding one type of temperament. Even though during the period when this temperament may predominate, the blood composition will also vary, on an hourly or daily basis, to express a range of temperaments.

So within the period of childhood when the blood composition is of a very definite kind and expressing a definite kind of temperament, the blood composition continues to go through smaller changes, producing a range of temperaments. These aid in the development of the body during the period of childhood.

The blood radiations, which result from the different blood compositions, influence the way that man experiences his environment and determine his temperaments. Even though people might have particular temperaments which seem to predominate during most of their lives on earth, they individually go through different periods in their earth-lives during which different temperaments predominate.

As a child, the sanguine temperament predominates and that is why children usually have a carefree attitude about them. During this period the radiations of the animistic predominate within the child, shielding the spirit core from the surrounding radiations. He functions mainly through imitations and by copying what he sees in his environment.

This gives way to the melancholic period or stage, when he begins to have aspirations and daydreams and is full of ideas and hopes. It is also during this period that the young man or woman begins to awaken to his responsibilities in Creation, when his spirit is able to make contact with the neutral creative power in Creation and also the different spheres of matter, so that he is able to generate intuitive forms as well as fully receive the consequences of past and present actions. This is the onset of his generative power.

After this period comes the choleric period, when he is ready and armed with acquired lessons to use his abilities as he further develops them in his actual work in life. The phlegmatic period comes in his old age when he is more reflective about his life, and when he starts to make preparations for his departure from earth in order to be born into the next segment of his development. He can also use this period to shake off any of the last remnants of the burdens which still cling to his soul.

This can also be likened to the seasons of the year in the temperate zones, where there are four main seasons, which correspond to the four temperaments mentioned above. The spring is like the sanguine period when the feeling of an awakening can be sensed throughout nature. Summer brings along with it the urge to activity. In the Fall fruits ripen and are ready for harvest. Winter gives off the feeling of transition and reflection, when one takes stock of the activities of the past year, looks forward to, and prepares for the new year and all that it might entail.

Just like the human being goes through a range of temperaments during the course of his life on earth, so does he go through similar cycles in the hour, the day and even in the week. During these periods he is under the influence of several radiations, which emanate from the various objects in his surroundings, and also from the stars, the planetary bodies, the sun, and so forth. He also receives the effects of the emanations from the different spheres of matter and from the Spiritual Realm.

When one lives according to the right recognition of the Laws of Creation, he must inevitably also adjust himself to the different temperaments and the seasons and adapt his activities accordingly, because these seasonal changes and changes in temperament are mandated by Law. They provide man with the right kind of transition from one kind of activity to the next and provide for him the basis for a healthy and productive life. He is able to draw the right kinds of radiations at the different periods of his earth-life when different temperaments predominate. He is also able to make the best use of the seasons of the year for his spiritual and physical development.

Just like his physical body, which also includes the brain that produces the intellect, he is to use the temperaments and the changes in the seasons as tools which can help him in the unfolding of his spiritual powers here on earth and in all of the material world, in a manner that will bring about the greatest benefit to all concerned. The timeliness of his activities will bring about peace and harmony because nothing will be done before or after it is due, but only at the right time. He will engage the species of his surroundings at precisely the right time because only that which has matured for an interaction with him will be attracted to him, or him to it, according to the Laws of Creation.

Here even the food that he eats will be consumed at the right time, because he would realize the significance of eating the fruits which are mature for harvest and consumption at their specific times of the season. The medicines, which lie ready for use in the different forms of nature around him, will also become more visible to him because he will come to realize the wide-ranging effects of their timely use and applications.

There are however further divisions within the four main stages mentioned above. And each of the divisions is also further divided into sub-divisions. Just like the different Spheres of Creation are further graded within the major spheres mentioned in this book. It is like this with everything in Creation because everything comes about through the working of the same Laws of Creation, which never change.

These stages of development can be further divided into seven stages, or up to twelve stages, some of which have already been identified in the different fields of activity of men, and by different peoples of the earth. So when man discovers something which seems to indicate a certain regularity in its working or its development, he has just stumbled onto another manifestation of the same Laws. These Laws govern every happening!

It is because of the above explanation that the development of man on earth has also followed the same course. Man developed from being able to see and sense the smaller elemental beings to being able to see the intermediate ones, and finally also the highest ones at the summit of the Animistic Realm, which lies between the lowest part of the Spiritual Realm and the denser World of Matter. The peoples who were able to see these beings or interact with them through seers, mediums, clairvoyants or clairaudients, also falsely regarded them as gods and often paid homage to them.

Some of these people include the ancient Egyptians, Romans and

Greeks. Men in ancient Africa, and also those who formally inhabited the Americas, were at different times quite familiar with other kinds of elemental beings which they also worshiped to varying degrees.

Because they did not know the workings of the Laws of Creation, these people thought that the actions of these beings, which include the changes in the environment which man refers to as catastrophes, like mudslides, volcanic eruptions, earthquakes, drought, famine, hurricanes, and so forth, were arbitrary. Men had deviated from living in accordance with the Laws of Creation and so could not see these activities any differently. Only man acts arbitrarily in Creation. Every other creature adapts its activities to the working of the Laws of Creation.

Man saw power in this "being able to act arbitrarily" because that was how he thought and acted towards his environment. Following the Fall of Man he was no longer able to connect the happenings in his earthly surroundings to their actual causes. He was only privy to the final ramifications of these causes and thought them to be arbitrary acts, the acts of some invisible being or beings with power and influence. This is because he viewed power and influence in the same distorted way.

But what they were able to see were the animistic beings who are in the service of the Will of God! These are distinct from the base forms conjured up by the intuitive perceptions and thoughts of men, which are known as demons and phantoms, and which torment those who have similar forms attached to them.

The animistic beings carry out their service to the Will of God with a kind of strictness that the human spirit cannot fathom, because he has neglected to adapt himself to the Laws of Creation under which influence these beings work! He has never been able to summon up enough inner strength to break away from selfish desires and focus his every attention on the recognition of the Will of God in Creation! Hence he never really understood the nature of the animistic beings either.

But he is meant to understand the nature of these beings, as well as that of everything in his surroundings, through adapting himself to the same Laws that they obey faithfully! Only by doing so could he be led upwards in his experiencing and understanding to the level of the Spiritual Realm as he matured within. His inner maturity would have been at the level where he would have been able to perceive from the Spiritual Realm in picture form through his active intuitive perception. After this would have come the next level, which is the ability to receive knowledge about the Primordial Spiritual Beings, after which he may then be able to know about the Creator.

He was given the opportunity and the help to develop in stages to the point where he would be mature enough to leave the confines of the World of Gross Matter and proceed upwards towards the Light. He was to gradually develop to this point only if he maintained the necessary connection with the Light, which alone could provide him with the needed guidance.

Man's development was forced to proceed in the opposite direction because of the state of his inner nature, in response to the attachment of base forms to his soul as he made his decisions under the influence of the Darkness, which works through the over-developed and one-sidedly cultivated intellect which man crowned master.

The spirit was not exerted and so it did not develop. Man ignored the Law of necessary movement and the consequence was a stifling of the spirit. This manifested in his physical surroundings in the form of a gross one-sidedness and a distortion of everything that was allowed to develop, because only that which was understood by the earthbound intellect was allowed to take hold. There was no balance in anything that he did because the knowledge of the other part of Creation, the part that remained inaccessible to him due to his self-imprisonment in gross matter, was lost to him. All the conceptions that he formed in his experiencing had to suffer from this. Consequently all the conceptions that he associated with happenings around him were wrong.

Men did not take into consideration the necessary stages of development because of their spiritual ignorance, and their interactions with their fellow men became based solely on force, envy, greed, aggression, fear and conceit. They did not focus on that which is the most important of all, which is to abide by the Laws of Creation in all activities. Rather men kept their eyes on goals that were always beyond their reach, or for which they had not yet matured.

They did not work diligently with what they had in front of them in terms of their current conditions and their immediate surroundings, like the nature of the radiations of their regions and their particular races, but kept their eyes on others whom they perceived were in a better position than they were, or perhaps were worse off and could not manage without their help. In the process of always looking to the outside men neglected the duties in front of them and sowed more dark seeds as a natural consequence.

They did not live in the present in order to develop harmoniously with their environment according to the prevalent radiations.

The only things that the peoples of the world had in common were the different attributes of the darkness. These base attributes drew them together in accordance with the Law of Attraction of Homogenous Species, and the result of such unions and mixing was destruction, disharmony, distrust, conceit, envy, greed, foul sensuality, hatred, and fear. There were also other factors which men shared such as the love of comfort and ease, and narrow-mindedness. Man's wrong conception of the reason for our being on earth and in the World of Matter led him to act wrongly and to further develop base forms.

There was no respect for the different stages of development of the different peoples in the world and so the most developed nations at different times sought to subjugate other weaker nations for selfish purposes. They conquered and looted in a bid to increase their influence on earth instead of providing supporting help. For this reason they also used high-sounding and confusing language and played on the weaknesses of the other nations. The conquerors tried to force the conquered to abandon their beliefs and take up the foreign ones which they brought with them, without the right understanding of either the belief system of the conquered or the teachings which the conquerors wished to impart to them.

The narrow-mindedness of men kept them from seeing the need for indigenous development of the different peoples, and they sought to make everyone adopt one culture for easy exertion of influence over the weaker ones, and for easy accumulation of wealth and power. This only fed the fire of hatred and envy, and the production of more base forms by all men.

Those who thought themselves disadvantaged, because they felt deprived of the "better things in life", the acquisition of which had become the goal in life for many, felt envy and rage against those who were seen as better off. Others who found themselves in-between the two extremes became lukewarm spiritually, not wanting to disturb things as long as they were somewhat satisfied.

This behavior on all sides led to a further cultivation of the intellect in a one-sided manner, and a further development of base forms which only served to keep mankind tied to the world of Darkness because of their weights. Consequently men have been circling around the World of Gross Matter for ages without being able to rise beyond its spheres and ascend into higher and more luminous regions. Men became earthbound through their cravings for those things which can only be enjoyed here on earth. These base propensities kept men down according to the Laws of Gravity and of the Attraction of Homogenous Species. Naturally this condition was a reciprocal action for what men willed for themselves.

Their volition has been directed mainly towards what is earthly and so the fruits of their labors have developed accordingly. Their surroundings on earth have also taken on base forms, which further serve to keep the blind from seeing. Clarity can only be derived from clarity, and distortion from distortion. The conceptions formed by man in response to the happenings around him have been wrong for ages and so the different cultures of the peoples of the earth have also developed wrongly. Man blinded himself through his own activities.

Only those things are seen as necessary by man, which can help in the acquisition of wealth and power and a life of ease! The development, which was to lead him to a better understanding of Creation, was halted and so man lost all knowledge of his reason for being.

He has held on to rigid doctrines offered by those who are just as blind as he because these lifeless doctrines, which reek of a gross lack of logic and sensibility, serve to pacify him when his intuitive perception tries to tell him that something is wrong. He fears change because he no longer has the strength to pull himself out of the entanglements which keep him slumbering towards spiritual death.

Only the individual effort of the human spirit, as he recognizes the

Laws of Creation and abides by them in his activities, can help him out of this. Only that can raise him up towards the luminous goal of returning to his origin in the Spiritual Realm. Similarly, only the indigenous efforts of the different peoples of this earth can allow them to develop their abilities, as nations and as races, so that they can finally contribute to the harmonious development of this earth.

This, however, can only happen when each individual focuses on himself and his observance of the Laws of Creation. Everything that he does then must result in beauty and harmony. For true beauty only comes from the strict observance of the Laws of Creation.

Just like the development of man in one lifetime takes him through changes in his physical body, as this body grows and develops, which allow for the right functioning of his spirit at the right time, so does he experience changes in the process of living through any period, be it a moment or a lifetime. These changes are supposed to bring about different radiations and conditions which aid in the experiencing and development of the human spirit. His development on earth and in the World of Gross Matter was also supposed to proceed in stages, with him receiving the necessary help for his spiritual advancement at the end of each stage.

They are steps which he must use in his ascent upwards. He must experience each step thoroughly in order to be familiar with it and in order for him to proceed to the next one. These steps aid him in his development. For this reason, he must pay attention to his particular environment at any given time in order to be able to fulfill his obligations in accordance with the Laws of Creation.

Only by rightly experiencing the different stages of development, at the times when they manifest, can man succeed in developing rightly. He cannot wait until these conditions have passed by before taking advantage of what they have to offer in the form of spiritual experience. Once he has lost the opportunity it is gone forever. His next opportunity to experience what he missed will be much tougher and will require even more exertion from him.

The different stages will also find him at different places or in different circumstances at different times. If he does not pay attention to the task at hand, the task of the moment, then he will fail to fulfill. For this reason he must stop looking at other people and their conditions, or trying to copy foreign traditions, which are not meant for his spiritual development but may be meant for that of others. He must concentrate on himself and on the present. Only in the present will he find what he needs for his development! Only in the present can he shape the future, because the decisions that he makes in the present are what shape his future! They determine how he experiences the future!

Man must reap what he sows; therefore he should concentrate fully in the present when he is doing the sowing. He alone is responsible for the fruits that arise as a result of such acts of sowing. So a child must be left to be a child, a youth has to be allowed to be a youth, and peoples must be left to develop based on their varied levels of maturity. Only the obedience of the Laws of Creation can help man achieve the right kind of development within any given stage of development. And only the right kind of experiencing during the different stages of development can lay the foundations for the development of the right kind of fruit.

When this happens, man will know where he is supposed to be and what he should be doing at all times. The current situation, where women have left their high positions on earth to participate in the coarse, manly and also mainly intellectual activities, will also come to an end. So will the current distortion of souls, which has resulted in the earthly manifestation of female souls in male bodies, and male souls in female bodies.

This has arisen as a result of the stifling of the spirit and its true volition, and the consequent misdirection of the volition of women and men towards correspondingly wrong activities. When a woman maintains the volition for coarse activity, she knots corresponding threads of fate in a manner that causes her to incarnate into a male body in her next life. This is in accordance with the Laws of Creation, which develop every act of volition to its fruition.

The coming into earth in a different body other than one which coincides with the chosen activity the spirit, the initial and one-time resolution of the spirit as it left the Spiritual Realm as a seed, is due to the type of weaving engaged in by the particular soul in its past incarnation. Because he always gets what he wills! If a man neglects his lawful duties as a man and directs his volition mainly towards the more delicate and feminine activities of the woman, then in response and as a reciprocal action for his volition, upon his return to earth, or upon the ripening of the fruits of this volition of his, he will come in a female body.

The reverse is the case for the woman who maintains the volition for masculine activities and who strengthens only that part of her nature. She will receive the fruits of living in a man's body in her next opportunity to live on earth.

One can see this in most countries today if one looks around. Such people who find themselves in this condition can only come to an awakening through living through such a condition. Because it is only in this way that they can grow to want to change their condition and return to those types of activities which coincide with the kind of soul they initially incarnated into earth with upon leaving the Spiritual Realm as spirit-germs.

This distortion is also due to the ignorance of why we are here on earth and how we must live and work in this world. There are also women today who are mainly engaged in the coarse field of activity, side by side with men in their field of activity, but who have not yet incarnated into male bodies, because the physical body is too dense for such a transformation to occur in one lifetime.

Such women can only prevent a future incarnation into a male body if they start in time to focus on those spiritual and physical activities which are womanly. It is the same with the men who are currently leaning towards feminine activity, neglecting their duties as men. Here, as well as in everything else, it is the spiritual activity that is of paramount concern. When the spirit leads the physical aspect of the human being's life will also naturally develop correctly, because the spirit leads upwards.

Woman can never become man, neither can man become woman. Within the individual will remain a feminine or a masculine soul, depending on the one-time resolution that the human spirit undertook upon leaving the Spiritual Realm as a seed-germ. When he or she returns in a body that does not match the activity indicated in that resolution, masculine or feminine, positive or negative activity, the distortion will visibly manifest and make itself felt.

As soon as one starts to strive towards recognition of the Truth, by experiencing and abiding by the Laws of Creation, he will receive the help to sever ties that would otherwise lead to the development of a worse condition. Such a condition could cause many to despair and to lose all hopes of redemption from their burden. For everything that is not in order today, and this includes everything associated with the present mankind, obedience of the Laws in Creation is the only way to get back on the path to the Light, that is, the right path.

If one strives to recognize the Laws of Creation in the experiences of the moment, and there are many such experiences every hour, and if he adapts his volition to that of these Laws, then he can step-by-step sever those ties that keep him connected to base forms and past karmic threads.

He will also not have any need to bother with the activities of another person who might have to experience something entirely different for his salvation. He would not interfere with the development of another because he would have realized that the person's own experiencing is absolutely necessary for his redemption.

He will become more understanding and broad-minded because in the closing cycles of his past decisions he will be exposed to the different ways that the Laws of Creation manifest. He will rise higher spiritually and become able to see over a wider horizon. He will also be able to further the development of his particular environment through his timely and gradual development. This means that he will experience things consciously as they happen, knowing their significance with respect to the working of the Laws of Creation, and not just after they have already happened and lie far back in the past. When he knows what is happening when it is happening, then he will be able to make the right decisions, which alone can bring about peace and harmony.

In his interactions with others he will act in ways that will show understanding for the persons' conditions and will act accordingly. His actions will then only lead to something beneficial rather than destructive.

By adjusting his activities to the Will of the Light he will live up to his name, which stands in the Law. He will live in accordance with what his name says in accordance with the Laws of Creation. He will take his rightful place in any setting that he is attracted to and will fit nicely therein.

Because in the unceasing movements caused by the activities of the Laws of Creation, he will only affect his neighbors in an uplifting way.

He will also see no reason to want to run away from his current situation but will work to find out how he must act in it and how the Laws of Creation work in it. He will then be more satisfied with what he gets because he would realize that he has asked for it in the way that he made his decisions in the period prior to the time of the happening. He will spend more time on his purification through the understanding of the Laws of Creation and the observance of them.

See to it then, man, that you always are focused on recognizing the lessons of the moment as you maintain a good and noble volition. Only then will you be in a position to act aright in all that you do for the maturity of your spirit and the ennoblement of your surroundings!

HELP FOR THE DEVELOPING HUMAN SPIRITS ON EARTH

Man descended down into the World of Matter as a spirit seed in order to develop into a fully conscious human being at the end of his successful wanderings through the developing World of Matter.

Just like in all other cycles of development which occur here in the World of Matter, and which show a material manifestation of the Laws of Creation, which drive all developments in Creation, the human spirit also completes a cycle of development when he finally returns to his origin in the Spiritual Realm. He can only return to the Spiritual Realm completely purified. In no other way will he be able to reach such heights because the Law of Attraction of Homogenous Species will never allow that he step into the Spiritual Realm with even a speck of an alien species attached to him.

So he must live off all that he allows to bind to him in the process of his wanderings through the World of Matter. It is in the course of his wanderings that he is able to know of the working of the Laws of Creation. He receives the fruits of his labour, of his thoughts, words, and actions, so that he may experience the working of the Laws, which bring him the finished products of the seeds of his desires, of his volition.

The more he is able to experience, the more he is exposed to the working of these Laws and the more he is given the opportunity to experience their immutability and their adamantine nature. If during this experiencing he aligns his volition to the nature of the Laws of Creation, i.e., if he always acts in the sense of these Laws in Creation, then he will receive fruits which reflect this, and which will bring to him those conditions which will increase his knowledge of the Will of the Light in Creation.

These conditions must bring about joy, peace, and harmony, even if for some time it appears as though everything is against him, because he has to live through the closures of all the cycles which he opened in the past through his actions.

At the same time he will also be able to witness the strict nature of the working of the Laws of Creation, and will grow to trust in their guidance and want to always obey them because of this knowledge. Since his knowledge of Creation will also be broadened in the process, because these Laws brought about Creation, being the expression of the Will of God, he will also always be aware of the dangers of not obeying them.

His understanding of the reason for our being here in the World of Matter and on earth will be increased in a manner that will correspond to his increasing understanding of the Laws of Creation. His spiritual horizon will be broadened because he will rise spiritually as he is pulled upwards towards those Primordially Created Beings in Primordial Creation, who bear all the virtues necessary for the lawful development of the rest of Creation, and whose activities have an attracting effect on all that is spiritual in Creation, including the developing human spirits in Subsequent Creation.

Thus he is able to constantly rise higher as long as he remains consistent in his compliance with the Laws of Creation. Everyday he will be able to add to his trust in, and his knowledge of the Laws of Creation, because opportunities to witness their working will continue to stream at him every moment. These opportunities will come by way of the ripened fruits of his past decisions, which may be good or bad depending on the way that he decided at the time of their sowing.

The nature of his decision will always be in accordance with the nature of his spiritual maturity at any given moment, which shows itself in the nature of his soul. So he creates the conditions which he lives under, and he also determines how quickly he ascends in Creation. He can decide at any time to start to pay strict attention to the happenings around him every moment, with a good volition and in humility. This way when the fruits which develop in response to his wrong volition return to him for harvest, he will be able to draw from them those lessons which can elevate him, and he will not be hit as hard as he would have been had he not changed inwardly beforehand.

So the only way to be certain that one is not setting oneself up for a fall, as one receives the fruits of the seeds of one's past, is by concentrating on maintaining a good volition in the present. Nothing else can help him. He must adjust his actions to the working of the Laws of Creation, because these Laws in their activities crush everything that does not.

But he who is able to live aright as is willed by God also benefits greatly and he is able to successfully complete that cycle that will end with him entering into the Spiritual Realm as a fully conscious human spirit. This is the goal of the human spirit who wishes to succeed in Creation, and with this he attains eternal life because there in the Spiritual Realm he need no longer have fear of evil because none can exist there. To be allowed to be there means that the human spirit no longer bears the type of volition that will allow for the generation of base forms, which currently torment the earthmen of today.

The fully developed human spirit will then be able to transmit Light from God in the purity of its species to the developing species below it in the order of Creation. He will participate consciously in the expansion of the Almighty's Creation. He would no longer take part in the hindering of currents of spiritual power, which are diverted in the World of Gross Matter towards the development of centers of darkness, leaving an open wound through which power is drained from the cycle of the spiritual current in Creation.

Within the mighty cycle of the development of the human spirit in the World of Matter or Subsequent Creation, there are many more smaller or shorter cycles. There are thousands or perhaps even millions of cycles, which play a part in the development of man, and to which he remains connected until he has severed himself from them and learned the lessons inherent in them.

These cycles are of varied lengths or durations and are specific for individuals and the different forms that are developed in the courses of these cycles. The final product, which then impacts man at the precise time that it must, helps to form the nature of his experiences and adds to what he calls his condition. But these cycles, many of which come to a close every hour, also bring to man the opportunities for recognizing the Laws of Creation. He must abide by these Laws if he wishes to be successful in his mission here in the World of Matter, but first he must know them. Within these cycles lie the opportunities to know these Laws. He receives help in these cycles because he is lost without these opportunities to ascend through the attainment of knowledge!

The impact that he receives at the end of every one of these cycles is always dependent on how he stands spiritually at the moment when it hits him. This usually depends on how he has lived and exerted himself in the time during the period of the development of the cycle. His knowledge of the laws of Creation depends on how much he is able to grasp at the end of each cycle. He must be spiritually alert in order to perceive spiritually the lessons of the moment, shown to him in the combined effects of the cycle-closures. And only spiritual knowledge can help him ascend, through the maturity of his spirit.

There are no gaps in Creation and everything affects the other in Creation, so man keeps attracting to himself the kind of condition that coincides with the nature of his spirit. If he is vigilant and strives earnestly to recognize these Laws then he will attract to himself the conditions which will make this possible, and which will also lift him higher spiritually. He must however keep at it if he does not wish to stagnate in his efforts and suffer retrogression due to the setting in of decay, which results from lack of vitality. He must remain spiritually active!

In every moment he is able to experience the guidance that reaches him through the working of the Laws. In his experiencing he receives guidance based on how he attunes himself, just like one is able to receive signals through a radio depending on how he tunes it. At the end of every cycle he is uplifted spiritually, remains on the same level, or he is dragged down.

It is his performance during these moments that determines how he fares in the mightier cycle that develops towards an end one way or another, to his origin in Paradise as a matured human spirit or as a spirit seed germ, which results from a long period of time in a torturous state where he will have to be dragged down to those spheres where he would go through the intense experiencing of all the evil that he has allowed to come into Creation through his base volition, and where he will be stripped of the opportunity of ever becoming self-conscious.

So each of the smaller cycles helps man develop because it is in them that he gains knowledge of the Laws of Creation. As explained in the previous chapter the development of the human spirit takes him through different conditions and lifetimes. He must go through these conditions because he put these conditions into Creation through the weaving of the threads of his volition, even if he is not conscious of this fact at the moment. While living through these conditions he must abide by the Laws of Creation, if he is to be successful at the ends of the various cycles experienced within the period of each condition, and also at the end of the period of the conditions themselves.

For instance, a man who has incarnated into a community in a country in Africa will derive the best benefit from his experiences while living in that African country if he abides by the Laws of Creation in all that he does during the hours and the weeks and the years of his life in that country. The benefit mentioned here is spiritual benefit and not material wealth or comforts.

If he spends a whole lifetime in the African country, i.e., if he departs from this world while still living there, then the nature of his soul at the time he departs from this earth will determine the conditions that he will have to live through at his next destination.

His nature at the time of his departure from his conditions in the country in Africa, however, will depend on how well he has been able to understand and abide by the Laws of Creation, because this is directly linked with his spiritual maturity. It is in the absorption of the right kind of impressions as a result of the experiences that we go through in life that develops the spirit. The closer the impressions are to the Laws of Creation the better the spirit develops, because then the spirit is able to develop in the best possible way, those gifts from God with which it descended into the World of Matter as a spirit-germ.

It is because of the necessity of the attainment of the knowledge of the Laws of Creation, in the process of the development of the human spirit in the World of Matter, that the Creator provided man with so many opportunities to observe the working of these Laws and to abide by them. They lead back to God because they came from Him and serve as the best guides for man to strive towards Him and His Help.

For this reason, at the various times when the earth experienced transitions from one period or age to another, which are termed Cosmic Turning-Points, during which different radiations set in to further the development of the World of Matter, Called ones and prophets were sent to earth in response to the volition of those few who had asked for them through their activities.

During these periods of transition the earth felt an increased pressure of the Light because it was able to penetrate the most at those times. Fruits ripened for men whose development they had nurtured in the past. Also at such times the animistic beings which had to develop the works of man received an infusion of Light energy which caused them to quickly develop everything that was due to be harvested and to hand the fruits to their originators.

The effects of this surge of power was also expressed in the destruction of things which had been formed wrongly due to the base volition of man, by the animistic beings responsible for the task. Some of these effects man has termed natural disasters and include the earthquakes, typhoons, hurricanes, volcanic eruptions, floods, wild fires, and so on. They work to attain that point in the development of matter that should have already been attained at the time of the Cosmic Turning-Point.

Man feels the effects of the so-called natural disasters the way that he does because he remains behind in his development and is not open to the warnings that over time could lead him to the experiencing of such happenings in more peaceful ways. Those who are struck in the process of such happenings are not struck by accident, because absolutely everything that happens must coincide with the working of the Laws of Creation.

But the so-called disasters, just like every happening in Creation, also hold for man an abundance of help from the Light. At those times people are often so shaken by the events that they are forced to pay attention to things that they would not have noticed had everything calmly gone along according to their own wishes.

Man is somewhat loosened from his connections to base forms because he is forced to exert himself spiritually at such times of apparent chaos. In his period of extreme grief or pure joy he is not as focused on earthly matters as he might ordinarily be. This gives him the opportunity to perceive in relative humility, for humility is absolutely necessary for an undimmed absorption of help from the Light. Without humility, the conceit of man and his pseudo-knowledge prevent him from seeing that which alone can help him.

Due to his distorted conceptions, which have become even worse following the Fall of Man, he finds it very difficult to be truly humble. But conceit, as well as other attributes of the Darkness like envy, greed, spiritual ignorance, fear and narrow-mindedness, seems to drive his every action today. When one is connected to forms of these attributes through his nature he also keeps himself from the possibility of receiving help from the Light, Which is of a different species, and so, in accordance with the Law of Attraction of Homogenous Species, cannot make contact with him through Its Rays. Man is always the architect of his fate!

So at those times of transition, during the long period of the development of the human spirit on earth, called ones and prophets were sent to the different regions of the earth, at different times and to different peoples. They incarnated into those regions which they were attracted to in accordance with what they had to offer. This incarnation had to agree with their natures and the natures of the peoples to whom they were sent. They grew up in the surroundings of those whom they came to help, and in the process of growing up they were guided by the Light to those conditions that got them ready for their mission of teaching the ways of the Light to those who were attracted to them in accordance with their own natures and in the course of their various activities.

These called ones were prepared for their mission before their incarnations into the various regions of the earth for the execution of their mission. When they spread the Word, as they perceived it, they gave it to the people in the manner that made the best sense to the latter, and in the manner that allowed them to perceive the Truth in the simplest of forms, because the Truth cannot be separated from simplicity. For this reason different prophets or called ones incarnated at different times into the different regions where the people spoke different languages, and they used different examples to relay their messages.

From the early periods, a very long time ago, help was always sent to the developing mankind. Before the prophets and called ones came the Created Ones whose origin is higher than that of the developing human spirits on earth, but lower than that of the Primordial Spiritual Beings. They are spiritual beings who did not have to develop to consciousness in the World of Matter first, but became immediately conscious of themselves in the process of taking on form in the Spiritual Realm. They came to guide and aid the developing human spirits on earth in the transition from one stage of development to the next. Necessary for this transition is the updating of the existing knowledge of Creation for the developing human spirits.

However, in strict accordance with the Laws of Creation, only those who had kept their spirits alert through spiritual activity, not the maintenance or development of intellectual acuteness, were able to recognize the messengers from the Light. This was in accordance with what they had willed for themselves in their everyday activities leading up to the time of the coming of help in the form of the teachings of the prophets. Those who allowed their spirits to fall asleep did not recognize these helpers who came to help man increase his knowledge of Creation and ascend. They all received what was due to them in the reciprocal actions of their past decisions. They remained in the dark and ignorant.

Already, at the time when the prophets came, man had fallen to his base desires and to the Darkness through his one-sided development of the intellect. He placed the intellect above the spirit in all his thinking and his actions. So he could not recognize what the intellect could not see or make sense of. He had decided that only that which the intellect, with all that has come from it, is able to understand and prove to exist will he also accept as true and as his reality.

Only very few people were able to take advantage of the teachings and the constant warnings of the prophets. Some listened to them but did not apply what they said to their own lives. The teachings did not become alive within them. These people's conceptions of what they experienced were not made to coincide with the wisdom of the prophets' teachings and so their interpretations of them were also wrong. Only through personal experiencing can one attain knowledge and conviction. They needed to experience aright what was taught in order to understand it.

The prophets brought valuable hints, which could help man attain knowledge along his path through the World of Matter, but man had to travel that path himself in order to get to true knowledge. This path is different for each individual however, so each individual must travel this path for himself and by himself in order to be able to understand the teachings through experiencing.

This means that he must respond to those reciprocal actions which we receive every moment in a manner that shows wisdom. In doing so he opens himself up to the Rays of the Light because he would be able to see what those closing cycles have to show him as soon as he is of the right nature to receive. He must incorporate the teachings into his activities! They must become a part of him! He must live them! Hence, they must become alive in him!

The prophets came to show man how to act in order to receive in humility that which Creation is constantly at the ready to give him. They could not just by their own actions make man knowledgeable. Man was to follow their hints, which came from the guided experiences of the prophets, if he wanted to walk on the right path, or along his path in the right way.

But most men derided the teachings and warnings of the prophets and scoffed at them. They regarded them as people out of touch with reality, because they had made their own reality only that which the intellect is able to understand. They put themselves, their spirits, under the rule of the earth-bound intellect. Those who listened to the prophets mostly received the teachings in a one-sided manner that caused them to only superficially and outwardly give the impression of understanding the teachings.

But they did not really understand the teachings because they did not make the teachings in their entirety become alive within them. They did not live in accordance with the sense of the teachings as they were brought. Rather, they perceived the lessons inherent in the teachings in the ways that showed their own inner natures, which had not been purified by their mere outward behaviour. They had not realized the reasons for most of what they did in the name of worshiping the Creator. They still held the wrong conceptions in their minds even though they outwardly portrayed something else to their neighbors in a bid to gain their favor, one way, or another. They lacked true understanding of the Laws of Creation, of the Will of God.

Their service was not to the Creator but to the intellect and therefore to the Darkness, because in their thoughts and in the way that they regarded their fellow men, they still planted those seeds which only led to the further development of evil forms.

They were still attached to those forms which draw evil currents from the dark centers in the depths of the Realm of Darkness. They still harboured envy, greed, spiritual ignorance, hatred, fear, conceit, and narrow-mindedness, and as a result they viewed their surroundings in ways that led them to further cultivate distorted conceptions. The base attributes clouded their sights and so they could not see clearly the Will of God in Creation.

When the returning effects of their past deeds came back to them, as they always will, they reacted in ways that displayed their lack of understanding of the teachings of the prophets. The fundamental issues remained the same. They had not rid themselves of the forms to which they had become attached during their previous lifetimes and before the coming of the prophets. They thought that they were automatically made special because the individual prophets or called ones happened to have incarnated into their particular regions.

Their conceited attitudes led them to think that they had to be special if they were picked to harbour such messengers, who, ironically, they often attacked with slanderous and malicious words at the time when they were still alive and trying to steer mankind away from the wrong course that they were on.

This feeling of being the only truly blessed ones, which stems from the vanity of mankind, made it difficult for men to accept the teachings of the other prophets who had not incarnated in their midst but had previously taught some other peoples in other regions of the earth.

They could not recognize the similarities between the teachings because they were particularly interested in themselves alone and how special they were for being the only ones to have received the "only true teachings." And since they had not done the necessary work of listening and making certain that the message was alive within them, they did not recognize the similarities between the messages of the different teachers. Also, those who had received the teachings in the other regions had not preserved them in their true forms due to their lack of understanding and spiritual indolence, making the teachings appear different.

The wrong conceptions borne by men also crept into the translations and transmissions of these messages so that the truth in them was further eroded and finally distorted. This was only a natural reaction because it cannot remain the same when it has passed through persons whose natures could not maintain the purity of the works of the prophets. Also, being mainly intellectual in their ways of understanding, men regarded the teachings of the prophets from the point of view of their earthly understandings, which were alien to the right conceptions that were intended by the Bringers of the Message from the Light.

Everything had to develop wrongly as a result. Only the human spirit who actually bestirs himself to see can see that the teachings all came from one Source and that the differences and distortions are the works of the darkened man. For he does not need to belong to any religious group or subscribe to rigid doctrines in order to realize the Will of God here on earth and in the World of Matter!

The prophets were here to help man continue upwards in his recognitions of God through His Laws in Creation. Man would have been able to rise higher in his recognitions and finally become able to see higher than the highest Animistic Beings, to the point of perceiving directly from the Spiritual Realm. And then in the process of the same upward development they would have at the right time been led to the knowledge of the Primordial Spiritual Beings, and finally of God Himself. He had to be led step-by-step, stage-by-stage in this natural process of development.

But due to his fall man put a halt to his ascent and held on rigidly to those things which had been passed down to him by his parents and others, who were often of a similar nature to him. The necessary activity of the spirit of earthman was lacking. He just accepted what he was told without questions, even when something within him told him it did not make sense. When his intuitive perception let him know there was something wrong with his conceptions of things and happenings around him, he tried even harder to brush it aside and act in accordance with the will of the intellect and all those people who serve the Darkness through it.

He did not realise that in his intuitive perception, part of which is his conscience, he could also perceive other forms of help from those who no longer exist in the physical body, but who have passed on into the next planes of experiencing, and who have as yet some cycles to close on earth.

Such people who may have cycles to close on earth, due to their past decisions, but who are not living in the material body of the earth and so cannot manifest visibly to earthman, can also help man while he is on earth through his intuitive perception.

These human spirits can help because they have been through those conditions or situations which they offer advice about. Often it will be in those areas where they once failed while they too were on earth. In their urge to help, out of true love, they receive the opportunity to offer advice through the intuitive perception of the person still living whom, through the attraction of homogenous species, they become attracted to in response to their urge to help and in accordance with their own natures.

By helping they can fulfill the Laws of Creation by closing those cycles for themselves which they cannot ascend without closing, and which may have bound them for sometime in the sphere of gross matter. They cannot force anyone whom they may be allowed to help to accept their advice. They have to let the person make up his own mind and make a decision one way or another, because man cannot be denied his right to choose, his so-called free will. They are able to share in the joys of those whom they are able to help make the right decisions, and also in the grief of those whom, despite their urgings, still go ahead and make the mistakes against which they are warned.

This experience also helps the one trying to help to resolve not to make a similar mistake again because he is able to see the anguish and the pain that it causes another whom he may be trying to help. His intuitive perception is able to make its way to the one being helped because of the ability in Creation of finer species to penetrate denser ones. Here, however the person who helps the other from outside the materiality of the earth-plane can do so because he has been through that particular experience and has learned the lessons therein. Only then can he help. He is not so much higher than the one to be helped that he can no longer understand him, but must be close enough to still understand the condition well enough to be able to help the one in need.

He is often half a step higher than the one being helped or on the same level as he. He is not some being from the Spiritual Realm or anywhere higher than the environs of the sphere of earth, but must be one who is close enough to understand and to offer the right kind of help to the man on earth in the course of his earthly activities. After he has helped him he must go along on his own path towards his own purification and ascent, just like the man on earth must do if he is to be successful.

Another human spirit then takes his place in helping the man on earth, who then has to deal with another circumstance which this new helper is familiar with, having lived through it at least once before and having been granted the opportunity to help and at the same time bring an end to a cycle which he must close on earth. This opportunity makes it unnecessary for him to incarnate on earth especially for that purpose, while he at the same time fulfils the Laws of Creation. For whatever originated on earth must be reaped on earth!

There are many such souls, which are ready to help man while he is still in the physical body on earth. Their urgings make up a part of his conscience, which he perceives in his intuitive perception. So the more he listens to and acts according to his intuitive perception, which is always a faithful guide, the more clearly he will be able to perceive the help that comes from outside the physical sphere. He must not, however, confuse the intuitive perception with the feeling, which is related to the intellect, as mentioned in the previous chapter.

The feeling is connected to the intellect while the intuitive perception is the expression of the spirit and is connected to it. By clarifying the intuitive perceptive capacity one also clarifies the feeling. This is because the thoughts that he will generate in response to some stimulus, in order to form a conception of the situation, will become more in line with the Laws of Creation and will also become more correct. Then his intellect, which helps to produce the feeling, can then be used as a tool of the spirit like it should have been from the beginning and ever since. Only then can he make the right use of his feeling. It must be led by the clarified intuitive perception.

He will also in the process learn to tell the difference between the thoughts produced by the frontal brain and the intuitive perception, which latter he will find to be connected to deep inner feelings, and comprise the first impression that hits the human spirit in any situation.

Here one can see the various opportunities provided man for a joyful ascent. He has help all around him but he is blind to them because he has formed a wrong conception of what he should be doing here on earth. He does not see the help for what it is and so he does not make use of it. He stubbornly insists on having his own selfish will prevail. The result is that he remains inwardly the same, despite the outward calculated changes which he may have made to present himself as one who is worth something to his fellow men.

Step by step man was supposed to develop to the point where he could be told about the Highest things in Creation and also about the Creator. This could only happen when he had successfully absorbed the other messages along the way in the process of building upwards.

Just like a child in school must go through the several stages of learning if he is to be allowed to go on to the higher levels in order to finally understand certain concepts which most adults already know about, so does man have to experience the Will of God in Creation in stages in the process of developing to spiritual maturity. In the case of the child he is tested before he is allowed to proceed in order to determine how well he has understood the lessons, and what he must still know before he is allowed to go on to the next higher level.

It was to prepare man and enable him ascend upwards to the Light that the helpers came to teach. They came to help him get ready for the time when there will have to be a final test, a Final Judgement, which will determine who ascends upwards towards the Luminous Heights and who must be left in the material world, which many have declared their love

143

for through their actions and their volition, so that they may go through the necessary disintegration with it, as must happen in the course of all material cycles.

Not everything could be taught at once then since the human spirits had to understand the lessons in stages. So every time there was a new revelation new ways of viewing the Truth were offered to the maturing mankind. New ways which in the past would have been incomprehensible to them due to their level of development at the time, but which at the present they would have to know if they are to continue successfully towards the Luminous Heights.

For this reason the Forerunners of the Light came to spread the Message of the Lord amongst mankind. For this reason Krishna incarnated in the region of India, and so did Buddha. Lao Tse incarnated in China and Zoroaster in Iran, all in a bid to respond to the needs of those who genuinely deserved to be helped with increased knowledge about Creation. The Prophet Mohammed, as the last of the Forerunners for the Light, incarnated in Arabia to bring this Message to the tribes of that region, and to all of mankind.

Also, Moses incarnated in Egypt in order to deliver the Commandments of God to mankind through the Jewish people at the time.

In the meantime however, as mankind was being prepared for this time which we are currently experiencing and whose effects must yet increase in accordance with the process of development in the World of Matter, mankind fell so low that they dragged the entire earth with them down into the realm of darkness. This made it even more difficult for man to form the right conceptions in the course of his experiences.

He became so deeply entangled that the words of the prophets and called ones no longer penetrated enough to make any meaningful impact on his spirit. He dragged everything down to the level of the intellect before he could even make use of it. But since the Message was meant for the spirit the intellect did not understand it for what it was and naturally transformed it into a form that will keep it (the intellect) in power. Every word was wrongly taken in and every conception distorted. Man was heading for spiritual death if nothing was done to wake him from his spiritual sleep.

The Light had to intervene if the few who were still worth saving and who still deserved the Almighty Grace of God were to be helped. So in order to save those ones from being lost to spiritual death, before the Son of Man was to come to bring the Judgement and the attendant purification of the World of Matter, the Creator severed a Part of Himself so that It may incarnate into earth and help them with the Power of Divine Knowledge.

So Jesus Christ, as the Love Incarnate of God, came to earth for the purpose of guiding those who still wished to be saved.

Prior to His coming the Called one, Moses, had been sent amongst the Jews who were in bondage in Egypt under the tyrannical rule of Pharaoh. At that time, as I have already explained, darkness ruled the greater part of the earth and the normal development of mankind had ceased. A lust for power and earthly pleasures was then the goal of the depraved men in most of the more developed regions. At the heights of their earthly powers such regions thought themselves invincible and sought to acquire more power in order to exert more influence in their surroundings.

The welfare and the development of the human spirit was not a concept that was understood by them, let alone considered. The objective of such peoples and their leaders was to acquire more power and maintain the status quo at all costs.

Their service was to the Darkness, which controlled the intellect to which these people had subjugated themselves. And so there was also very little concern for the welfare of those who were considered outsiders and slaves. There was really no concern for the welfare of the human spirit. Greed, narrow-mindedness, fear, hatred, vanity, sordid sensuality, lack of shame, love of ease and earthly comforts, and spiritual ignorance ruled over mankind, and also through the leaders of such peoples. And such was the condition also in Egypt under the rule of the then Pharaoh.

Under the rule of Pharaoh the Jews at the time, through their intense suffering, which was also a reciprocal action for their past neglect, came to perceive the nature of their oppressors and also of their own vulnerability, laying the grounds for the type of humility that came with broad-mindedness and reduced conceit. In this state they became able to perceive a Supreme God to whom they prayed and asked for help. Help came from the Creator through the person of the called one, Moses.

He responded to his calling and proceeded to show the Egyptian ruler why he had no right to keep the Egyptians as slaves and to torture them so, and demanded at the same time for their release. His trust in the Creator was strengthened by his own personal experiences, which followed earlier preparations that took place before his incarnation amongst the people in Egypt at the time. In the process of fulfilling his task he also gave the Egyptian ruler the opportunity to see the error in his ways, for the Truth that he had perceived was not just for those whom he was trying to free but also for all men who could still help themselves through It.

Their liberation from bondage also gave the Jews the impetus to awaken from their spiritual slumber and energetically embrace the truth about the Will of God in all their actions. They received the best help for this through all they were allowed to experience. Through Moses they received the Ten Commandments which, when strictly abided by, would lead any willing and earnest human spirit upwards to the Luminous Heights. This happening also at the same time helped prepare the soil for the incarnation of Jesus Christ centuries later.

But before He came, the Jewish people at the time had once again slipped back into base attitudes which were against the Will of the Light and once again found themselves under the tight grip of the then powerful and influential Romans. The Romans were at that time at the stage in their development when they had developed to the point that, as was the case with the Egyptians before them, all the attributes of the darkness were nourished to devastating degrees, due to conceit and the lust for power and earthly comforts. They channeled the neutral power in Creation towards the development of base forms, and being so developed at that time that they had influence over those in the surrounding regions, they were able to spread the effects of these forms as far wide as they could.

This has been the trend with this mankind. Whichever group of people were able to rise in earthly power and have influence over the rest of mankind or their neighbors, effectively developed to over-ripeness the

146

base forms that plague earthman, and in the process exerted a negative influence over a wide region of the earth through their activities.

They spread the rottenness of their ways aboard, far and wide, as they subjugated other weaker peoples in various ways. This behaviour has resulted from the gross conceit of man and his ignorance as to why we are here on earth. This phenomenon can be noticed on earth today in all the spheres of activity and in the relationships between countries and peoples, even between individuals and groups of individuals.

It has prevented the absorption of help from the Light by those who have become too narrow-minded and too conceited to receive in humility. They become lost in lust for earthly power and influence and so cannot consider anything else to be of importance to them.

At around the time when Jesus Christ incarnated on earth the Romans were exerting their influence and power on their surroundings and the people in them, these included the Jewish people of that time.

It was under the rule of the Romans that some of the Jews at the time were able to develop inwardly, to come closest to the right understanding of the Laws of Creation. They however were still far from rightly fulfilling these Laws, but they came closest amongst all other men at the time to their rightful understanding.

Because of their experiences they were the ones who were most open to the radiations from the Light. Compared to other men they stood closest to the Light in their attitudes and understanding. It was because of this that the Son of God incarnated amongst them in accordance with the attraction between homogenous species.

Here it is a question of the Jews at the time forming the best conceptions about the working of the Laws of Creation, the Will of God, when compared to the rest of the people on earth. They however were not pure or lacking in base forms or spiritual ignorance. Theirs was just not as dark or as base and distorted as those of the other peoples on earth at that time. And since the Son of God could only come along the path of Purity for His High Mission, He incarnated amongst those who came closest in grasping the right conceptions of the Will of the Light, which alone lead upwards to the Light.

He came to earth from the Light and not from the surrounding spheres of the World of Matter where developing human spirits have to go for a time in order to further develop and to live through the conditions which they caused to arise through their activities while on earth. And from where they also return to earth in order to live through the conditions that have ripened for them here and also to develop further.

But He came from the Creator Himself for the purpose of, for a time, forming a direct link between mankind and the Creator so that, with the Power of His Divine Knowledge, He could cleave through the entanglements of the Darkness and give deserving men the *opportunity*, through His teachings and His Word, to detach themselves from the base forms that they have attached to themselves and ascend upwards.

In order to do this He came to live amongst men so that in the process of fulfilling the Laws of Creation He could tell men the truth. By virtue of His high Origin, He had the power to objectively present the Truth and live It amidst the surrounding Darkness. Only One such as He could deliver men from the entanglements in which they had bound themselves, by showing them the way through His Teachings and through the personal example of His own earthly life.

Prior to His coming there had been several prophesies concerning the coming of a strong Helper Who would bring man the knowledge that can help him disentangle himself from the base forms that keep him weighed down in the World of Matter. However, this promised One still had to go through a period of preparation, during which He accustomed Himself, through personal experiencing, more thoroughly with the nature of mankind to whom He had been sent, and amongst whom He would have to do His Work of giving the knowledge of Creation to deserving ones.

He had to thoroughly know the evil that has the human spirit bound in the World of Gross Matter in order to help him get out of it. In no other way could He help the developing human spirit, but through the personal experiencing of all the forms of this evil. He was still being prepared for this High Mission when Jesus Christ had to incarnate, for the sake of the few who could be saved and who could be further helped at the time when this strong Helper, the Son of Man, would come to earth bringing the Judgement with Him.

The coming of Jesus Christ was an Act of Emergency for the sake of those ones who deserved it! He came knowing of the dangers that He might face amongst the men who served the Darkness. But He is the Love Incarnate of the Creator, the kind of love that mankind has never been able to understand, and which he would still not be able to imagine at his most luminous form in the Spiritual Realm. This love is the perfect kind, which comes from Perfection and so oversees all of Creation. It guides to the Light all those who express their wish to be led to the Light. This wish they have to express in their activities.

To such people the Son of God came to show the ways that man must act if he is to save himself. These ways will lead him over time to the right understanding of the Laws of Creation. But he must do the work himself since he can only experience that which he has brought into Creation through his volition. He must travel along that path that will bring to him the fruits of his past deeds so that he may reap them and learn from them. The Son of God brought man knowledge of the ways to live in order to be able to sever the ties to wrong conceptions and base forms, in the process of which he would also know of the Laws of Creation and mature.

He brought Light into a world of Darkness so that those of the right nature could see their ways out of the Darkness! Without His coming the human spirits developing on earth, and who were already slumbering towards spiritual death, would have surely lost all hopes of being able to attain self-consciousness and return as fully conscious human beings to the Spiritual Realm. They would have had to undergo disintegration with matter.

He did not come to do anything as unlawful and as impossible as to take away the sins of the guilty man of this earth. He knew that He might have to suffer under the hands of guilty mankind, since He was descending into the World of Darkness, where He would be open for attack by the Darkness through its soldiers. His coming despite this knowledge meant that He was prepared for and accepted whatever might befall Him in the process of fulfilling in His Mission of Love! This way the Laws of Creation were also fulfilled because He came already prepared for the possible dangers that He faced, for He was armed with the Truth, Which is the same as Divine Power!

But this does not mean that He came so that He could die and be sacrificed for the conceited earthman, so that his sins would be washed away through the act. No such thing could be possible in the Will of the Light! This base assumption is the product of the base volition of man, his conceit, which causes him to see himself as more than he actually is!

In his need to maintain this falsehood he pictures himself as one whom the Creator needs, instead of one who needs the Creator. He knows of the work that is needed in order to become more like one who is deserving of the Love of God, so he chooses to think that it is the other way around, that the Creator Himself needs him and so will go against His own Laws in order to make the little earthman happy, so that he can continue in his old and diseased ways, affecting his surroundings in quite negative ways and bringing about nothing but destruction, only in the end to throw the burden of his guilt on the Son of His Creator and ascend to heaven!

Man indeed has reached the peak of his conceit and narrow-mindedness if this could sound logical to him. And the Laws of Creation are always logical. They are logic itself! There cannot be anything more logical than these Laws, which express the perfect Will of the Creator! Anything that is wanting in logic cannot be in accordance with the Will of God! It cannot be in accordance with the Laws of Creation, because they come from Perfection!

So Jesus came not to die and take away man's sins but to help the deserving ones, i.e., those who could still become active spiritually, to find their way out of the Darkness. He used parables to illustrate the happenings in Creation, but the vanity of men did not allow them to thoroughly scrutinize themselves by putting themselves in the position of the sinner, so that they could get rid of that attitude which makes them like those whom the Son of God spoke against in His parables.

The teachings were taken too superficially because men could not bring themselves to experience intuitively what was talked about in them. They did not see themselves as ones who were in need of change. They always thought that somebody else was being talked about in the parables with which Jesus Christ taught. But He was talking to all men, for none is without sin. It is only the conceit of men that keeps them from strictly applying the teachings to themselves objectively.

The people who led in the temples at the time saw Jesus Christ as a hindrance to their ability to keep a firm grip on those whom they had influence over. They feared for their reputations and their positions in the society, just like would be the case should Jesus Christ come to earth today, or should anyone dare to throw some light on the dark practices of today's mankind.

They knew that their rigid doctrines, which they had passed on to those who happily accepted them so that they did not need to exert themselves further, would soon come tumbling down, especially since they themselves did not really know why they did what they did. The true knowledge of the Will of God can only be attained through personal experiencing of the working of the Laws of Creation, and this knowledge is not known to anyone who cannot recognize the Truth in the teachings of Christ, or who can make such comments as is made about the Mission of Christ by the churches.

The teachings of the prophets were to help man with this experiencing so that he did not continue to form wrong conceptions and fall deeper into the trap of the ever cunning Darkness, which uses the intellect as its tool. However when the teachings are not lived, i.e., when the hearers of such teachings do not live in strict accordance with the right sense of the teachings, then the teachings themselves can do nothing for them.

They would remain sealed to them because men would just bring the teachings down to the level of perception of the intellect as they try to understand it with dull spirits, and this at best will lead to the distortion of what the teachings actually say. Only the active spirit can understand what is meant for the spirit. Only through experiencing can one come to actually know something. Everything else he does not really know, he merely may have heard of it or learned about it using his perishable intellect.

And what the spirit has not assimilated through experiencing not only remains behind on earth after the physical death of man, but also does not change the way that he experiences life, the way he forms his conceptions about the happenings around him.

It is like dressing up a goat in clothing worn by human beings and expecting that that is enough to transform its behaviour. The goat will remain a goat and the human spirit with wrongly formed conceptions will always remain just that, until he severs his ties to that which negatively influences the way he thinks and acts, and recognizes the Laws of Creation in the process.

And the only way to know the Laws of Creation is by rightly experiencing the happenings in our surroundings here and after we leave the earth. So when the teachings from the Light are not assimilated through the right kind of experiencing, then the human spirit does not mature and the same mistakes are made over and over again, bringing about worse conditions in the reciprocal effects of the wrong decisions.

Calling oneself a servant of God just because one works in a temple or a church does not make one a true servant of God. The person only serves the church or temple and falls with it if it does not adapt itself and its activities to the Laws of Creation.

Only obedience of His Will can make one able to truly serve God. This is because he would be able to transmit light, which is undimmed by the darkness of the soul, to his surroundings, and bring the glory of the Creator to his surroundings through his works. In order words he must strive for inner purity in order to be able to serve God. In the reciprocal actions of this only harmony and peace will arise.

The leaders of the temples of the Jews at the time when Christ incarnated amongst them were guilty of spiritual ignorance, just like the men around them and all around earth were. They showed this clearly through their actions, their works at that time.

They put a lot of effort into discrediting Jesus Christ and His activities and as a final act of fear, hatred, envy and gross vanity, they served Him up to the authorities of the time, with lies and slanderous talk, so that He could be removed from their midst and stop agitating with His teachings the sedated crowds which they exerted their power and influence over.

This happening, which resulted in the physical death of Christ, was not just due to the acts of those who actively and physically tried to stain Him and His reputation, but it was due to the darkness of the souls of the various individuals who have fallen to the Darkness in the process of developing in the World of Matter.

Those who were there and who actively participated in the heinous acts were merely the executors of the volition of many. Each person would have to receive his just measure of the reciprocal action for this crime against the Light as has already been explained in the different chapters previously.

Upon His discovery, through His experiences, that His disciples could not understand most of what He had to tell them, He promised that the Spirit of Truth, the Comforter, shall come and will lead them to all truths. This Person of Whom the Son of God spoke is the Holy Spirit through Whose Radiation Creation came about. It is He in Whose Name all the happenings in Creation are fulfilled because He is the Beginning and the End of all happenings. All cycles open and close according to His Volition, for He is the Living Will of God Whose Laws brought about the entire Creation.

It is because of His activities, which keep Him linked with Creation, that He bears the title the Son of Man. He is also a Part of God the Father, the out-born Son of God, because in His activities He remains at the boundary of the Divine Realm. He is the Divine Will of God the Father and for this reason everything in Creation is fulfilled in His Name, has to succumb to the Laws of Creation, which come from Him.

He is the beginning and the end of all happenings, because He is the starting point of the Radiations that formed the entire Creation, and He will be the last One left should everything in Creation have to shrivel up and disintegrate. It is His presence at the boundary of the Divine Realm, unimaginable distances above the point at which the Primordial Beings were able to take on form, which makes it possible for Creation to remain in existence and with a constant supply of Power from God. He is the Alpha and Omega!

Through His activities the entire Creation receives Power for the maintenance of all that has been created, on the Day of the Holy Spirit, of the outpouring of power by the Holy Spirit. Those who are open to receive it experience the outpouring of this Power every year here on earth, as do other creatures in the rest of Creation. This Power revitalizes all those who can consciously experience its radiation, and they become energized and strengthened in their Light-willed activities. It was this outpouring that was experienced by the disciples of Jesus Christ Who had gathered in commemoration of their ascended Lord, following the death of their Master on the cross.

He also It is Who comes at this time of the Final Judgement as already prophesied about by many servants of God. And He has come, and the Great Purification, which is a part of the Judgement, can already be felt all over the World of Gross Matter, of which the earth is a part. This period brings to men the fruits of the seeds whose development they have nurtured through their volition and actions over thousands of years.

Through His activities He draws corresponding undimmed Light-Power down to this part of Creation, and He is able to pave the way out of the Darkness after personally experiencing its effects during His period of training. With His help men can find their way out of the entanglements in which they have bound themselves through the expression of their volition.

At this time the cycle of the appearance of the Radiant Star is closing, the Star of Bethlehem, which heralded the birth of Jesus Christ, now returns, filled with spiritual power from the Primordial Spiritual Plane. Through its Ray Light-pressure like never experienced before on earth can be felt, and this is causing the rapid and never-experienced speedy closure of all cycles which remain open, so that men can be Judged through the experiencing of all the evil which they have placed in Creation through their thoughts, words and actions.

It was to prepare men for this period that the Son of God Jesus Christ came. His teachings were to prepare men for this time, because if they had been absorbed in the right sense then, men would have already started at that time to change their ways and sow more good seeds, as opposed to the wrong and evil seeds that they have been sowing since the departure of Christ from earth.

But His teachings were not well understood, not even by His disciples, because the separation between they and the Son of God was too great. His core was Divine Unsubstantiate (i.e., of the same nature as the Creator Himself Who is without form) while that of men is spiritual. The distance between the two are unimaginable by the human spirit because he can never attain to the Divine Realm, let alone to God Himself. The Son of God means a Part of God, incarnated in flesh through an unbreakable Radiation. He departed from His disciples, knowing that they had not understood all that He had told them.

Before His death He promised them and His other followers the coming of the Son of Man, the Comforter, the Spirit of Truth. He asked them to have faith in what He had taught them so that in living according to His teachings they would sow the kind of seeds that will make it possible for them to receive salvation in this time. In the reciprocal actions of their deeds they would receive knowledge about the entire Creation, which they would need in order to resurrect themselves from the World of Matter, because He is the Resurrection and the Life, since He bears the Living Word within Him.

However, He said that the faith must become living within these people. For this to happen men had to live in accordance with His teachings. In the process of doing so they would have attained a level of conviction that would have made them more steadfast in their knowledge of the Laws of Creation. They would have developed more trust in these Laws and more confidence in their protection as they made the right decisions in the process of their development.

But the teachings were not properly assimilated and became grossly distorted so that today what is left of the original teachings of Christ, as they are taught by those who think they know, are rigid doctrines and traditions which have nothing to do with the worship of the Creator. These traditions are passed down from generation to generation in a manner that prevents the entry of any knowledge of the Truth into the person trapped within these base entanglements.

This lack of understanding of the teachings of Christ have shown themselves in various ways in the past two thousand years and have led to the alienation of masses of people from the true knowledge of Creation. In trying to spread this limited knowledge of theirs, which shows no signs of life, men have disrupted the natural development of many tribes and peoples, because they did not understand Creation well enough to know how and when to help. For two thousand years man has fallen deeper into the world of Darkness and stands to reap much that is ugly.

In this period the cycle of the coming of Christ would also come to a close, bringing with it reward and punishment for those who have been allowed to make their decisions and contribute to developments of various forms during the period of development of the cycle. Man will be rewarded according to how he has been able to assimilate the Word that Christ brought to mankind in the face of immense hostility from the Darkness. The proof of this will be in the way that he has acted in the past two thousand years towards his Creator and His Will.

This will of course be in addition to all other fruits which man has yet to reap, whose seeds he still must atone for, seeds which he has sown in Creation since he came here to the World of Matter.

Wake up, man, so that you may experience consciously the working of the Laws of Creation in this period, so that you are not lost to disintegration together with the maturing World of Matter!

SOME OF MY EXPERIENCES BEFORE WRITING THIS BOOK

I was born on June 17, 1975 in the city of Edmonton in the province of Alberta in Canada. My parents had decided to move back to Nigeria, where they were born and where they grew up. So when I was six months old and my older sister was one and half years old, we all moved to Nigeria. My father was a medical doctor who specialized in obstetrics and gynaecology.

He had been away from Nigeria for about twenty years having lived and studied in the United Kingdom for a great part of that time. When we got to Nigeria, he worked in a general hospital run by the government of the state in which we lived. My mother had studied microbiology and completed her masters program in a university in Nigeria after we got to Nigeria.

We lived in the city where my father worked until I was about 5 years old and it was there that I attended nursery school and the first grade of elementary school. We got along quite nicely with the neighbours that surrounded us. Also, there were about three of my older cousins on my father's side of the family who mostly lived with us in the different parts of Nigeria where we eventually lived in.

These cousins were not as fortunate as I was to have parents who could pay for my schooling, so my father took care of that while they lived with us and helped out with activities around the house. This included taking care of us children while my parents were out working or tending to other issues. This is the way things usually are in Nigeria. There is no welfare system and people usually live with relatives when their own parents are not in positions to educate them.

I grew up with about two to four of such cousins throughout my entire stay in Nigeria. All of these cousins were female cousins except one. At some periods during my life in Nigeria, there were altogether eleven people living in our house. While in the first city that we lived in my mother bore two more girls. So at this point I had three sisters, with one older one and two younger ones.

I played with my sisters, the neighbours and my cousins. During the last year of our stay in this city, my father worked in a hospital in another city close by. My youngest sister was born in 1980 just before we moved to the other city to join my father. In the next city, I enrolled into one of the best elementary schools, together with my elder sister and an older male cousin. I remember being usually quiet at school and in the midst of other children, but I was generally happy and performed well in the school examinations.

While in the second grade I met a boy with whom I became friends. I found him to be different from the other children in the class and I was able to forge a relationship with him. We sat next to each other in class because of this reason and we were still friends when we found ourselves together in the same class again in the fourth grade. We had so much in common that when the teacher asked us to all keep silent for a period of time so that she could elect the class prefects for the year, we were the only ones who took it seriously enough not to say a word during that period. He was made the class prefect and I the assistant.

After the first term of the fourth grade I transferred to a semi-private school for the children of the staff and faculty of a nearby university. The headmaster of the school was from my village (every native of Nigeria should have a village where his or her ancestors hailed from) and was close to our family and so I, with my sisters, called him uncle. There were some people in the school whom I knew before attending that school and I met others for the first time while at the school.

Two of the friends that I knew prior to attending the school were actually my second cousins (they were brothers) and we were all in the same class. I was not the most notorious boy in school but I was also not unknown in the school. In the final year, the sixth grade, I was elected to be the head prefect of the school. I also participated in certain activities such as the school drama presentations during one of which I played the part of an employer who attempted to accept a bribe from a job candidate.

Towards the end of the sixth year of elementary school, every pupil is expected to take a series of exams for acceptance into a secondary school. One gets to pick one's first, second and third choice of schools and then will gain admittance into one or more of those schools depending on his or her performance in the entrance examinations. I took the examination for this process and I also took the examination to get into the Nigerian Military School.

The idea of going to a military school was thrilling, partly because the location of the school was far from home and partly because it seemed like it would be an interesting experience. It certainly was going to be different from the schools that some of my friends were interested in. The interview for the military school exam was held at the site of the school and it lasted two weeks.

Since we had to travel to the school, which was far away from home, my mother, who accompanied me and the younger of the cousins in my sixth grade class, had to stay with her uncle who lived in a city close to where the school was. She also had time to visit ("by chance") the widow of a very prominent Nigerian military person whose son had attended the same military school and who, according to her, had been put through a lot of misery and torture.

At the end of the two weeks my mother was all too happy to get me out of there. We left for home after taking advantage of my great uncle's family's hospitality, and without my mother mentioning anything of what she had been told by the widow of the prominent military figure. After we got home life went on as usual.

Most elementary school kids in my city usually attended evening lecture sessions after returning from school and having lunch. I was on my way out to such sessions when my parents called me to the table where they were having lunch and showed me my name in the newspaper, as one of those who had been admitted into the coveted military school. I was one of top students in my state according to what I saw in the paper and I was delighted. I practically ran to the evening lecture session that day and, of course, I let some friends know about my good news.

Before I left home my parents asked me what my decision was concerning the school that I would attend. I had already gotten the results of the other examinations that I took with many other students and friends of mine, and I had been accepted into the school of my first choice. So I had two schools that I could attend and which were ready to take me. They were both federal boarding schools and quite prestigious in their own rights.

The military school, however, seemed more interesting to me because it stood by itself while the other school had one or two sister schools in many of the states in the country. The fact that the military school was the only one of its kind (although there was another for the Air force), and existed in only one city, made it stand out in my view at the time as the obvious choice.

But my parents, especially my mother, did not share my enthusiasm. They however, did not say why they were concerned about the choice I had made and left it at that.

Power outages are common in Nigeria and it was also common in the city that I lived in then. During one of many power outages, I was sitting by myself on a couch in a corner in our living room, thinking about going away to school. As I thought about this I pictured myself living approximately two hours away from home and a certain nostalgic feeling came over me. The fact that it was not well lit in the room at the time did not help with this feeling that later turned into a sad one.

The thought of leaving my loved ones to go and live in a school with other strangers, two hours away from home, was disturbing to me. This was the first time that I had actually deeply reflected on the matter. Then it dawned on me that I had actually decided to go to the military school in the city that took almost a whole day to get to.

I was still sitting on that couch when my mother returned home. I ran to her right away after she came through the door and told her that I did not want to go to the military school, which I was so bent on attending. I told her that I had changed my mind and that I wanted to go to the closer school. I had decided within myself that a closer school with more people whom I already knew sounded much better than a very distant one with no elementary school friends.

I made this decision myself even though just recently my mother told me that she did not intend to let me go to the military school. It was only recently that she told me what she had learned from the widow of the prominent Nigerian figure whose son had attended the same military school. I was silently thankful to her for the fact that she let me make that decision.

So off to the closer boarding school I went with all the provisions and other requirements such as a broom, a bucket, a jerry can, a cutlass (for cutting grass), two white bed sheets, two white pillow cases (for making the bed in the mornings before the daily and Saturday inspections), a coloured bed sheet and pillow case, two sets of two kinds of uniforms (for classes and afterwards) and some other things.

The edible provisions included things like powdered milk, sugar, biscuits (cookies), cereal and a few other things. My things were inspected at the gate of the school and I was helped into my hostel by the captain of the house in which I was placed. In the hostel I was assigned a dormitory. The hostels were designed to have two parallel bungalows with four dormitories in each building.

At one end of the buildings was another shorter one which was perpendicular to the parallel buildings and which connected the two buildings. This shorter one housed the toilets and the showers. They never worked so we bathed outside from buckets.

In between the two buildings and the perpendicular toilet building was a quadrangle with pine trees and some shrubs and hedges. It was the duty of the students in the school to keep the premises of the school clean and tidy. It was for this reason that we all had to have our cutlasses, for cutting and trimming, and our buckets, for fetching water used for cleaning the toilets, inside the dormitories and the gutters that led water away from the front of the dormitories (since we did not have the type of underground drainage systems found in North America, for instance).

The bore hole, which was our only source of potable water, was about fifteen to twenty minutes away from my hostel (one of four hostels) if one did not get stopped or harassed by a senior student on the way down. All activities were regulated by a bell, which was rung twice before the final ring that was not supposed to catch any student in the wrong place, or outside the building that housed the announced activity.

As a result of this, every activity was tightly regulated and students had to work really hard to get their laundry done, dishes washed, clothes ironed and water secured for bathing in the evening and the following morning, all between activities.

In addition to this, junior students had to avoid most of the senior students as the former did their chores, because the senior students had the authority (not mandated by the school but was customary) to make any student below them in class or grade do anything for them. The first and second-year students were most often picked on and I was in my first year.

With the little time that we had between activities to do our chores, it was doubly hectic having to handle doing laundry and securing bathing water for one or two other individuals. It was because of this that people generally attached themselves to senior students for whom they would do chores and who would in return protect them from being harassed or bullied by other senior students.

It took me a while to finally settle with one senior student because there were very few available in whose corners I cared to stay in. Also, I mostly liked being independent, although I realized that I had to compromise due to the conditions in the dormitories. I finally attached myself to one who was the sanitation prefect at the time and who already had about four students in different years of study under him in his corner in the dormitory.

His corner was already fully packed with the bunk beds of the students under his protection. I therefore had my bunk bed (which I shared with a friend of mine who was asthmatic) outside of his corner. I was able to stay outside the corner of this prefect and still enjoy his protection. I was one of the students responsible for getting his bathing water or his food from the dinning hall (getting food from the dinning hall was against school policy).

Having joined the *family* of this prefect, I grew closer to the other members of this family, some of whom were already my friends, including the son of the headmaster at my elementary school. We started to move together and formed something of a clique.

While taking a walk with a senior friend and another member of my clique, the senior student (he was also the labour prefect at the time) asked my friend if he wanted to have the older student's little female friend as his girlfriend. My friend said that he was not interested. The girl in question sat right in front of me in class and had come into the school a bit later than the we had. My response was yes when the senior student turned to me and posed the same question.

I later on ran into the girl on our way to get water and we discussed the situation and from then on I had a girlfriend. All the girls in the school stayed in one hostel although they were also placed into different houses or groups (just like teams). The school was a mixed school, with both boys and girls attending classes together but residing in different hostels.

There were three other hostels occupied by boys apart from mine because there were more boys than girls in this school. Other girls that wished to attend such a school as mine did so in schools that were comprised of only girls.

In order to speak with my new girlfriend I had to get someone who was going into the girls' hostel to call her and then we would meet in the classroom area. This went on for a while and after some time we gained some notoriety because we appeared to be the only ones who were officially together (if it could be called that) amongst the first year students in the school.

Her clique, or group of close friends who she always walked around school with, also became quite popular. But then came a time when I thought things had changed between us. She no longer came out when I sent for her, citing one excuse or another or no excuse at all.

When I felt I could not take it anymore I wrote her a long letter which I ended by stating that she was not the only one around and that there were "other fish in the sea," and so she should make up her mind about us. I gave her the letter in class and went back to my seat. She read it and asked to see me outside. While outside, she wanted to know whether or not I meant what I had written to her.

I was surprised that the letter upset her that much. The way things were going before I wrote the letter I could not believe that she would be upset by me giving her a chance to break things off. I really wanted her to be the one to say that she was no longer interested so that I could stop wasting my time and hers by sending for her and waiting in vain for her. So I was really taken aback when she went back to her seat and put down her head on her desk. I got the impression that she was crying and that confused me even more. But I started to think that she did not have to cry since I clearly stated that the choice was hers. I was convinced that I had done nothing wrong and so I remained in my seat.

My bravado did not last for too long because I started to feel that maybe I had gone a bit too far and should try to fix things between us, especially since I may have misread the situation. When I went up to talk to her about it, after a few days or weeks (I cannot remember exactly) she did not seem enthused by the idea of us getting back together and burying the hatchet, so to speak. Again I was somewhat confused. She told me that she was going to need some time. I agreed and left her to it.

Days later (or weeks later), I went back to her and I got a similar response as I had received the previous time. I went back again to her the next term, by this time we were in our second year in the school and I was thirteen or fourteen years old. I had heard that someone in the third year level was interested in her as well and that that could have been the reason for her reluctance to give me a definite response to my questions.

I made that the last visit and I told her that I was not going to bother again if she said no. She said no. I never spoke to her again, until our final year at school. Our cliques (groups of friends) had become quite close, with my friends being quite friendly with hers. I did not feel comfortable talking to her friends because of what had happened between us and in fact I did not want to talk to any girls at all.

To me it just was not worth it. I became even quieter in public after that experience and withdrew more into my studies. The other aspects of my life in school remained the same. I was the class prefect of all my classes from the first year class to the fifth year class. In my sixth year, I became the captain or prefect of my house (or hostel); the one I described earlier.

I was in the drama club and the press club, although I did not actively participate in the activities of those clubs. I participated in the production of the press club magazine and helped in the organization of some events for the club, but I was not interested in gathering the news and presenting it in front of the entire school every Monday morning.

This did not stop the outgoing president of the club from appointing me as the succeeding president and so I was president of the press club as well in my final year. I was lucky to have as the vice president, my asthmatic friend, whom I shared the same corner (in the dormitory) and class with throughout my stay in the school. He was up to the task of gathering and presenting the news and so was my cousin, who had gone to the military school interview with me.

In addition to gaining admission into the military school, he (my cousin) had also received admission into the Air Force school that I mentioned earlier and the school in which we all ended up. He was the editor-in-chief of press club in our final year.

At the beginning of our final year at school, I was told by different friends of mine that my former girlfriend (mentioned above) wanted to talk me. I always thought that they were just saying that to try and get us back together and so I did not listen to them. Besides I had made my last move as far as the entire affair was concerned. I felt that if she wanted to talk to me she knew where I was and could always let me know directly. That was how I felt because at that time I had managed to forge a different life for myself at school, one that could operate without any special person in it to cause me to worry. I was not going back to that state, not when I was quite comfortable with the way things were.

It was our final year and I had to focus on the university entrance examinations and was just in the right frame of mind to devote myself to my studies. Finally, she sent a friend of mine to call me outside during a cultural dance rehearsal at night, while the rest of the school was studying. When I got outside to meet her, we both noticed that I had become a lot taller than she was. She commented on that fact and on how she had never stopped liking me. I let her know that I also still liked her even though we had been apart. And it was as though we had never stopped being together. We were back together in our final year and the song that had been made up for us in our junior days was dug up again by our friends.

The final examinations came around April in 1992. It signaled the end of secondary school days and the beginning of the struggle to get into university. Getting into university was the ultimate goal of most people in secondary schools in the southern part of Nigeria because there were very few jobs to be had without a university or college degree.

Attending a university also carried with it some social benefits since it indicated the graduate's intelligence and opened up opportunities for him to meet with all sorts of people from varied backgrounds. Nigeria is an amalgamation of numerous tribes and each of these tribes has something unique to offer to the others. Attending a Nigerian university is therefore an opportunity to take advantage of the multifarious nature of the ethnic backgrounds of the students and gain a wealth of experiences.

I was happy to learn that I performed well in all the subjects that I needed in order to pursue a medical degree in a university in Nigeria. The next examination was to determine which schools I would be qualified to gain entry into and which areas or fields I would be allowed to enroll in.

I had wanted to study medicine because I liked the idea of being able to take care of people, especially my family, like my father did with us, and also because of the prestige inherent in the profession. Also, I saw it as a noble profession and having being raised with the Grail Message in our house, I wanted to make sure that I chose a profession that would allow me to do something noble while in this life. That was my goal.

Medicine was the key to this the way I looked at it. The fact that my father is also a doctor also helped nourish this idea and made it seem more like a matter of fact.

We had grown up, as little children, going to a protestant church with some of our older female cousins. My parents stayed in bed while we went to church in the mornings. This went on for about two or three years after we had moved to the second city that we lived in after returning to Nigeria.

Then my father started going out somewhere to worship and later introduced us to the Grail Message. My mother read it after my father had read it, and my elder sister soon after started to read it also. This was happening before I went to secondary school and so I was still too young to start reading it.

I, however, with my younger sisters, attended the children's classes where we were taught about the Elemental Beings that tend to flowers, trees, the soil, fire, water, rocks and so forth, like the elves, the gnomes, the water sprites and others. After getting into secondary school I started attending a reading class where I read the Grail Message with some other people in the presence of an experienced person who could guide us through the readings.

I finished reading the Grail Message and became sealed to the Light, just like my parents and older sister before me and my younger sisters after me. I was not able to get into my school of choice to study medicine. I did not get a score high enough to allow me to study medicine either. This was not uncommon as many people had to take one or both of the required examinations more than once before gaining admission into a university to study in the fields of their various choices.

I was able to get into a different school, however, and was allowed to study biochemistry. I had the intention of switching to a medical school after my first year and after getting good marks and so forth. I started school about three weeks late in the university that allowed me to study biochemistry.

The process of gaining a university education is very chaotic in Nigeria due to the fact that the corruption in the nation is deep-seated. Nothing was maintained in right order due to the country's inability to handle its resources and the corruption that is in the nerves of the nation. I now know however that this is a fruit of the adoption of foreign ideas and cultures by a people who are developing under different general conditions.

As a result I cannot say much about the quality of education that I received in this particular school, which had not even been completed before we were forced to occupy its premises. I can however talk about other experiences that I had while living amongst other students in this school.

There exists in most or all the Nigerian universities groups of fraternities that might have been formed in an attempt to imitate the fraternities in North American universities. These groups however, do not function in the same way as fraternities do in North America, even though I am not here endorsing any of the North American fraternities in any way.

The ones in Nigeria, however, are essentially gangs that terrorize each other and others who may not belong to any of them. The situation is so bad that first-year students are sought after to join these groups so that the group with the most people or the "best" type of people for certain jobs then become the most powerful and so can "rule" in the school. I was one of the targets for such recruitment efforts and people I knew prior to getting into the school were targeting me. These people were in their final years in the school and I was in my first. I knew that I could not join such evil organizations and yet I could not find a way to tell these people, who were nice in their approach, that I wanted nothing to do with their organizations, without at the same time getting them upset and possibly starting something ugly.

I decided that I was just going to act friendly towards them until I transferred to another school to study medicine. This was not an easy thing to do, nor was it the best decision on my part to maintain a relationship with those people, because in no time at all, one of them thought that he had actually convinced me to become a part of his crew.

As a result of this, I was able to look into their world in a way that had not been possible prior to that time. I was able to see how they had totally invented reasons for wanting to keep the turf wars going and for wanting to increase the size of their army. I could not justify in any way why any sane person who had been given the opportunity to exist would want to make his life that of crime and violence the way those people did. I saw that I had absolutely nothing to gain in partaking of any of the activities that related in any way to what I had experienced.

I saw the wastefulness inherent in spending even a single second in the types of activities that they partook in and the way that it trapped them into that world which they willfully created for themselves and which they could not leave because of similarly stupid reasons. There was absolutely no reason for the existence of such groups in Nigerian universities, or anywhere else in my opinion. I heard that some of the members of such groups felt a sense of power while walking around their campuses. They worried about their abilities or lack thereof to go to this or that party or to talk to some girl or another. But that was the bulk of it.

I also noticed how only those who paid attention to such people and their interests felt really threatened by them. Only by allowing themselves to buy into the fear imposed by the thugs could they be frightened. Only by engaging in such activities as the thugs could they hope to cross paths with them and possibly become harmed by them. In other words it was entirely possible to go about one's life on campus without concerning oneself with the activities of the thugs.

They were only able to affect that person who reached out his hand to them. I sent a prayer upwards that I would leave the presence of those people and it was answered. After the second semester of the first year, my parents told me that I was to leave the country due to the fact that lecturers at universities and other schools were going on too many workers' strikes, and that the strikes were bound to delay my education.

After studying a world map they decided that I should go to Baltimore, Maryland where I had a cousin who could offer me a place to stay and help me get on my feet while I went to school. They did not want me to go to Canada (my country of birth) because they did not have any one like this cousin in Canada. My cousin was the best I could have asked for. He and his family welcomed me into their home where I was treated like part of the family.

It took a few months for me to adjust to the loneliness of being in North America, with the knowledge that I was on my own and would have to soon start fending for myself in the absence of my parents. In Nigeria it is generally the tradition that the parents pay the ways of their children from nursery school through university, and in fact until the children get jobs.

The idea of working to fend for myself did not scare me. I actually welcomed the challenge. I felt that I had already been trained to be a survivor in different circumstances through having to go through boarding school and a year of university in Nigeria. I had essentially started to train myself towards independence since I was 11 years old. What was a bit frightening was the fact that I had no more holidays and no more breaks from being worried or concerned. I felt myself passing into a new stage in my life.

While in secondary school we used to return home for holidays and that used to be a period of attending house parties or just driving around visiting friends. We walked around or rode in taxis to friends' houses or favourite snack places. It was during one of such holidays that I taught myself to drive my mother's car, which was a manual transmission vehicle, just like the majority of the vehicles in Nigeria.

I had started off by cleaning the cars in the mornings (my father's and my mother's) and then it graduated to starting the ignitions and warming up the cars, which led to eventually driving the car out of our driveway.

When I became really interested in learning how to drive I started bothering my parents to teach me, while at the same time watching the hands and feet of other drivers as they drove. I decided that if everyone who wanted to learn how to drive achieved his goal, including a girl whom I had seen handling a large vehicle in an expertly fashion, I could learn to drive without too many problems.

I began to watch everyone whose car I happened to be in. I watched taxi drivers as they switched gears while depressing the clutch and I watched my friends who could drive as they handled their parents' vehicles. I also bought a small British driving book for beginners and I used it to study the subtleties involved in the movement of the feet, even though the directions in this British book were the other way around, compared to the driving and traffic situation in Nigeria. This is due to the fact that one drives on the other side of the road in Britain.

One morning, after cleaning my parents' cars, I eased my mother's out of the driveway and was out on the road before anyone could take notice of my actions.

I went through a busy part of the city and circled quickly back home. I gained more confidence as I repeated this act in the mornings that followed. The day I was caught was the day my mother decided to wait for me to return with her car, on the balcony overlooking the driveway. She apparently had wondered where I was and had gone to look for me where I was supposed to be but could not find the car or me.

After I got back and noticed that she was already there waiting for me, I pulled into the driveway and braced myself for the worst. She, however, calmly asked me where I had been and why I had taken the car without permission. I replied that I wanted to show them that I could drive by taking the car out. I then described to her the route that I had taken. She made me promise not repeat it without a licensed driver in the vehicle. The legal driving age in Nigeria was 18 and I was just 17 and without a license.

When my father found out about it he explained to me the dangers of driving without knowing all that is involved in driving. He then explained to me the things required by the police following a traffic stop, amongst other things. He, however, got me to drive him around sometimes when he went on errands. I later on took possession of the car as my means of getting around during the holidays together with some of my friends.

So I was in Baltimore, Maryland, and I had to resign myself to the fact that I had no more holidays and I was going to start going through life's other experiences. I asked my parents not to send me any money because it would be quite a strain on them and would make it difficult to provide adequately for my sisters who were still in Nigeria. I also saw myself as being in a position to make money more easily in Baltimore than was possible in Nigeria without a university degree.

I got a job working in a fast-food restaurant after months of searching for work. I had on me my Canadian passport but could not get a job legally without the proper work visa. I did not know about that and all the other laws that operated at the time in North America regarding work, and so I had to learn slowly and made do with what I could get.

The job in the restaurant was obtained somewhat illegally since I did not have the permission to work provided through a work visa. My cousin made a lot of sacrifices that included waking up in the middle of the night to pick me up from work after the restaurant had closed.

I was accepted into a University in Baltimore to study medical technology. I still wanted to study medicine but I had learned that I had to start off with a pre-medicine course before proceeding to medical school. I decided to make that my plan, to finish my degree in medical technology and then proceed to medical school.

I had initially wanted to enroll into a microbiology program or something similar, but it was not offered at that university so I settled for medical technology, which sounded similar. As long as it was pertaining

171

to medicine, it was fine by me. I later found out that it is actually quite different from microbiology.

I did not do a lot of research after I left Nigeria, I just went where the tide took me. As long as I stayed focused on the final goal of studying medicine, I was fine with the things that came in between. For some time after that my days were occupied with school material and work. I worked full-time and I took close to a full load of courses each semester. I was not able to take full course-loads every semester due to the fact that I had to work a lot in order to pay for school.

I was not eligible for loans because I did not have a student visa, having arrived the United States straight from Nigeria as a Canadian citizen. I had very little time for anything but school and work as a result of this. As time went on, I was further encouraged to continue struggling by the fact that my grades were good and I could still keep medical school in my sights.

I made some friends while I was in Baltimore and they helped make things easier for me. Knowing that I had friends who could support me in time of need also helped me face challenges and overcome financial and other obstacles that came my way.

I still could not get other jobs to supplement the one I had at the restaurant, where by the way, I had been made a shift manager after about three months of working there. Most of the friends that I spent time with did not have to work because they had money sent to them from their parents who lived in Nigeria. Others that I knew were living with their parents or in close proximity to them. I was able to relax a bit and forget about the stress of work and school in their midst.

I also had some other friends in Virginia at the time. It happened that about two weeks after I arrived in Baltimore, two of my friends and their family came over from Nigeria to join their father, who had been living and working in Virginia as a psychiatrist. Their father had gone to Virginia four years prior to their trip out of Nigeria to re-establish himself and pave the way for his family to join him in Virginia.

These two friends of mine were brothers. The older of the two was the boy whom I had shared a seat with in grades two and four of elementary school, the one who became class prefect when I was assistant class prefect. His younger brother was about my age while the boy himself was

172

a year older than we were. These two people also attended my secondary school. The younger one was in a different house from mine but in the same year as I was. We had not become close at that point. I still only knew his older brother at that point. But he was one year our senior in the school because he had left elementary school from the fifth grade instead of the sixth grade. This means that he took the entrance examinations and passed them while he was in the fifth year of elementary school.

Due to this fact, when we were in secondary school together he was mostly with people in the same year of study as he was so we did not interact much. After secondary school was over, however, we had some time to get together and renew our friendship. It was also at this point that his younger brother and I became quite close friends.

I took quite a few trips to their house in Nigeria in the car I had managed to ease off the grips of my parents. They had five sisters and they all, with their mother, joined their father in Virginia about two weeks after I arrived in the United States. I went to visit them several times since our arrival to North America.

They also were part of my support group. I did not keep in touch with my friends a lot because I had become used to being by myself but it was nice to know that they were around if I needed their help. I also did not have a lot of time to spend with them when school was in session. I eventually moved out of my cousin's house and into a place of my own, after living briefly with one of my friends.

My place was a bachelor or studio apartment with one bathroom and one living space with the kitchen space provided within the living room. There was no bedroom, but the living room was big enough and I was by myself. It suited me well, although I could never really get out from beneath the pile of debt that I had hanging over my head and furnish the place.

I had been introduced to someone who worked in the accounting department at my school and he had agreed to help me out with my tuition payments. He allowed me to pay in installments instead of paying everything at once. It was not easy to get that type of help since I was not even supposed to be in school without a student visa. I only found this out after I learned more about the laws governing such issues in the United

States of America.

My most important financial concern was making those payments and staying in school. By moving out on my own I had essentially added to my list of worries and so the heap of debts just kept getting higher and heavier. I had discussed moving to Canada with one of my close friends in Baltimore but I never could get myself to take on the trip to a far away land that was completely unknown to me. I knew that I had to leave the United Sates of America for Canada at some point but was very reluctant to leave my friends and the comfort of having them around. There were several reasons why I had to make the trip to Canada. One of the main reasons was the fact that I was living a lie by working illegally in the United States of America. Everything else was bound to act as a burden as a result of this.

I was a bit scared of making that bold move that I knew deep down I had to make. It had to take a stronger stimulus to get to me finally see reason and move.

In 1997 I received the stimulus. I had been getting good recommendations at work and had passed all the required tests that would get me promoted to the position of assistant manager. I would have been in a position to run the store and have only one supervisor who would have been in charge of my store and another one.

My supervisor was also somewhat fond of me and tried his best to make sure that my promotion was hastened. And indeed it was, I was finally ready to go for the final interview that would determine whether or not I got the promotion.

I went through the interview and came out with flying colours, according to my supervisor. I was told the good news over the phone when I called him to find out how I had fared. During the telephone conversation he informed me that I had to come in the next day with all my personal documents again so that my personal information could be changed in the database to one that reflected my new position within the company.

I became speechless, but later managed to thank him and hang up the phone. I had just been informed that I had to present my documents all over again. I was not told that I would have to do that or else I would not have agreed to all the tests and the interviews. I, however, had to present the information if I was going to start my training the next day at a different store, a part of which process would have involved the re-entry of my information under a different status.

My supervisor had really worked hard to get me to the level that I had just attained and so I stood there by the public telephone and contemplated the implications of my situation.

There was absolutely no way that I was going to present my information to the company because the information that I was working with was not valid, at least it did not go together with my actual legitimate documents. If anything bad came out of the revelation of this fact it might have seriously harmed the individuals who helped me get the job in the first place.

The worst thing that could have happened to me, in my opinion at the time, would have been deportation to Canada, which did not seem that terrible compared to prison. So I made up my mind on the spot to leave the United States of America for Canada. It was a good thing that I had already thought about leaving for Canada prior to this event. It was for me to be prepared in my mind for the decision that the thought of leaving had already occurred to me. Had I listened to the urging of my intuitive perception I might have started the process of moving to Canada earlier.

It was fear that kept me from acting on my intuitive perceptions earlier. I imagined that I had to know how I was going to fend for myself before making the move, since I knew no one in Canada whom I could trust to help me. I was also reluctant to leave Baltimore, because there I was surrounded by friends whom I would have left behind. These, in addition to other mundane material factors, caused the inertia that made me postpone the decision to leave Baltimore. But at this time the reasons to leave outweighed the reasons to delay my departure.

I immediately called my cousin who I consulted before making any serious moves and told him that I was leaving and that it was the right time to do so. He had also witnessed my hardships but offered that I stay with him until I had raised enough money to make the trip with. I convinced him that I had to go because it made very good sense for me to leave at that point.

I held back from paying my rent, which was due for that month, in order to conserve money. I moved all my belongings to my friend's apartment and spent the night there. I also called my friends in Virginia to inform them of my decision. They invited me over to spend some time with them before leaving; they were even upset that I was contemplating such a move without seeing them first.

At this time I had spoken to one of my friends (the one with whom I discussed moving to Canada) about accompanying me to Canada. He was not able to leave his responsibilities right away and he explained that he needed about a month to wrap a few things up. I decided to go without him since I could not afford to remain in the country for a month.

When my friends in Virginia invited me over to their parents' house, it was just in time because I had nowhere else to go. The friend who allowed me to store my belongings in his place had his sister visiting from Nigeria and I did not want to crowd up the apartment for them. So I accepted the invitation and off I went in a 1984 Subaru station wagon, which I had purchased before deciding to leave the country.

I bought it from a co-worker who had just bought a new car. Trusting that the vehicle would get me safely to Virginia, I set out for the four-hour drive south on the Interstate 95 highway. I was welcomed with open arms by my friends who did nothing but take care of my every need while I was with them.

They were, at this point, living in their father's house in Virginia since their father had moved to Kentucky where he lived with the rest of their family. It was a very relaxing period and I was able to calm down before embarking on the trip to Canada. While I was in Virginia, I joined their family on a trip from Kentucky to Buffalo and Niagara Falls in New York. I drove part of the way during the trip to New York and back to Kentucky, and in the process I received a few tips on navigating the United States highway.

I also knew that Canada could not have been as far as I assumed it was because on the other side of Niagara Falls in New York was Niagara Falls in Canada. I learned all this during the trip and I became more confident about my trip. I learned how to acquire specific directions from a company that helps people with directions and other travel details. I also learned how to read the maps and be able to travel anywhere in the United States of America by road.

After about three weeks, I returned to Baltimore. By that time I had sold most of my things, leaving behind my fairly new television set, some pots and pans and my clothes. I stayed at a friend's place until my traveling companion was ready to make the trip to Canada. At this point no one could convince me that my 1984 mode of transportation would not take me all the way to Canada. I had taken it to Virginia and back and that was enough to convince me of its strength. So we left for Canada when my friend was ready. I drove all the way to Canada because the car had a manual transmission and my passenger could only drive ones with automatic transmissions.

Upon our arrival in Canada, we were informed that I had to pay import duty on the Subaru since it was purchased in the United States of America and was being imported into Canada. I had told the customs agent at the inspection booth that I was a Canadian citizen who was returning home. That statement, and the fact that she could see my belongings through the window of the car, made it quite clear to her that I was coming back to stay and not just to visit.

In addition to the duty that I had to pay, I was also informed that I would have to pay tax on the purchase price of the vehicle. After expressing my frustration at the customs officials I agreed with my friend that it would be better not to make any trouble and try to pay the money. I gave them most of the money I had on me, and my friend put the rest of the bill on his credit card.

We were able to get some information about the cities in Canada at the Canadian border. We drove to Hamilton first and I was amazed at how neat the streets were and how nicely arranged and pretty the flowerbeds were. We found a Salvation Army shelter and I registered with them.

We drove on to Toronto and, as we drove closer to downtown Toronto on the Gardiner expressway, I knew that I wanted to settle in Toronto as opposed to Hamilton. I also felt good about what I saw because I felt that Toronto was not going to be very different from the cities that I had become used to in the United States of America.

We drove along Yonge and Bloor streets in downtown Toronto because they were the busiest and most obvious streets that we saw. We found the Social Services office and I registered for welfare assistance. I felt like I could do anything that I wanted in this city because it was in Canada, I had a Canadian passport, and for the first time in over three years I felt free. Also, the people were very nice when giving directions, even though they all seemed to speak differently.

The streets were clean and once, after I came downstairs from inspecting an apartment for rent, I noticed that one side of the street had been washed. It felt incredibly nice to be in Toronto. I registered in a nice and clean homeless shelter and looked around for a job and an apartment. We spent the night in a hotel paid for by my traveling companion, and in the morning I saw him off at the Greyhound bus terminal. I was once again alone.

My first move after my friend left was to try and secure an apartment for myself. I had been informed at the Social Services office that I would need to find a landlord who was willing to rent to me and get some confirmation of this fact from him before receiving any rent cheques.

I drove around the city all day that Tuesday just like I had done the previous day. At the end of the day I retired to the shelter that I had been directed to at the Social Services office.

I had gone to the shelter to register and was pleased to find that there was vacancy and that I was qualified to stay there. It was a nice, well-kept shelter, which was privately run but funded by the government. I was warned not to let go of my guard while on the premises of the shelter since people from off the streets of the city occupied it. I let the proprietors know that I was used to the sort of atmosphere that they were trying to warn me about because I had spent six years at a boarding school in Nigeria, in comparison to which the shelter in question was a classy hotel.

I checked in on Tuesday night after driving along Yonge and Bloor streets for most of the day. These two streets are two of the most popular streets in the downtown Toronto area. Bloor street could be seen as the beginning of the downtown region when approaching it from the northern part of the city, while Yonge street is the dividing street that separates the east from the west side of the city. It has been reported to be the longest street in the world.

Since Yonge street was right in the middle of the city, becoming familiar with it got me closer to recognizing the grid-like formation of the city. This pattern was not present in Baltimore and I found it to be quite helpful, because it allowed me get around without having to know the city very well.

I also picked up a map of the city to help me get around. I used the map to get around as I searched for a job and an apartment. My stay at the shelter was comfortable. I had made up my mind before leaving Baltimore that I was going to do whatever it took to settle in Canada, even if it meant sleeping in my car and working on some farm.

I got a lot better than that because I stayed at this shelter, where I was fed with specially delivered food (maybe from a restaurant or hotel) and allowed to watch cable television. I showered in a clean bathroom and slept on clean white sheets. I could not ask for more.

After the third night I was able to find a room in a house in the eastern part of the city and was able to receive my first check from the Social Services office. I later found work as a courier driver for a private company that just happened to be desperate for drivers.

They hired drivers who had their own cars and paid them a percentage of the delivery cost of each package they delivered. There were many advertised courier jobs in comparison to the other listed jobs in the classified section of the newspaper where I did my job search. I might have called one or two courier companies before calling the company that eventually hired me.

The latter asked me to show up ready to work, and when I did they loaned me a map book since all I had was a one-sheet flat map. It was nice to know that all I needed was a map book and I could navigate the entire city. The grid formation of the city also helped me find my way quite easily.

They learned that I had just come from the United States of America and did not know the city well. They let me know that they were desperate for drivers and were hiring me for that reason. I had no objections to that.

Everything worked out well on both sides. With the map book and the radio that they gave me, I set out on my first run. I had gotten myself a job.

After driving around the city all day I went back to my room in the house that was home to four other tenants, and I watched cable television. I was beginning to settle in. I was delighted when I got into my new room and plugged in my television set to find that there was access to cable television in that room. Having settled to the point that I had a place to stay and a job to pay for it, I started to worry about the next immediate concerns.

One of these concerns was the idea of working with a car that could break down at any time, and the fact that I could have a serious cash flow problem if that were to happen. The other concern was the fact that I wanted to get back to school but could not do so without my transcript from my other school in Baltimore.

Because of my sudden departure and the fact that prior to that departure I had failed to pay for a full year's tuition, I did not settle issues financially with my former school. I also found out that the release of my transcript was not going to be possible without me paying what I owed the school. I expected that to be the case but hoped that an unofficial transcript, which I had obtained from the accounting department, would somehow suffice.

It did not suffice, and after visiting the only two schools that I knew existed in Toronto, York University and the University of Toronto, it became clear to me that I was going to need to obtain my official transcript. Getting my official transcript meant that I had to pay over C$5,000, which was about US$4,000.

I had lost some of my money in a bad investment in the summer before my last full semester in Baltimore and so could not pay the tuition for that semester. I also had some outstanding debts to the school which, when added to the tuition totaled up to $4,000. I decided to take care of the smaller problem first before thinking about what I could do about getting back into school.

I bought some tools for working on the car and I bought a manual to help me do work on it myself. In a short while I was able to change the brakes, spark plugs, and a few other things in the car. I also became more confident in trusting that I could drive the car for work and fix it when minor problems arose.

I later decided that it might be a good idea to get a second job just in case something did happen to the car and I could not fix it in time before the next day of work. Also, the car could have got so badly damaged that it might have required more money than I would have been able to afford in order to fix it.

At this time I was already visiting a particular nightclub every Saturday night. That was the only avenue that I knew through which I could be around other people. I still was quite private and mostly kept to myself, but I needed to get out of my room at least once in a while.

I also liked the idea of going to the club where I could meet people and even dance with girls, but not have to worry about communicating with them afterwards. It was at this nightclub that I noticed for the first time that the security men at the clubs in Toronto were not as big and fierce-looking as the ones I had seen in Baltimore.

The idea of working as one of those security men occurred to me and I though about it for a while. I was at the nightclub every Saturday night and on some Friday nights and so it occurred to me that I could make some money at the same time while I was there. Instead of paying the cost of parking my car and the entrance fee, I could be making money that could supplement the cash flow from my courier job.

I also could rest better knowing that if something big did go wrong with my car I would not necessarily have to be out on the streets. I contacted the supervisor and after a brief meeting I was employed by the security company.

At this point I had the courier service job in the daytime and the nightclub security job at night on weekends. I had one more major problem to address and that was the question of where to get money from for my Baltimore school transcripts.

Prior to getting the job at the nightclub, I had met a girl whom I became friends with at the same nightclub. She lived with her parents, worked and went to school part-time. When she heard about my dilemma she offered to lend me money from her savings to help me out. We agreed that I would pay her back from money that I was going to get from loans and other sources.

I was reluctant in accepting the money but then realized that the money that I was hoping to get for the release of my transcript from Baltimore was not going to fall from the sky but was going to come to me in a way that had to be natural and logical. There I was being offered more money than I had ever held in my hands at once, from someone whom I had not known until just a few weeks before.

I had to realize what it was that was happening and make good use of it. I made certain that she was not going to need the money any time soon and she assured me that it was okay to take it. I then promised her that I would pay her back with interest, which she did not seem interested in. A few days after that conversation I had C$5700.00 in my pocket.

During all of this I had been meeting with a lady in the University of Toronto admissions office to get her to accept my unofficial transcript. After it was clear that she would not accept it, I got her to give me an extension on my admission into the school to study microbiology. I needed an extension because I started to get help from all around me after the deadline for the submission of documents had already passed.

She was able to get me an extension, according to her, because my grades were good and she was able to convince the panel that sat over such proceedings to grant it to me. When everything was ready for my admission to be complete, all that was left was the C$5,700 that I needed to get my official transcript from Baltimore. It was at this point that my friend offered to lend me the money.

I was beginning to experience miracle after miracle. I was convinced even more about the lack of arbitrariness in all that was taking place regarding my move to Canada and the help that I was getting in seemingly impossible situations. The fact that Canadians appear nicer than I had expected also greatly enhanced this buoyant feeling.

It was because of this feeling that I wrote to my parents in Nigeria about Toronto being "a breath of fresh air," in my first letter to them after my move from Baltimore.

With the money in my pockets, I set off for the border of the United States of America and Canada, south of Niagara Falls. There I was asked why I had been in the United States of America for so long as to have had the time to attend a university for almost two years. I was informed that there was no way that they were going to let me go back to Baltimore until I had obtained Canadian documents, such as a driver's license, and had kept them for six months.

I was two hours away from Toronto and I had just been asked to go back without my transcript. I was even searched at the border because of the perceived discrepancies between my story of trying to go to Baltimore to retrieve my transcript and return to Toronto, and the United States of America documents (driver's license, Morgan Sate University school documents, etc).

I was fortunate that the money for my transcript had been in my pocket throughout the trip. I had at one point thought about putting the bulky envelope containing the money under my seat. That, in retrospect, would not have looked good to the officials searching the vehicle. I probably would have been suspected of selling illegal drugs between Canada and the United States of America.

I was also fortunate that the officials were not permitted to search a driver's person during their efforts. I made the trip back to Toronto, a bit dejected but still optimistic. I had learned through my experiences that things can always turn around in the very last moment. One might not expect it to because one might not yet be wise enough to be able to see the different possible scenarios that could play out in a given situation.

With this in mind I drove back home and decided not to try the other border west of the city of Toronto, at Windsor. I decided to call my cousin in Baltimore and ask him to pick up and deliver the transcript for me. I was going to send him the money via Western Union, have him pick up the transcript and deliver it to me via express mail. I did not like to bother my cousin or anyone else for that matter, but I had to learn to do so when situations called for it and so I did.

I sent the money to my cousin and he fulfilled on his part as usual. The transcript was finally in my hands and, thanks to the lady in the admissions office, in time to be accepted by the panel in charge of admitting me into the University of Toronto to study microbiology.

Microbiology was just a science course that I hoped would eventually lead me to study medicine, which was still my goal. I was finally in school and did not have to watch other students going off to school while I drove around the city delivering packages. I saw getting back into school as a step towards attaining the goal which I had set for myself.

I could not foresee a situation where the goal of studying medicine was not attained, because I could not think of my life turning out differently. It seemed so logical to me; I was to go to school and be trained in a noble profession like medicine because that seemed to be the prescribed path for most people I knew. There seemed to be nothing else as important in life as fulfilling these goals and establishing oneself materially. Hopefully one would later start a family and his offspring would have to repeat the same process over in his own life.

I arrived in Toronto in August 1997, got into school in the summer of 1998. I still had to deliver those packages in order to survive. I delivered them between classes and on the days when I did not have any classes. I still kept the nightclub security job for the same reasons that I took it. I received the Ontario Student Assistance Program loan and I paid my tuition and bought books with it. After everything was settled I barely had any of it left. I had to keep the two jobs if I was to keep school and everything else going smoothly.

So I had taken care of most of my big concerns and it looked like Toronto was going to be my home, at least for a while. I felt I had lost a lot of time while trying to get to where I was. I had started University in Nigeria soon after secondary school in 1992 and was still between second and first year in the University of Toronto in 1998. This was because I did not take my Nigerian University transcript with me to Baltimore. I felt it was going to be too much of a hassle knowing the state of confusion that the country and its schools were in at that time.

Also, the thought of transferring my credits did not appeal to me a great deal because I had never really known how I performed in my last semester at the school. I did not want to know because of the chaos under which I had taken my final examinations. When I transferred to the University of Toronto, some of the credits that I had earned from Baltimore were not accepted and I had not taken some necessary prerequisite courses while in Baltimore, so that I lost some more time trying to make up for the lacking credits.

I was beginning to grow weary of the whole idea of staying in school for as long as it was going to take me to finish a medical degree. Sometimes I briefly considered whether or not I really had to study medicine. It was already taking me a long time to finish my first degree. At that point, when doubts about my eventual study of medicine crossed my mind, I knew that I could not dismiss it, having grown up with knowledge of the truthfulness of the inner voice.

I knew that it was not carved in stone that I should study medicine. So I used the idea of studying medicine to help me strive to get through microbiology with descent marks. If in the end I did not get into medical school I might still have the grades to do something else. That seemed like a good enough strategy for me and so I went with it. I also decided to put my best effort into doing well since I was already feeling somewhat disadvantaged.

I was still taking courses that I thought I probably would have done better at if I took them right after secondary school. I was working at the two places of employment while taking those courses and it always seemed as though I needed money.

My main concern was with school and I was not doing as well as I did when I was in Baltimore. There was also talk about the Canadian university materials being tougher than the American ones. I saw some truth in that, but that was not my problem. My problem was that something was always going wrong.

Things went wrong during examinations where I momentarily would forget something vital to a particular question in a test or I would be sick with influenza-like symptoms. I felt that if I stopped for a second to think that maybe there was something wrong that I should have known about, or which was preventing me from escaping the "misfortunes" that I had during examinations, I would not have put in my best efforts.

So I decided that since there was no way for me to magically stop whatever was wrong, I was going to put in my best so that come what may, I would have no regrets and would be able to say that in spite of everything I did my best. I felt that that would be okay with me even if nobody else understood what I really went through.

So with that sense of determination I strove on ahead. There was never a course that I did not understand. I even liked some of the courses to the point where I learned from them and did not just study to pass them. I gained knowledge but it was not always reflected in my grades. The testing methods were also made a bit tricky so that one required more than just knowledge to do well. One had to also be able to spot the tricks and always be on the alert for them.

Maybe it was the fact that one has to often just regurgitate information in order to do well in some of the tests that negatively affected my performance sometimes. But in all I enjoyed the process. I really exerted myself and whatever setback I suffered made me more resolved to face the next one. I felt I had no choice but to do it and I was going to do it as long as I was given the chance to.

It was in the midst of some of these struggles that I received word about my elder sister coming to Canada from Nigeria. She was born in Edmonton like I was and so had a Canadian passport just like I did. I told my parents that getting money together for her trip would not be a problem.

I wanted to help with some of the money because it would have been easier for me to get it while in North America than it would have been for those in Nigeria. I was still living in the room that I first rented when I arrived in Toronto.

When my sister finally arrived, we lived together in that room. We later moved to a bigger but still small bachelor or studio apartment. She was able to get work and start school taking a part-time course. She had finished a law degree in Nigeria but did not want to take the certifying exam because she was not interested in practicing law.

It was nice and beneficial to be living in such close quarters with my older sister. While we were young she always did different things from us, her younger siblings, and was usually at school or with her friends and away from the three of us. The period that I spent with her served to make up for a long time of us being apart from each other so that I got to learn more about her and she probably got to find out about my own idiosyncrasies.

It could also be said that she helped me stay out of trouble. This is because, after I found myself all alone and had resolved the issues concerning school, work and a place to stay, she served as a check to make sure that I acted in the same way as I would have, had I been back home, close to my parents.

With my sister around I was also reminded of the time when I was still in Nigeria and my mother told me that everything that I did outside of the house would get back to her. They often did get back to her, and so I began to watch my actions more closely, and avoid those things which I did not want to get back to her. My sister brought that feeling back and helped me to stay more focused on important issues.

In the year 2001, I was in the third year of studying microbiology. I heard of opportunities to intern with professors in the summer of that year prior to getting into the fourth year of the microbiology program. At that time I was beginning to get worried about what I was going to do in the future. I knew that I might not end up in medical school and had heard of stories of people who became dejected after not making it into medical school.

I decided to do the internship so that I could increase my chances of doing something meaningful, even if I did not get into medical school. At this point I had decided to keep my mind open to other ideas about a future profession and just focus on doing the best that I could in the present.

I decided to try getting into the laboratory of a particular professor who was new to the school. When I went to his laboratory, he informed me that he was leaving for a vacation that summer. He then referred me to a fellow professor across the hall from his laboratory. When I went to see the other professor, he told me that he wanted to hire me but that he was low on funds and could not afford to pay me. He referred me to a third professor next door, down the hall from his laboratory.

The third professor said that he already had someone who was interested in the position but that the position was mine if that person did not show up. I was not very impressed with the way things had gone but I stayed optimistic. I knew that I had no choice but to stay optimistic. I now understood the benefits of optimism. One does not have to see the results of optimism to have it.

Some days or weeks later, on my way from picking up some letters of recommendation from the head of my program, I stopped by the third professor's laboratory and learned that the other student, whom the position had been reserved for, had not shown up and that the position was mine.

I spent most of the summer in the laboratory working with this very meticulous professor, whom I learned a lot from. The things I had learned in theory, and had only been able to practice in the laboratory classes, became clearer to me as I learned and used molecular biology techniques to do research and carry out some experiments.

I was able to pick up some of the basics in research work in the three months that I spent with this professor. The experience that I gained in the summer helped me a lot in the next year, which was the fourth and last year of the program. I read a lot of scientific papers and expanded upon what I had learned in the previous years.

I became quite familiar with molecules and compounds, such as DNA (deoxyribonucleic acid), and with some of the microorganisms that surround us. I also learned of the different microorganisms that plague us, of others that help us, of the differences between some of them and their developmental cycles. I improved upon my understanding of vaccination and the idea of immunity to certain diseases, amid a host of other things.

After the fourth year I could not graduate yet for a number of reasons. I still owed the school some tuition money. I also still had to take a summer course because I had taken too many first year courses, and had to replace one of them with a higher-level course. I could not pursue a master's program in any field because I had to graduate before I could commence the program.

In addition, I also had to travel to Nigeria and had not determined how I was going to pay for the trip or when the trip was going to commence. I wanted to travel to Nigeria because my sister was getting married there and I also wanted to see my father after more than seven years of being away from home.

I had to buy tickets for my trip some months ahead of the travel time in December because Nigerians around the world usually go back home to Nigeria at Christmas time. Due to the large number of people that travel every year during that period, it is usually advisable that a person purchase tickets to Nigeria many months before the travel time in December.

I decided that I would register for some more classes so that I could use part of the money that I would get in student loans to pay for the tickets. I registered for some interesting and enlightening courses and I got the loan, as well.

I later on got a job with a biotechnology company and worked there for about three months under contract. I worked as a laboratory technician in a big lab with other technicians and a few other people with graduate degrees in science.

The work was too monotonous and did not really challenge me. I was glad to have it, however, because it looked good on the resume (curriculum vitae), and I could make some money for my trip back to Nigeria.

It was while I was working at this company that I decided to try obtaining a Master's degree in Business Administration. I was told that the head of the company that I was working for did not have a science degree but was running a science-based company. I decided that I could do what he did so that I could retain some freedom, as opposed to the position that I would be in if I became a doctor.

I had lost the passion to pursue a career in medicine. The driving force that had taken me through university, and all the events in between, had dropped away like an old coat. The reality of being a doctor was very different from the image that I had in my mind about the profession. I decided that I wanted to be able to move back and forth between Toronto and Nigeria, so that I could do business between both places in a way that would benefit my family back in Nigeria and me. So with this idea in my mind I left for Nigeria in December of that year.

I enjoyed my trip to Nigeria. I was able to spend time with my parents and I got to see my father again. I had seen my mother in London in the December of 2000 when I went visit my two younger sisters, who live, work, and attend school there. My elder sister's wedding was well-attended and I got to spend some time with people that I had not seen in a long time.

I was also reminded of the chaos that exists in Nigeria. I was taken to the police station after I was stopped while getting a ride in a car with my two younger sisters and two of my female cousins. We were taken to the police station because we had the photocopies of the vehicle documents that they requested.

Usually that is their way of extorting money from the operators of vehicles. I decided that I was not going to make Nigeria my home for a long time to come, even though I wanted to be able to visit it once in a while. The incident at the police station was resolved when members of my mother's family came and retrieved us from the police station. I visited relatives whom I had thought about a lot while away from Nigeria. I returned to Toronto after three weeks of enjoyment and experiencing, and I started my job search again.

I had hoped to get work soon after returning home to Toronto. I went to a few job interviews but none of them yielded fruit, each for a different reason. The frequency of the job interviews was approximately one interview in a month, with some months passing without a single interview.

I had to rely on the nightclub security work, which I had kept since I came to Canada as a part-time job. I never really stopped working at nightclubs because I always needed the extra money that it provided. The owners of the nightclubs that I worked at said that they particularly liked the tactful way in which I did the job.

I never really wanted to get involved in fights and so I had to use the tactic that I knew best. Besides, many of the fights that break out in nightclubs happen because the security guards often get easily excited. I had been fortunate to experience the behaviour of people from a wide spectrum of backgrounds, and so was able to use the knowledge gained in the process to keep from aggravating the clientele.

Working only at nightclubs afforded me the time to revisit some of the things that I had pushed to the background due to school and work. I started practicing my drawing again, and spending time in the park as I did the drawings. My drawing skills were getting better every time I went at it. I was becoming really relaxed and did not see the need in worrying too much any more.

I felt that things were just gong to take care of themselves when the time was right and that I just had to wait for that time. I decided to take things a day at time. I could no longer communicate with most of my friends and members of my family. I was reluctant to communicate with people during this period because I did not have any news for them. I did not know what I was going to do the next week or the next month, and people always seemed to want to know that.

A big factor that helped me stay relaxed was the closeness of my girlfriend. She was Hungarian, but she lived in Yugoslavia until she was about 15 years old. We had known each other for about two years, but I had only just made up my mind to get closer to her than I had previously been.

I had started staying at her apartment, in a tall building that is close to the downtown of Toronto. I did not stay at my apartment anymore because I was spending a lot of time with her and it made no sense to go back to my apartment only to return to hers the next day. I was able to really enjoy myself for the first time since I left Nigeria. I had always been involved with school and work since I started school in Baltimore and I had to deal with problems that often came up in between, while still focusing on school and work. I was finally able to relax and think of very little else but the next trip to the park.

I have never introduced any girl to my parents because I have always felt that the woman that I introduce to them as my girlfriend should be somebody that I can see myself spending the rest of my life on earth with, and not just a little while. I had to be sure that I could do just that with my current girlfriend, and so I could not let my family or friends know about her until then.

I had to resolve some issues about both of us, within myself and between us, before making such a move. My parents, on the other hand, have always allowed me to make my own decisions, which include the person that I eventually end up with as a mate.

There has, however, always been a slight taboo associated with a black man marrying a white woman in Nigeria. I grew up in Nigeria knowing about this. I also felt that my growing up in Nigeria gave me a strong advantage over those people who may not have a solid connection with their roots.

I felt that one could draw strength from knowing where he comes from because I did draw strength from it. As a result of this, I did not want to knowingly place any offspring of mine in a position where he or she will be at a disadvantage of any kind. I thought that if I wanted to settle down with a woman of a different ethnic background and race from mine, then I had to resolve the issue of the possible fate of my offspring.

I knew that if I were to make such a decision without carefully weighing everything against what I had learned from the Grail Message as I grew up in Nigeria, I would be risking bad reciprocal action against me in the future.

I had to be sure that it was okay to stay with her and that I could live with it, having grown up in Nigeria, with all the different negative attitudes towards the idea of marrying from outside one's ethnic background. Some of these attitudes could have sprung from the innate sensing of the boundaries set by race, which are actually important and need to be heeded.

At present, I understand why different peoples should develop according to their own natures and at their own pace in those regions where they were born. I also understand the dangers of not heeding the boundaries set by race. This almost always ends up in disaster because the wrong attributes borne by the different groups and races, which mix indiscriminately without regard to the Laws of Creation, attract the groups together and create the conditions for the further development of the base forms and the consequent manifestations of their effects.

When races mix indiscriminately they bring with them their faults, which become the homogenous features through which the different groups or races attract one another, in accordance with the Law of Attraction of Homogenous Species. These features or dark attributes are then multiplied through the activities of members of both groups, because the foundation for the mixing or interactions was not based on the obedience of the Laws of Creation.

Forms of envy, distrust, hatred, fear, conceit, arrogance, spiritual ignorance, love of comfort and ease, greed, narrow-mindedness, one-sidedness, and others, are cultivated to great degrees due to the interruption in the healthy development of the races and nations. This hinders spiritual development as well as leads to physical health disorders as a part of the ramifications of this neglect.

The normal process of development is breached, so that the unions of the different peoples result in chaos and disaster just like any decision made without taking into consideration the Laws of Creation.

Only when people come together for the right reasons and are individually motivated to fulfill the Laws of Creation, will such unions and associations become beneficial, no matter the nature of the unions or the persons involved in them. This is because they will occur at the right point in the maturation of the different groups of people or individuals, who will work to make certain that their every action is prompted by the urge to fulfill the Laws of Creation. It is only this volition that can bring about harmony within any union.

Where there is not this volition, all unions must result in the development of base fruits, no matter what the make up of the union is. Those coming together to unite for any reason will not be attracted to each other for the right reasons and so will not produce good fruits.

When those striving towards a union strive to fulfill the Laws of Creation, then they will be drawn to those people or groups who will best cooperate with them in the fulfillment of their goal. This will also happen through the Law of Attraction of Homogenous Species. In this case, as in every other case, the nature of the spirits of the uniting parties will be the determining factor in the attraction. Only when they can help each other fulfill the Laws of Creation will they be able to bring about peace and harmony through their union.

The striving to fulfill the Laws of Creation must be the paramount volition, which will then allow for the natural and harmonious attraction of forms, individuals, groups or people

This I know now. But at the time I had to work with what I knew of the Laws of Creation and how I felt about the issues that tugged at my conscience.

I had to make my decision based on my understanding of the Laws of Creation at that time.

I was trying to make the decision based on how I was affected by it, and how I felt I would be affected by it in the future. When we started seeing each other, I had told her that it might become a problem for us to stay together, and that we might have to separate sometime in the future. She said that she was fine with the idea. But every once in a while, we would go back to that topic, because we would have grown closer than we were the last time that we had the conversation.

Within myself I also knew that I could not ask for a better partner if I were to choose one, and so I was also going through a quandary of my own. I made more compromises so that we would stay together whenever she brought up the topic. I did not yield too much because I still felt that I owed it to her, my offspring and myself, to consider the issue very thoroughly before making a firm decision. At the same time I thought that telling her exactly how I felt about her would complicate things for her, and might make it more difficult to do what I thought might have to be done at some point in the future. I had not realized the futility and the wrongness in planning.

She left for Hungary on vacation in July of 2002 and I remained in Toronto, still looking for a job and practicing my drawing in the park. In my thoughts, I often went over the idea of staying with my girlfriend and possibly getting married to her. I just could not get over all the obstacles that I thought would make the whole thing impossible. I also did not know if it would be right and in accordance with the Laws of Creation.

I had told her that things would work out if we just hoped for the best outcome and waited. This I said to her when we discussed the difficulties that were sure to arise when we had to separate in the future. Somehow I felt that everything would work itself out if we did not worry about it and focused on the present.

In her absence, I felt closer to her. One day, while I was leaving her apartment and walking towards the elevator, I heard a voice within me say, " it's futile." I heard that while I was thinking of the situation between my girlfriend and me, as I walked towards the elevator of the building. The voice was so clear that I could not mistake it for a thought from my brain.

I had always known about the intuitive perception from reading the Grail Message as a younger person, but I had never really heard my inner voice speak so clearly, or been able to so clearly distinguish it from thoughts generated by my brain. I shuddered at the thought of having to make the decision, which I knew was right, because it had come to me through my intuitive perception, which is never wrong. I had to make a decision.

I knew from childhood as well, that one always has to listen to one's intuitive perception, because that is how one can be warned of dangers that lie ahead, or of a mistake that is about to be made, and that it is through it that one receives guidance while here on earth. I later found out that my girlfriend had sent me e-mail saying that I should call her in Hungary the next day.

When I did, she sounded really worried and seemed somewhat shaken up. She said that she was really feeling terrible because of the arrangement that we had between us, and that I had to make a decision as to the fate of our relationship. Fortunately, I had been forewarned the previous day and so I told her that everything was fine and that I no longer had any reservations about us being together.

She also added that she would boldly face her parents, and anyone else who had a problem with us being together. I was already sold on the matter, and after I made that decision I felt a huge weight drop from my shoulders, and I knew that I had made the right decision.

I reached that decision after thinking of the fact that I had decided to remain in Toronto, in the country of my birth, for the foreseeable future, and any offspring of mine would have to experience life in Toronto, or at least in the same zone as his place of birth, during his or her childhood. It will be the most natural thing for the child to grow up in the zone in which his physical body was formed because it is in that zone that it will receive the radiations and nourishment from the stars and the environment for the most beneficial and natural kind of spiritual and physical development.

Man has continually transgressed the natural Laws in this regard, because they have not realized that it is in the zone in which the physical body is formed that the best development of that body can be achieved. This also means that the spirit will develop best in this zone because it is able to work through a body that has developed in the most natural way.

I realized later on that it was not an accident that I had returned to my place of birth, which would provide me with the best opportunities for the development of my physical body, which will have to be in good condition if I am to experience my physical surroundings in the way that best suits the development of my spirit. I had gone through a cycle that brought me back to the place of my birth in time for me to work actively with the radiations of this zone of my birth for the most beneficial results. I could use the experiences that I gathered in the time when I was away from this zone in the work that I will now have to do in this zone.

Also, my offspring would have to go through his or her own experiences that would have to be different from mine. I had always known that my offspring did not have to share my exact experiences, but I had not been able to let go of many other issues that surrounded my particular situation, or my conception of what is right or wrong regarding the issue of where I finally settled down and with whom.

I had just discovered that I have to make my decisions in the moment and for the moment, bearing the Laws of Creation as I understand them in mind. When that has been done the future will unfold in accordance with such decisions. I found out that this lays emphasis on adapting oneself totally to the Laws of Creation because the more one adjusts one's actions to the Laws in Creation the better and more harmoniously his future will come together. Just like a plant which develops and blossoms under the best daily care while receiving a good daily supply of sunlight. He will also let go of so much that is unnecessary and that burdens the soul.

One cannot know what the future holds for one because one shapes it in the present. In the present he determines through his decisions how the fruits of the future will taste. There cannot be any planning because such will be based on what is already in existence in the world of forms due to the thinking of mankind for millennia. Planning or scheming is always based on that which man has already experienced or learned. Man cannot however accurately guess how the multifarious effects of the Laws of Creation will shape his future with respect to the decisions that he makes in the present, and so he cannot plan for this future which is yet to unfold. He must concentrate on making the right decisions in the present if he wants a peaceful and harmonious future.

I know that the thinking of mankind for millennia has been devoid of Divine Wisdom since man has mainly allowed himself to be guided and ruled by the calculating and exacting intellect, which became the tool of the Darkness. This means that I cannot then plan for the future if I do not want to make similar mistakes as have been made countless times in the past.

Knowledge of the Laws of Creation helps one in deciding correctly in the moment, and deciding correctly in the moment helps one recognize the Laws of Creation in the future as he experiences the returning effects of his past decisions. It was based on the above experiences that I made my decision to stay with my girlfriend.

While she was in Hungary, I had a seizure and had to spend about four days in the hospital. I had been working at an event where Catholic pilgrims had gathered to meet the Pope. I was doing crowd control duties under the hot sun for about twelve hours, and had done the same duties for four straight days. I was sunburned, hungry, and tired after the fourth day. I put some potatoes on the stove to cook, and took my lunch dose of insulin (I became diabetic in November 1999) after I got back to the apartment.

I had to eat my meals thirty minutes after taking the corresponding dose of insulin, according to the requirements of the type of insulin I was taking at the time. I decided to take a bath while I waited for both the insulin and the potatoes to get ready. I must have dozed off because I awoke next in the hospital, a day or two later.

Apparently the water in the pot had evaporated causing the potatoes to burn, and the smoke from the burnt potatoes set off the fire alarm in the building. The superintendent of the building was alerted by the alarm and discovered me in the bathtub when he came into the apartment to investigate the cause of the alarm. I was able to put together what had happened from what he told me afterwards, and from the way everything was positioned in the apartment. I still cannot remember the last few minutes before I went to sleep. It was not the first time that I had taken insulin before the meal to be eaten was ready, so it makes sense that I did exactly that in that particular situation.

When I left the hospital everything outside felt fresh and new and I noticed parts of the streets that I walked on for the first time. I felt really refreshed and ready to go right back to business as usual.

My girlfriend sent an e-mail to say that she might be returning earlier than she had planned. She then sent another e-mail to say that she could not return early, like she had said, because she had started meeting with her cousin and others in Hungary to learn about spiritual issues. She told me that she also learned a little bit about how to do certain things, such as feeling her aura and those of others, using the lessons she was getting.

She often spoke of her dream to heal people and that made her even more interested in what she was being taught. It was not easy, but I waited for the time to pass and she was back in Toronto when her return date came around. I was very glad to see her again and we discussed the spiritual issues that kept her from returning earlier.

She purchased a book that was recommended by the people from whom she was learning in Hungary. Prior to this time I had often spoken to her about the Grail Message, but only up to the level that I was able to understand at that point. It was, however, still enough to enable me to draw her attention to certain truths about Creation and the Laws that operate in it.

I began to read the book that she bought and I could tell that it touched on some issues that I knew to be covered in the Grail Message. The Grail Message gives the Truth to mankind through providing them with a survey of the entire Creation and the Laws which operate within it. It contains all that man needs to know today for his salvation from his self-willed entanglements. I wanted to see what the book which she brought had to offer. Besides, it had been quite sometime since I settled down to read any material relating to spiritual issues. I had spent quite a lot of time dealing with school material and work. They left me with little time for anything else.

This clearly showed me how we have completely turned our priorities upside down, by considering what is earthly and material to be of more importance than the spiritual. It is only because of this that more emphasis is laid today on university education and the like than on the study of that which alone lives within the human being developing on earth—his spirit. But no amount of erudition can give to man that which he needs in order to mature spiritually and to leave this part of Creation for his origin in the Spiritual Realm.

In accordance with the Law of Attraction of Homogenous Species, only spiritual knowledge can lead to the path to the Spiritual Realm. Spiritual knowledge however is not attained in the universities or even in the religious practices of today, but through the personal experiencing of that person who has the volition to serve the Light and to tread on the path which leads thereto through obedience of the Laws in Creation.

I finally concluded that it would be better if I went back and read the Grail Message, since I then had more time on my hands than I had had for the previous eight years. I had often read certain lectures from the Grail Message but I had not read it as an adult from cover to cover, in sequence as it should be read if it is to give to the reader the necessary help. I proceeded to read the Grail Message and to try my utmost to heed its teaching, and by the time I was done reading it, I felt as though I had just climbed out from underneath a heavy cloud of Darkness. I felt detached for a while from everybody around me, and in my mind, I could picture people chained together at the head, as if huddling together.

I could not see any chains, but I could distinctly see the unifying factor that held them all together. I could sense it. Every one of the people that I pictured was walking along the street or sidewalk, motivated only by attributes of the Darkness. I could see that they were either worried about money or they were motivated by the need to make money.

I could also see the arrogance in the eyes of some and the conceit in others. I could see that in the absence of the knowledge provided in the Grail Message, it would be very difficult to even explain to those people what they were doing wrong. I felt a detachment from everything in a way that made me then wonder why I was still alive. I later prayed that I be told what I had to do if I was being kept alive for a reason. For I had no motivation within me towards any of the activities in which I had previously partaken.

I felt like I should not still be alive because I felt no attraction to things that previously made sense to me, or which previously seemed important. It is a feeling that cannot be adequately described in words since it is a feeling that seems alien in a world where the Darkness has ruled for many ages. It is an experience of the spirit, which lies higher in the order of Creation than the World of Gross Matter where words take on form. It is also a personal experience and so might not make the same kind of sense to everyone. Each person would experience it in his own way.

I actually shouted out loudly as I laughed when I realized that such a feeling was possible and that I had felt it. The peace that comes from this feeling of detachment is like one from "out of this world." It follows the removal of the scales from the eyes of the person going through it, so that he can see how the world has been going in the wrong direction for thousands of years, and how he has been paying too much attention to mere trifles for most of his life on earth.

It also should not take long for anybody who is serious about it to achieve that type of detachment and peace, through the knowledge obtainable by severing oneself from the wrong desires of this world, and the striving for what is good and noble. The Grail Message helps the reader or hearer to know how to wander in Creation. It helps him see what it is we are here for so that he can quickly and easily stop nourishing those forms that keep us anchored in the realm of darkness. It helps one see, through becoming knowing in Creation, because it teaches about Creation in a manner so comprehensive that it has no gaps.

The next thing that I had to worry about was pressure from the Darkness in the form of temptations. I then had to constantly try to stop using my brain to think because it really should not lead, but the spirit should. The brain is not for one-sided thinking, but must be used as a tool of the spirit for the transmission of the impressions of the spirit, i.e., if one wishes to produce those thoughts that do not anchor him to the world of darkness.

When he uses the brain in such a one-sided manner and acts on the thoughts generated through the process, man only ends up carrying out the volition of the Darkness, because he only makes contact with those thought-forms which are the result of the similar one-sided thinking of others. This I have already explained in the preceding chapters of this book as being due to the Law of Attraction of Homogenous Species.

Through this way of thinking one can *fall* in times of temptation because he attracts to himself those base desires which have been cultivated for centuries through the same one-sidedness. He is shielded from the right way of acting, which comes to him in his intuitive perception, which is the expression of the spirit, because his volition is steered towards only what is base and material, and what has developed in the absence of spiritual guidance.

When you allow thoughts to be formed by your brain without guidance from the spirit through the intuitive perception, and without weighing every thought against the Laws of Creation to be certain that they agree with them and will lead upwards, then you can have hundreds of thoughts that do not swing harmoniously with the Laws of Creation, and the forms produced will develop and return to you for reaping. Also, you would be creating a channel for the Darkness to reach you, through the connecting threads that you would generate every moment during the period of your uncontrolled thinking.

As you make these connections you will inevitably be dragged down to the level of the base forms to which you willfully bind yourself. At such levels your perceptive horizon will be correspondingly reduced and you will understand even less of what is spiritual.

It occurred to me that I should write a book that includes my experiences, and which will point men to the existence of the Grail Message as the source of the necessary knowledge for all developing human spirits who truly seek the Truth in this critical stage in the development of mankind on earth.

It is because of this that I started to write this book. I later stopped working at nightclubs because of the implications of such work. I had experienced a lot about the nature of man today during the times that I spent at the nightclubs. I was able to see the ease with which man is distracted from that which is paramount in the existence of man on earth, the development of his spirit.

Every opportunity is sought by men today to keep from thinking about this issue and they jump at the first available chance to indulge in all kinds of activities which may serve to temporarily cause them to forget themselves and "let loose." But during these periods of "letting loose," when one's primary objective is to ignore all responsibilities and "let oneself go," one is constantly and inevitably entangling oneself in dark threads of fate, which form conditions that one *must* live through in order to again free himself and ascend.

Man's preoccupation with one-sided earthly activities which wear him out and cause him to tire, also lead him to search for diversion and avenues where he can act irresponsibly, simply because such activities may be sanctioned by the State. His concern is not for the well-being of his spirit but for the indulgence in irresponsible acts. He seeks to shirk his responsibility by acting in the most shameful manner under the guise of progress and sophistication. But he cannot shirk his responsibilities because the Laws that govern all happenings in Creation are adamantine in their working. They connect him to his works and develop them for him to reap at their maturation and ripening. But man seeks to follow the wide easy road because he has made, through his past actions, the road to the Light difficult for himself. He seeks opportunities to act irresponsibly and indulge his selfish and base desires.

And so the entertainment centers, clubs, and bars exploit this weakness of man and readily provide him with the opportunity to satisfy his base urges, all the while filling up their pockets with the financial proceeds. No one cares what happens to the spiritual development of the individuals who visit these places. As long as the man-made laws are not being broken, man has no problems in engaging in those activities that harm the soul.

He does not see the part he plays in the decadence that is promoted through such activities, through the forms which are generated every moment during those times when he wishes to indulge in a wanton manner in all kinds of immoral and loose behaviour. The wrong conceptions formed over the ages by man about the Creator, the worship of Him, and what life on earth should be about has led to this.

But the responsibility of the individual lies in his development of those abilities which he came into the World of Matter with. Man must decide for himself what he wishes to do with the power of decision given him by God. The ability which he has to channel the neutral power of God in Creation towards the generation of light or dark forms! He alone stands to reap the fruits of this decision!

I decided to sever ties with the nightclubs and such activities as are part of that industry, because only then could I effectively sever the ties to the base forms which I attracted to myself in the process of working there, participating in and being involved in the activities at the clubs. Also, only then could I discover the other possibilities that were to develop in accordance with my decision.

I also was no longer interested in furthering my university education because I found it to be unnecessary for the experience which I need in order to know and fulfill the Laws of Creation. For no formal education is needed to observe the workings of the Laws of Creation and attain the right recognition of the Will of God. One simply has to channel his volition towards what is light and to the fulfillment of this Will and he will be led to those activities that will aid him in this, and which will help him develop those talents which he came to the World of Matter with.

I thereafter decided to make spreading the truth my main vocation. I deeply sensed that I should write about the Truth and what I had experienced, and so I did.

One of the reasons for my writing about some of the experiences that I had prior to beginning this book is to illustrate to the reader or listener the dangers of forming the wrong conceptions while here on earth.

We have become so used to certain ways of thinking and of doing things that we have essentially narrowed our abilities to perceive, and have confined them to this World of Gross Matter. Only that which traditionally has been passed down to us as worth doing do we consider worthwhile.

I tried to show how I had been taught to strive for a noble goal in life, but during the course of my experiencing before writing the book, my goals were more material than spiritual. I made my decisions based on what, at the time, I thought was right. But this was always confined to what I considered important based on what I had learned and what I had experienced while growing up.

But in the end I still acted with little knowledge of the truth of why we are here on earth, because the picture of Creation had not become clear to me. My goals were still too material, and so my decisions along the way were equally limited to the material sphere. Not until I made some realizations after reading the Grail Message again as an adult, and after trying hard to heed its call, did I realise the futility in most of my activities with regard to the actual reason why we are here on earth. It was only then that I decided to make my every decision based on what will benefit my spirit because only this will impact my environment in a way that will not be harmful but will help in its ennoblement.

It was only through striving to understand the teaching in the Grail Message that I could know what is good for my spirit. Only through this could I make decisions based on what will benefit my spirit. And only when one makes decisions in ways that benefits one's spiritual development does one sever those ties that cause one to adhere to traditional and customary beliefs and act accordingly. Only then can he stop worrying about mere trifles like I had done and concentrate on the only thing of importance, spiritual development and ascent. When man makes his priority the fulfillment of the Will of God through obedience of His Laws in Creation, this will also yield material fruit that will benefit him as well as his surroundings, because he cannot fulfill the Laws in Creation without action on his part.

It is to show those who wish to know the way back to the Light, by pointing out to man the reason he is here on earth, through the revelation of Creation and its Laws to him, that we have been provided help in the great Work: In The Light Of Truth—The Grail Message.

To succeed man has to become individual in his thinking and actions. The art of independent thinking has been lost in the process of trying to conform to one lifestyle or another. Men do not bother anymore to consider the necessity of their actions but blindly follow the masses because of shared wrong conceptions which are passed down from generation to generation.

Man has acted as a slave to his intellect for thousands of years and has caused everything that was meant to develop here on earth and in surrounding spheres to develop wrongly. Consequently he has created problems for himself which he encounters in the reciprocal actions of his past wrong ways of thinking.

Due to his steadily increasing narrow-mindedness he has sought to remedy these problems in mainly intellectual ways because he has steadily withdrawn from the Light and has increasingly lost his connection to the guidance therefrom. Simultaneously he has over-cultivated the frontal brain that produces the intellect, and has passed this deformity down to his offspring as the *inherited sin.*

This deformity which has been passed down now gives those incarnating on earth, from the various regions of the World of Matter where they had to go in response to their weaving while previously here on earth, a fertile soil on which to cultivate more evil and wrong conceptions. It does not force them to commit sin but provides the fertile soil for this to happen quite easily.

The already abnormally enlarged frontal brain makes it easier for the incarnating souls to follow in the trend of their predecessors and continue with the over-cultivation of the intellect. It prevents the impressions of the spirit from being clearly expressed because it has also brought about the stunting of the hindbrain, which serves as the bridge for the transmission of spiritual impressions to the frontal brain. Or better said, the lack of spiritual activity has led to the stunting of the bridge across which spiritual impressions are meant get to the frontal brain for the formation of thoughts and execution of the will of the spirit.

This deformity provides the platform for the exaggeration of material instincts, like the sexual instinct or the need to needlessly accumulate wealth, because the conceptions formed by man in this state are primarily directed towards what is of this earth, and what will continue the development of the already generated base forms here on earth and in the surrounding ethereal environment of the World of Matter.

The wrong seeds are then continually planted irrespective of the disastrous outcome of similar practices and behaviours of men in the past. Man continues to experience problems and continues to try to remedy these problems using this enlarged and malformed brain and the associated over-cultivated intellect. His conceit, narrow-mindedness, and one-sidedness continue to grow and cause him to even press harder on the downward trend. He is unable to receive from the Light the help he needs to extricate himself from his entanglements because he cannot bring about the necessary humility required for such a reception.

Downward he progresses while all the time thinking that he is making good progress. He does not realise that only the forms of the conditions change but the core of the issues remains the same. He is devoid of knowledge and continuously sows the wrong seeds in all his actions. This is because with his downward-acting intellect at the lead, through its one-sided development, everything was bound to develop wrongly and out of rhythm with the natural Laws of Creation. These Laws maintain balance in Creation and require balanced activity by the creatures of Creation in order for them to abide by the natural Laws. Man has removed himself through his actions from the necessary balanced swinging in Creation, and so he continuously experiences the adverse results of his wrong decisions.

He invests time and resources in the development of the conditions that will make him more comfortable and which will allow him to live a life of ease because he has never yet realized why he is here on earth. He imagines that he can solve his problems with technological advancements, because he is only able to survey the last ramifications of the working of the Laws of Creation, and so he only feels the bitter end result of the wrong seeds which he has sown for millennia. He thinks that using his brain even more can normalize the harsh conditions under which he finds himself, and so he thinks some more and tries to outdo the past generations with his pseudo-knowledge.

He attributes the problems of the past to a lack of intellectual acuteness and he strives to sharpen his intellect even more. In the process he relegates all matters of the spirit to the background. He does not learn from the past actions of men before him who also thought like he does now, but who in the end fell like others before them. He refuses to learn from history so he repeats the mistakes of the past. In place of true knowledge is a false picture of what life should be about as presented by the Darkness with the help of its numerous satellites here on earth.

During the course of thousands of years the base attributes of the Darkness have had time to develop to gigantic proportions. Envy, conceit, greed, distrust, narrow-mindedness, and fear rule the world. Man responds to them in kind. He becomes darker in the process, because during his striving for false goals he attracts these base forms to himself

206

and he nourishes them with his every thought, word and action.

This becomes his reality. He can no longer make sense of what the Callers sent by the Light have to say. He wants that which he pictures as the ultimate goal in earth-life. He craves power, influence, and a comfortable life and he does all that is in his power to achieve these. With his eyes fixed on these base and earthly goals he ignores every warning on the way to their attainment. He strives towards their attainment at all costs!

The earth has developed wrongly in every respect, due to the failure of man, who was supposed to cooperate with its development towards the Light, towards becoming a Paradise on earth. He was supposed to make the earth a reflection of the Primordial Creation, because the Paradise that is his origin is also a corresponding reflection of the Primordial Creation, as should all spheres in all of Creation which took on form following the formation of the first Creation.

He can only attain this goal by adapting himself to the Laws of Creation, which brought about the Primordial Creation. Only this can bring about peace and harmony in Creation. Nothing else can! Since everything has developed wrongly, it would be wrong to continue to contribute to this wrong development through the same kind of activities and ways of thinking that have prevailed hitherto!

I have written this book to call out to mankind and draw their attention to the fallacy that is the way of life of today's mankind. I have presented a story of the experiences that I had prior to starting this book partly in order to get the earnest reader or listener to look at his own experiences and ponder the reasons for the decisions that he has made so far in his life. Did he have in mind the fulfillment of the Divine Will as he made those decisions or was he following already existing traditions? What is he willing to do about his realizations?

He will also be able to see the results of his past decisions and recognize the working of the Laws which bring to him the fruits of the seeds he sows with his every decision. He might then become able to consciously experience the working of these Laws in the present as he strives to do only that which is in accordance with the Will of God. Because he will realise that the decisions he makes in the present will determine the outcome of his future conditions, which are the fruits of the seeds sown in the present. But in this he should not limit his attention to this earth alone, but realise that he experiences simultaneous radiations from the different planes of the World of Matter. He forms his path through these planes, as he strives upwards to the Spiritual Realm, with his volition while he is still in his physical body. The path is light when his volition is directed towards what is light, and it is dark if his volition is dark.

Only when the Laws of Creation are abided by, that is, when the fulfillment of the Divine Will of God is the basis for a decision, can there be beneficial fruit. This Divine Will manifests in every happening and shows man how to live in this Creation so that he can be fruitful, as well as happy. They govern everything that takes place in Creation and are also responsible for the development of the forms of nature. They are the Language of the Creator in Creation because they express His Will in Creation.

To act according to this Will requires that this Will be known. The more one strives to act in accordance with It, the more he opens himself to the knowledge of It in his experiences. But this means that he will have to make changes in the way that he lives his life, from the smallest things to the biggest. "Everything must become new" was the admonition of the Son of God Jesus Christ. This means that everything is wrong. The new cannot be built upon what is already wrong, but the wrong must be uprooted and done away with as it is replaced with the new.

With the *new* will come the development of the right conceptions and the right kind of activity. Man will then be able to develop the spiritual abilities that he left his origin with as a spirit-germ. He will no longer hinder their development due to his pursuit of base desires, or through the adoption of alien opinions which do not originate from within him and so do not rhyme with his intuitive thinking.

The way the earth has developed so far has left mankind with apparently limited options as to how to channel the power of God in Creation. In channeling this neutral power towards wrong ends due to the wrong conceptions passed down over the ages, he prevents the development of his real abilities. He does not get to realise his true worth and his real potential. He remains dependent on the opinions of others, never being able to stand on his own feet.

Man must make his goal a great and high one if he is to realise his real potential. Being spiritual this goal lies in spiritual activity and not in the material. With a high spiritual goal he will be able to unfold much more of his abilities than would be the case if he strives for earthly or material goals only. He would be forced to exert his spirit and so would be able to draw strength from higher and more luminous spheres for his activities.

Consequently he will be able to achieve much more than hitherto. Also, he would not have to worry about material issues the way he does today, because in the outworking of the effects of his spiritual volition his earthly conditions will correspondingly come together in a way that only serves and uplifts him.

Then men would become more individual in their thinking and reintroduce into their lives the necessary vitality that is needed in the harmonious development of this earth. This can never be achieved through the imitation or copying of foreign ideas or behaviours. Man will learn to decide for himself through personal exertion which leads to conviction. His spirit will be strengthened in its growth, leading to the possibility of higher recognitions.

He will at last drop the burden that is a result of the feeling of the need to conform to one way of thinking or another, which may not coincide with his sense of justice and beauty. He will learn to become one with his intuitive perception and in the process become more spiritual in his actions. All his actions will then be just and bring about beauty.

Finally, I have presented some of my experiences here in an attempt to dispel the wrong conceptions about what it is to be spiritual. Man is spiritual at his core. He cannot run away from this or choose not to be spiritual any longer. He cannot decide to separate the spiritual from his everyday activities because earthly activity is only the result of spiritual activity. The more noble the spirit is the better his earthly efforts will materialize and the better its impact on his surroundings.

He can decide to bury its abilities through non-exertion of his spirit, but he cannot stop the machinery of this Creation, which still sees him as a creature of Creation with a core of a spiritual origin, who has a corresponding responsibility in accordance with the Laws of Creation, and who stands inevitably to reap the fruits of the seeds that he has sown using the power made available to him by God.

Maybe with this the reader or listener can also set about the unfolding of his own abilities through using all his strength to form the right conceptions henceforth in his experiences. May Almighty God grant us the strength to fulfill!

THE WORLD OF CYCLES

In the previous chapter I provided details of some of the experiences that I went through prior to beginning this book. I included those details, among other reasons, to show that we all have to travel along different paths according to our past decisions whose cycle-closures bring us the experiences that we need in order to mature spiritually.

Within these conditions we find challenges which only strengthen us spiritually when we confront them with the volition to do good and to fulfill the Will of the Light by spreading the volition of the Light through our actions. The conditions which materialize as a result of our decisions, come to us as the fruits of the seeds which we sow with every decision. This sowing is done using the neutral power of God in Creation, which we channel towards the generation of light or dark forms in accordance with the nature of our volition.

By experiencing the results of our decisions we are able to recognize the working of the Laws in Creation which present to us a picture of the Will of God. The more we are able to experience of this working the more trust we will have in the strictness of the working and the perfect justice that lies in it.

The experiences of every individual are for that individual alone and the Truth should make sense to that person according to the experiences that the person has been through. It is widely accepted by people that everyone has to travel a road that is distinctly for him, during his wanderings on this earth. The same also holds true about the road one has to travel in the entire Creation.

If one can see the truth in that, then it should make sense that all of one's experiences are unique and serve a purpose for the spiritual ascent of the owner of those experiences. It is those experiences that are meant to teach and help us individually in understanding our intuition. The more we make decisions for ourselves and rightly experience the outcome of such decisions, the more we mature and are prepared for the next challenge that will require a decision from us.

It is only by doing this that a person can then trust that inner voice that helps direct him on the path that he has to follow for the benefit of his spirit. It should be clear then that diversity is actually necessary in our communities and amongst individuals, even amongst friends and family members. Since we are all individual human spirits, who came into our respective homes and neighbourhoods due to the Primordial Laws of Creation, it follows that in our activities, our thinking, and our speech, we should remain individuals. And as individuals we cannot then be the same within, but must express our individualities through the development of our different spiritual abilities and gifts.

I also wanted to show with the presentation that we become inclined to follow certain guidelines or rules already set out here on earth, prior to our incarnations into our current earthly existence, which are directed towards very narrowed and earthly goals, because we see all around us the established rigid forms that maintain this wrong way of thinking.

Thus we go through life trying to attain some earthly goal or another without ever having the time to stop and question the rightness of it all. Out of fear, we march on along the paths rigidly paved by the intellect so that we can participate in the maintenance of the wrong volition of the Darkness, which uses the intellect as its tool. So we remain in the dark as to the reasons for our misfortunes and our sufferings, because in the course of the pursuit of our earthly goals we forget about that which alone actually matters, the Will of God.

We lose our individualities in this process and so are not able to make sense of our hourly and daily experiences for our ascent. We see everything through the lens of the lowly intellect, and get drawn closer to disintegration together with the base forms to which we remain connected, and which we nourish every moment. We are constantly drawn away from the recognitions that should bring us closer to the knowledge of the Will of God.

But only this knowledge can help one navigate this world and successfully make his way back to the Spiritual Realm where he came from as a seed, as a spirit seed. This knowledge can only be attained through the personal experiencing of the Laws of Creation. With this comes conviction, which is living faith in the Will of God.

We reach convictions on our own because we all have the ability to do this. It is impossible for a person to attain spiritual maturity by following the path taken by another. To stubbornly try to go against the Laws of Creation, which govern all the happenings in Creation, would be to expect disappointments and even destruction and catastrophe for the errant soul in its earth life, or later in the beyond. Such a soul would have to remain incapable of journeying well through the worlds that it has to traverse on its way back to the Spiritual Realm, because it would not know the Laws that it would need then. It would not be strong enough for the journey which it must make through the planes of the World of Matter. Because it spent its earth life pursuing material goals and never was able to gain trust in the Laws of Creation through experiencing.

It is because of this fact that I have to draw the attention of the reader or listener once more to the idea of concentrating on oneself when searching for faults that need to be rectified! During the process of purifying himself man gains knowledge of the Laws of Creation, because he needs to exert himself spiritually for this. This can only happen along his own personal path of experiencing. The strengthened spirit is then able to perceive the spiritual currents which constantly permeate the World of Matter.

We face numerous problems on earth today because people are constantly looking to the outside and worrying about what the next person is thinking about, or what he is doing or saying. There is so much of this going on that people have forgotten how to look within themselves for faults. Man today constantly seeks someone to blame for all his misfortunes. He does not realise that he is the architect of his own fate, that the path that another person follows is the concern of that person alone. Along that path that person will receive his reward or punishment for his past decisions. The focus of our critical gaze has been misplaced.

That person who gets excited about the faults of others you will find to have the same faults within him to a greater degree. He gets excited and irritated by them because of his own familiarity with these faults, because of the existence of these faults within himself. He is able to draw this from the person whose faults he gets excited about, through the attraction of homogenous species. A simple examination of this statement will prove this to anyone who makes the right effort while observing the goings-on in his surroundings and with his neighbours.

By constantly thinking about the faults of the next person we spend our time and energy contributing to the development of forms of conceit, distrust, fear, hatred, envy, narrow-mindedness and others. We are planting seeds that will have to mature and bear fruit. The fruits, however, will have to go back to the originator of the thoughts, greatly multiplied.

Ignorance of this fact will not prevent it from happening because the Laws that govern this happening are immutable and do not cater to the opinions of men. Ignorance itself is a fruit of neglect because the person has not made the right kind of effort in the recognition of the Laws of Creation, which never pause in their working.

When you do not form a bridge by which you become connected to evil of any nature, then you will not be affected by evil of any nature. One is only affected by what one draws to oneself in accordance with his volition. Every thought, action, or speech opens up a cycle which must close. The closing of such a cycle could bring with it good or bad situations.

But even a seemingly bad event that occurs with the closure of a particular cycle could be used for the ascent of the originator of the act that opened the cycle. That person, however, has to realize the purpose of the experience. He has to know that it was not arbitrary and that there is a spiritual lesson to be learned from that experience.

He has to be able to see his contribution to the developed fruit and make a change in his attitude so that he does not sow more similar seeds as brought about the distasteful fruit. The person then has the opportunity to take advantage of the Grace of Almighty God Which gives him the opportunity to ascend through being able to recognize His

Divine Will in the closing of the cycle.

He could get redemption from past actions, thoughts or words, and he could also learn and grow spiritually in addition. The person, however, who does not know about the Laws that govern Creation, may not realize the significance of the experience, and could become more frustrated, and delve even further into wrong actions that open up more cycles. The newly opened cycles will, in turn, have to close and bring about more frustration to this one who is not yet enlightened.

Here, this person will not benefit from the closing of the cycle and, worse still, simultaneously opens up another cycle and thereby increases his days of hardship and darkness. He also encourages and supports his spiritual indolence by not taking advantage of the opportunities presented to him to close cycles and proceed to the next liberating experience.

If we do not pay attention to our every single utterance, thought and deed, then we are going to forego all the opportunities given to us, through the Grace of the Creator, to atone for past actions. We will also trifle away our time on this earth while looking at other people for change.

Since all that we do, think or say, comes back to us manifold in modified forms, it is best that we stop creating these wrong thoughts, actions, and speech. We are today reaping the fruits of the seeds that we sowed in the past days, years, decades or centuries. In the chapter dealing with reincarnation, I mentioned how we are able to reap the fruits of the seeds that we sow in future earth lives, or between earth lives in the beyond.

By "beyond" here I mean the planes in the World of Matter that we cannot see with our physical eyes, but which are one with this part of Creation and the activities of which penetrate the coarse material of the earth and influence its surroundings. If a particular fruit has not matured enough to be reaped in one lifetime, then it might be reaped in the next one, or in-between earth lives after the soul of the individual human spirit has left its physical body and is living off the conditions which it caused to arise for it in one of the other planes of the World of Matter. Many of us have been reincarnating for thousands of years and have still to reap some of the fruits that are yet to mature from some of those years.

Some of these fruits might bring misfortune while others bring joy. The reason that certain situations in our lives might appear arbitrary is because we have not paid enough attention to the Laws of Creation in a way that would allow us to recognize the root-causes of our present conditions, so that we can embrace our conditions, good or bad. For only then can we live through such conditions and consciously learn from them.

Only through recognition can the cycles we opened with our past decisions and actions be closed, and liberation from the binding threads be achieved. If we were quite familiar with the Laws of Creation we would not have to keep coming back for additional chances to close cycles and mature. We would not try to go around the issues which need to be addressed by simply dealing with the symptoms of the real issues that plague us on earth.

We despise problems and setbacks and we try to push our own selfish earthly agendas ahead of that which is beneficial to us and to the world in general. We lack the right conception of why we experience the things that we encounter in our daily lives, and so we do not develop like we should and end up returning to earth many more times than would have been the case had we obeyed the Laws in Creation.

I am calling your attention to these Laws now because it is only through their knowledge and adaptation to their working that man can live peacefully, in joy and harmony, and in a way that shows gratitude to the Creator. We glorify Him when we live according to His Laws in Creation.

For our own benefit we are mostly not aware of all that went on in our past lives, and so we often cannot see the need in examining ourselves and finding out why we are where we are on this earth. We have particular earthly goals that we have set for ourselves and we just want to march on until we achieve them. As we do this we stumble over or even totally disregard all those opportunities intended for the maturation of our spirits.

By following the rigid paths, which have been laid out by the intellect, we miss the opportunities for personal spiritual growth because we expend all our strength in the fostering of the goals of the intellect, which currently serves as a tool for the Darkness.

We turn against one another because of the wrong conceptions of what life on earth should be about, what success on earth should be like. We get into a state of senseless competition where we destroy our bodies and darken our souls for the sake of fulfilling a false goal. But this we do only because we live in ignorance of the Truth. We live in darkness. We have blinded ourselves with our actions, and we have shunned the liberating Light.

Many people who are worried about being in the wrong fields of activity are afraid to leave them, because they would not be able to live up to the earthly expectations that they set for themselves and their families. The points in their lives when they have to learn and make major changes to their lives are then missed, due to ignorance, conceit, envy, and greed, all of which are attributes that serve to chain one to this plane of Gross Matter, and so are anti-Light. They hinder the necessary ascent of the spirit by chaining it to the World of Gross Matter through misdirecting the volition of the spirit towards material ends.

Everything in the World of Matter goes through cycles. The movements in our solar system and the cycle of the seasons could be used as starting points for recognizing this. There is a precise moment for everything to happen and this moment occurs at a particular point during the cycle that brings it about. A certain degree of maturation must be reached for the various stages of a cycle to commence or end. Our journey down to earth for our development and our return to the Spiritual Plane, where we came from, is also in a cycle. We have all taken a long time in the completion of this cycle because we came down to earth in the World of Matter, lost sense of our mission, and became stuck in this region.

It is because of this fact that most of us have been circling between the earth and the planes within the World of Gross Matter, without ever getting to the point of our origin, or even up to the finer and lighter species of the World of Matter. We no longer even remember that we should be striving to get back to our origin in the Spiritual Realm. Worldly issues have so taken over that everyone is busy minding the business of the next person without realizing that he, himself, does not have a clue as to why he is here on this earth. He does not know his true goal and so his every action bears an element of destruction within it.

In a previous chapter, I used the example of an apple dropping to the ground after ripening, to illustrate our mission on earth. The apple seeds go into the ground and a seedling germinates after the necessary development of one of the seeds has occurred in the ground. It is, however, only after the necessary development of the seed has occurred that it emerges from beneath the ground and proceeds to grow into a tree. It is the same with us human spirits, except that being spiritual, we have correspondingly higher responsibilities here in the world of our own development.

We came as seeds into the world of development which is matter. We would only be successful if we are able to return to the Spiritual Realm as self-conscious human spirits. Our resurrection from the World of Matter would be like the germination of the seedling from beneath the surface of the ground. We can then continue to grow and mature as we spread light to the World of Matter from the Spiritual Realm as fully conscious beings.

According to the Primordial Laws of Creation, our development should coincide with the ennoblement of our environment. Therefore our failure to mature as human spirits over millennia has caused the destruction and degeneration of our environment. We have not only neglected to develop ourselves, but have also, as a natural consequence, neglected the earth and, in fact, the entire World of Matter.

This is due to our wrong decisions, which, when put together, can be called our collective volition. Our volition has been dark for ages and so we have burdened ourselves with dark attributes. We have fallen deeper and closer to the regions of Darkness and thus have taken the World of Matter down with us. We have not behaved like we should and like other creatures in Creation always do.

The apple tree supplies its surroundings with fruits and shelter and plays an uplifting part in the process of the development of the World of Matter. Being under the care of animistic beings it goes through its cycle of development while helping sustain its surroundings. In the course of man's developmental cycle he has brought ruin and devastation to his surroundings because what comes out of him, in the form of his various works, his thoughts, words and actions, leads to the destruction of his surroundings in every respect. He has dragged it down to low and dark depths.

Our closeness to the regions of the Darkness makes it easier for this world to be enveloped and surrounded by the Darkness. It makes it easier for the Darkness to rule in this part of Creation. The magnetic pressure exerted by the Darkness on all that is dark, keeps us in a comfortable slumber, one that we have been in for ages. This grip of the Darkness on the earth has become so uniform that man can hardly notice its effects. He has become comfortable in his ignorance and his love of ease. He only senses discomfort when he tries to resist the influences of the Darkness.

The reign of the Darkness in this world could not be more clearly shown than in the events surrounding the murder of the Son of God. Jesus, the Son of God, the Love Incarnate of God, came down to earth without any guilt, to show us how to live and try to wake men up from their spiritual slumber, after we had ignored and debased past teachings by others sent to help man before the inevitable closure of the cycle during which man was to develop on earth.

The cycle of the World of Matter is approaching the point of disintegration and so the human spirits developing in it must hasten to resurrect from it. For this reason man must hasten to separate himself from matter through spiritual maturity, if he wishes not to be caught in the process of disintegration.

Man should have already reached a much higher level of maturity at this point in his development on earth. That he has not done so is his fault alone, because the Light sent help through messengers at all the times when such help was due. Also man, at any time, can take advantage of the ability to help himself through the recognition of the Will of the Light so that he can perceive more of Its glory through his experiences. He alone chooses not to pay any attention to the warnings. He finds it more important to dwell on earthly matters. The fruit of his volition is his present condition.

We have had quite some time to mature, but due to the fact that we started to rely quite heavily on the intellect, we lost the ability to receive guidance from above. Due to our one-sided use of it, the intellect put a seal on our receptive abilities, and has kept us from fulfilling our mission here on earth. But this was only possible because we empowered the intellect to rule over the spirit through our negligence, our slothfulness, and our conceit.

Men started to rely on the intellect for everything and naturally became totally lost through it. They are just like blind mice running around in a maze. When things go well for them they have no idea why, but they try to fashion out a reason by theorizing and making wrong assumptions. Sometimes they thank the Creator, but, in a way, that is insulting to Him.

They consider themselves fortunate and deserving of His blessings when they meet with good fortunes, and become frustrated and often angry when they encounter hard and difficult times. In this, man clearly indicates his conceit. He imagines that he does not deserve what he gets when conditions do not correspond with his conceptions of how things should go. He displays his ignorance of the Laws in Creation and their strict and quite objective manner of working! He does not see how he gets back the fruits of his actions.

Those who do not believe in the existence of a Creator attribute their good fortune to the magnificence of their intellect, or to luck or chance. They look for someone to blame when they meet with unfavourable conditions. This just clearly shows man's lack of understanding of Creation because he assumes that there is arbitrariness in the happenings in Creation. His conceit keeps him from recognizing that the fault lies within him. That he has attracted the conditions to himself. Again, this only points to the ignorance of the Laws of Creation among mankind, a lack of understanding of the Will of God, and a lack of trust in His Perfection.

The Laws of Creation operate without fail throughout Creation and take care in directing the matured fruits of man's volition back to man, the originator. Here, in the perfection of the Creator, everybody gets exactly what he deserves. He gets back manifold what he placed in Creation because it develops in accordance with the Laws in Creation.

The thought, action, or word that you put out goes around its elliptical cycle and receives reinforcement on its way as it develops. When it returns to you at the end of that cycle, it would have gained reinforcements from other similar forms, and it would hit you with a blow that corresponds to the nature of your spirit at the time, and also according to the nature of the original act. Just like when you plant corn you do not get only a seed of corn at the end of the cycle at the time of harvest, but a whole cob of corn.

Those men who have material wealth should know the Laws of Creation so that they would be able to realize how best to put their wealth to good use for the ennoblement of their spirits and environments. And also so that they do not through their activities attract to themselves harmful conditions in their reciprocal effects.

Those who do not have a lot of material wealth should know the Laws of Creation so that they can best know what field of activity would best benefit their spirits, as well as those of the people around them. In their individual ways they will contribute to the joyful and harmonious development of the earth. There is no injustice in Creation. Man may think that there is because he is the only source of arbitrary actions and all forms of injustice. But even then, he still receives his just measure in the reciprocal action of his deeds. As soon as he starts to look at his surroundings in the new light brought by the coming of the Son of Man, he will see things as they really are and not as he imagines them to be. He will then be in a position to spread light around him.

Ennoblement of one's environment, which goes hand in hand with spiritual maturity, cannot be done without one ennobling oneself first. In this world where darkness has reigned for so long it is necessary to point out to those who wish for it the way back to the Light.

Due to the Law of Attraction of Homogenous Species you attract people of the same spiritual nature as yourself. As you strive towards the Light you will be brought together through the Law of Attraction of Homogenous Species to those people who are drawn to you for mutual spiritual and material benefits. There is always some giving and some taking and the cycles that bring about the opportunities for these are continually closing.

It is then imperative that everyone pays attention to the experiences that he or she goes through every moment of the day. Since the Laws of Creation are immutable and will go on working whether or not we know of their existence, it is advisable to stay alert so that no more wrong seeds are sown. Knowing the Laws of Creation and placing oneself within them, and swinging in harmony with them, is the only way to start avoiding the opening of more evil cycles.

This way man can concentrate on experiencing the closures of the already opened cycles of the past as he experiences the working of the Laws. He will no longer have fear about the future because he will know that he deserves and needs the experiences that it brings for his spiritual development. He will know that it is the only way that he can sever himself from the ties to those forms which have caused him to remain fettered in the lowly regions of Creation.

It has become quite difficult for people to find any reason to put aside their bad habits and heed the warnings about the dangers that will result from their old ways. With everyone else doing whatever he or she pleases, why should you care? Man wants to know what is in it for him. He thinks only in the material sense when the issue of obeying the Divine Will comes up. He may have to then wait until he has lost all opportunities for a timely turn around, when the forms which he nourishes with his volition will have to be crushed in the Judgement, together with all those still connected with them.

Man has for a long time now given up his individuality. He wants to do, wear, say things that are in fashion or that are trendy, no matter how ridiculous and wrong certain things appear to him. He supports leaders who clearly make policies that cause serious harm to his people and to those in other countries, and joins in the slander of people whom he has never met before. He does all this just so that he can maintain his own comfortable condition. He cannot see beyond his own narrow world. Consequently, he sows his seeds accordingly.

He remains linked to all his actions, including his thoughts and words, and also to those who help nourish them as they develop, through their spoken or written words or in their thoughts.

In this way all the people who contribute in any way at all to actions that are considered wrong in the view of the Light, will have to share in the fruits that such actions will bring about when their cycles end. Everyone must receive what is due to him, be it great or small. In this there can be no mistakes. Minutely, the Laws of Creation hand man back the fruits of his labour.

It is for this reason that I have to stress that everyone has to become individual again. It is only in becoming individual that you can make beneficial use of the Grail Message about Which I write, in order to avoid being swept away towards destruction during the imminent Purification that has to precede the closure of the earth's cycle, and the cycle of the development of the human spirit on earth. Because it offers man knowledge of Creation, without which he can no longer attain the conviction necessary to make it through this period.

The wrong deeds of past years opened up cycles that have to close now. They have to close now because the earth is approaching the end of its cycle, within the bigger cycle of the World of Matter, which is heading towards its disintegration. This is a natural process and not an arbitrary one. Just like everything else that has to develop in the World of Matter, there is a point at which disintegration must set in, in order to allow for reformation from primordial seed.

Since the World of Matter is approaching its disintegration, it becomes necessary for the human spirits still developing on earth, and in different parts of the World of Matter, to hasten their separation from all that is material. This must be done prior to the time of disintegration if the human spirits do not wish to go through this disintegration process together with matter.

Different celestial globes in different parts of the World of Matter would have to go through this process of separation and disintegration at different times depending on their various levels of maturity, and how close they are to the Light above. It is time now for the separation to occur here on earth, so that those who are able to can make it out of the World of Matter in time to avoid being sucked into the disintegration process, whereby they will lose all that they have been able to acquire in terms of experiences, with which alone they are able to form themselves into mature and conscious human spirits.

Those who are not able to separate themselves from matter because of their volition and their love for what is material, will be drawn along to the depths with those forms which have to undergo destruction, so that new forms can develop from the primordial seeds of matter, which will be fresh and ready to serve as coverings at the right time for the species that in future may become mature enough to incarnate in them for the purpose of their own development in the World of Matter.

These people will be those who do not take the time to sever their ties to base forms which they nourish with the neutral power that courses through Creation, of which the developing human spirits are a part. Since they remain attached to these forms through the connecting threads, they will have to be drawn along with them to their fate, in accordance with their volition at the time when the Ray of Purifying Light will strike them.

The separation from matter of the human spirits who grasp the help from the Light and make use of it, will be preceded by the Great Purification, which has already begun, during which the Darkness will be destroyed together with all those attached to it. This will be followed by the period of a *thousand years of peace*, of the reign of the Son of Man, Imanuel, which means God with us.

This is the period of the *Millennium*, which has been prophesied about for thousands of years by Called ones and prophets of different kinds, through the ages and all around the different regions of the earth. During that time of the thousand-year reign of peace, those who make it through the Purification will be schooled in the ways of God, under the Leadership of the Son of Man; Whose Radiation will so penetrate the earth that no evil will be able to exist. The reciprocal actions of the decisions of man will return to him with such a quickness as to reward or punish each act instantly, never giving evil the breathing space to develop itself.

During this period of Purification, which has already begun, the fruits of all the wrong done in past decades and centuries will quickly ripen and be reaped. It is during this period that people will judge themselves. This has to happen if the ones who have decided to change their ways are not to be soiled once again by those who hang on so tenaciously to the old.

It will be a self-judgment because the fate of a person in these times will reflect that person's inner nature and thus judge that person. The crushing blows that are landing on individuals and on masses and nations all over the world today are a sign that the time has come when the Purification has to hand people back the fruits of what they sowed in past years. It is also at this time that the Darkness is going to put up its greatest fight, and try to take as many people as it can down with it. It will try to keep mankind from perceiving the Truth. It will work through its servants here on earth, those who will strive to oppose the spread of the Truth here on earth.

During this time when all that exists as a form in Subsequent Creation will be forced to mature under the intensity of the increased Light-pressure, the dark forms will ripen and fall on the laps of their originators. All evil that has been thought of or spoken of will have to be lived off as well. It will have to manifest physically, so that through itself it will be destroyed.

Through the Law of Attraction of Homogenous Species evil forms will come together and destroy one another, while good and noble forms will be strengthened through the actions of one another with help from the increased power of the Light in the World of Matter. Man will attract to himself the fate that he has woven through his volition, whatever it might be. All that is slumbering within him will be awakened and be judged. The slumbering spirits of men will now be roused in the Judgment and be forced to move. Their movements, which will be the same as the expressions of their volition, will determine how they will be struck by the Sword of the Light.

Those who wish to ascend will be able to do so at a rate never before experienced in the World of Matter. Those who neglect to take advantage of this help, and who persist in their old ways will be crushed and dragged down to those regions where they will have to painfully live through all that they have caused to take on form through their base volition.

The separation will be complete and it will be thorough! It will occur precisely in accordance with the nature of the individual human spirit at the time when the Sword of the Light strikes him. See to it then that you always stand aright!

THE FINAL JUDGMENT

I gave a brief picture of the process of the development of mankind here on earth in the chapter, "The Development of the Human Spirit on Earth," and described it as one that had to occur in stages. This had to be the case since the developing human spirits in the World of Matter had to develop in accordance with the Laws in Creation from seed-germs.

For this to happen they had to go through the different stages of developing from seeds and maturing to the point of harvest or decay. They had to follow the same process as can be witnessed in the development of a plant, which develops from a seed, matures, blossoms, and bears fruit. Their development in the World of Matter had to be so because it could not have been any other way. It had to be in accordance with the Laws in Creation, which express the Will of God.

The human spirits who had expressed their wish to develop self-consciousness were immersed into the World of Matter as spirit seeds, through the activity of the Holy Spirit, the Divine Will of God Who granted their petition to become self-conscious.

The only road open to them for this was one that led them down to the developing World of Matter because at the time they were in a similar state of maturity with this World of Matter. Being spiritual, however, they bore within them the striving towards the Light, which expressed itself in the urge to become self-conscious.

This urge, which exists in all that is spiritual, was supposed to lead to the development of the human spirits from seed-germs while simultaneously ennobling their surroundings in the World of Matter. This way they were to participate in the development of the World of Matter, which is without inherent warmth, as they themselves matured towards self-consciousness.

In the process of having to subsist in this coarse part of Creation they were to awaken through self-exertion. This would have strengthened them spiritually, and they would have been able to draw help from above which always lies in wait for the spirit that is able to receive it in humility.

Since they would have had to exert their spirits in the process of wandering through the immense World of Matter in the process of maturing, they would have inevitably produced forms, which would have impacted their surroundings according to their nature. If they abided by the Laws of Creation they would have created a peaceful and harmonious world around them as they matured and ascended out of the World of Matter into the Spiritual Realm from where they descended.

But this development had to follow the process of development that exists here in the World of Matter, in accordance with how the Laws manifest in this part of Creation. So man had to go through this process so that he might gain the necessary knowledge of Creation through the experiencing of the Laws operating in it. Since these Laws express the Will of God, he would have gained knowledge about the ways of God through his experiencing of His Laws in Creation.

Only after such knowledge had been attained could he be allowed to enter the Spiritual Realm, into Paradise, as a fully conscious human spirit who is able to withstand the pressure of the Light in that sphere in Creation, through being knowledgeable of the Will of his Creator, because being self-conscious in the Spiritual Realm is synonymous with being knowledgeable of the Will of God and abiding by It in the Spiritual Realm.

He was to receive knowledge which corresponded with the expected level of maturity of the human spirit, at different points during the process of his development. If he had stayed alert spiritually and fulfilled on his part then he would have been elevated through the absorption of new knowledge at each of the points in the course of the cycle of his development, which he could have added to what he already knew up until then.

Finally, he would have reached the point in the cycle where he would

SAMPSON IRUOHA

have had to receive the final bit of knowledge, with which he would have
completed the picture of Creation, and which would have then allowed
him to perceive from the highest realms in Creation and act accordingly.
He would have then been ripe for departure from this part of Creation,
and as good fruit would have been admitted into Paradise at the end of his
wandering through the spheres of matter. For only when completely
purified and free from all alien species could he be admitted into the
Spiritual Realm, since the Law of Attraction of Homogenous Species
would not allow for any non-spiritual species to get into the Spiritual
Realm.

But man fell and diverted his efforts towards the development of the
intellect, and those forms which are primarily concerned with matter.
This one-sidedness cut him off from the spiritual currents, which were
meant for his own development. And since he was no longer receiving
these currents undimmed, all that he willed in the World of Matter was
already diseased and destined for destruction from the start. They were
destined for destruction because they were not in line with the Laws of
Creation, which are only upbuilding in their working.

The Laws of Creation will destroy all that is hindering to the harmony
in Creation. Those things which are not in line with the Laws of Creation,
that is, which are opposed to the Will of God, must lead to destruction
because they cannot receive the necessary help to further their
development when they reach that point in their cycle of development
where they have to be either strengthened or destroyed.

They are destroyed because they bear poison within them and are not
worth being allowed to exist in Creation. They poison the rest of Creation
with their effects and cannot lead to anything of use in Creation. So from
the instant they are sown they already developed towards destruction.
They show their barrenness at the time of harvest and have to be cast
aside, like a farmer will discard useless and decayed fruit at the time of
harvest.

It is the same with the human spirits who were allowed to develop here
in the World of Matter. When they succumbed to the false principle of
Lucifer, and strengthened this principle through their base attitudes, they
sowed seeds which inevitably would lead to destruction.

228

They distorted the normal order of things and turned everything upside-down in their activities. Not only were they unable to recognize their mistake but also they were unable to make use of the help that was sent time and again during the various turning points in the course of their earthly development.

While this was going on the World of Matter, which they were supposed to help develop, suffered from neglect and poisoning, due to the base forms which they introduced into Creation as a result of the wrong conceptions which they formed while living in darkness.

Their actions were based on these wrong conceptions and so they always acted wrongly. Even those with the will to do good could no longer recognize what was good for them because they had developed in the midst of wrong conceptions and wrong ways of living.

As reciprocal action for their deeds, men suffered greatly in different ways. But being so narrow-minded and so full of conceit, they sought to remedy their problems by relying even more on the misguided intellect, which naturally led man to those decisions which would keep it (the intellect) in power and in control. Consequently man always directed his efforts and his thinking towards the maintenance of material wealth and earthly comforts. His conception of what man is on earth for was completely distorted. Consequently, he always sunk deeper into the realm of darkness because he lacked the humility to receive guidance from the Light. His conceit was boundless.

In the direction man was going he was sure to end up being destroyed at the end of the period allotted him for his maturity, or even before this time. He was fast becoming overripe and diseased and had harmfully affected the harmonious current of spiritual power that was supposed to circulate between the World of Matter and the Spiritual Realm, like blood does in the physical body. He diverted this power into the development of base forms as he dragged the World of Matter downwards through his activities.

He allowed for a wound to develop in the Spiritual through this diversion of power and, through this, Spiritual current was being drained. This wound was felt all through Creation. To block this wound would mean to destroy all that is wrong and all that contributes to the existence of this wound. All that cannot swing in the rhythm of the Laws of Creation would have to be destroyed, because it does not allow for the proper circulation of this current and for the right expansion of Creation. But this was going to happen anyway at the end of the cycle of the development of these forms, and also of the part of the World of Matter that has become overripe due to the existence of these base forms. It was going to happen through the working of the natural Laws of Creation.

Included in what would be destroyed are the personalities developed in the meantime by human spirits who were allowed to develop in the World of Matter, but who no longer could get themselves to swing in the rhythm of the Laws of Creation. These were the ones who helped in the multiplication of the base forms which caused the World of Matter to sink towards the Darkness.

In order to help those who could still be saved from this fate man was sent help in the form of prophets and teachers, who had been prepared for their tasks in more luminous realms, and who had asked for the opportunity to serve the Light here on earth. Very few people were willing to listen to them because mankind had become so far removed from the natural obedience of the Laws of Creation that they no longer recognized what was good for them.

Full of distrust, fear, conceit, greed, and spiritual ignorance, they scoffed and jeered at these helpers. In some cases these helpers were even murdered by the same men to whom the help was sent.

From the position of the Light It can see the various points or stages of development which the developing human spirits must yet pass through and what they must yet encounter along their course of development if they maintained a certain course, because the Laws that bring about this development issue from the Light and constitute Its Will. So the Light knows of the various points in the normal course of development and could see that mankind were headed for total destruction if left to go along their chosen wrong course.

But for a few who deserved help from the Light, it would have happened that this mankind would have been left to destruction for the sake of all that is Spiritual. Because the Light will never take away the freedom to decide from man since it is a part of his species. In accordance with the Will of the Light expressed in the Laws of Creation the human spirits developing on earth were given free will.

It is because of the few who could be saved and who still had some light in them that the Light severed a Part of Itself so that It may descend into this darkened world and bring them undimmed Truth, as a guiding light out of their entanglements. This was a sacrifice on the part of the Light because It risked the animosity of the Darkness and its soldiers, who were likely to resist this help and attack the Envoy from the Light.

But the Love of Almighty God is absolute and inconceivable to men. It will not allow any human spirit who does not deserve it to suffer unjust destruction with those dark ones who work for the Darkness. In fulfillment of His Divine Love, the Son of God was sent by Him to help the deserving few, those who still had a spark of longing for the Light within them, who had not allowed this spark to become extinguished.

But at the same time preparations were being made for the coming of Another in case the base humanity of this earth made it impossible for the Mission of the Son of God to be completed. Already, it could be seen how dark men were and how badly the Son of God was being received by base humanity. Men could reject the Truth and Its Bearer because they would always have the freedom to decide, the so-called free will.

This other One, however, was being prepared in such a way that He would come prepared with personal experiences that made Him more knowledgeable of the weaknesses and faults of men. Envoys from the Light have to experience through living amongst men in order to know how to help them, because evil is alien to the Light. Only through experiencing can anyone ever know anything. This is also true for an Envoy of the Light.

Jesus Christ came directly from the Light and spent very little time in the Spiritual Spheres and the intermediate spheres where He absorbed little spiritual experiences. His coming was an Emergency Act of Love without which it would have been impossible to save any of the errant human spirits from destruction.

Upon sensing of the evil in men the Light started to make preparations for the coming of Another, Who would be armed with the experiences which will allow Him to hit at the core of what keeps man entangled in the

Darkness. In order to do this He had to personally experience all the evil that binds man, and this led Him through quite painful and sorrowful experiences.

It also meant that He had to take a longer route than did the Son of God Jesus Christ, because He had to spend more time in those spheres connected to the developing human spirits in order to acquire enough experiences. These experiences were to form an armour around Him and aid Him in His work of bringing the Truth to mankind.

When the end of His life on earth was approaching, Jesus Christ promised His disciples that Another would come Who would lead them to all truths. He said this in full knowledge of the Laws of Creation and of the opportunity for a final attempt by the Light at helping those who could still be saved.

The Son of Man, Who is also referred to as the out-born Son of God, because in His activities He stands between the Divine Realm and Creation, as the Holy Spirit at the Summit of Creation, would come to the earth and explain Creation to us. With this He will give mankind all that they need to complete their development and be resurrected from the World of Matter in which they are currently immersed. The knowledge that He is to bring will be the final one, which will complete the picture of Creation for the developing human spirits, for it is through the Radiation of the Holy Spirit that Creation came about.

But like all the other helps which the Creator gives to His Creation, only the deserving shall reap this help, can absorb this knowledge. In order to reap this help one must be open to receive it. He must be able to put aside his pseudo-knowledge and his wanting-to-be-clever intellect and receive in humility.

Because of this, Jesus already admonished His listeners to make His teachings come alive within them, for only then can they recognize the Envoy from the Light, the Bridegroom. For they will have to recognize Him through His works, through what He brings to mankind.

Making the teachings of Christ alive within one simply means acting in accordance with His teachings, and this is not restricted to Christians only. Anyone who is able to live strictly in the sense of the Word brought by Jesus Christ has already fulfilled this commandment. Coming from the

Light Jesus Christ paved the way for the salvation of many with His teaching, anyone who travels along that path aright must benefit from it. He need not be a Christian or belong to a specific sect or group. The Message brought by Christ was for the individual human spirit and not for any particular groups.

In the same way the coming of the Son of Man will only benefit those who bestir themselves spiritually and who strive to receive of His help through the maintenance of a steadfast good volition. Through the Law of Attraction of Homogenous Species he will attract to himself the necessary help, which must travel along the road of purity. So man only needs to strive for purity in order to benefit from this. It is solely an individual effort. In this no one can do the work for another, no matter what the earthly standings of those concerned are.

The prerequisite for the reception of this help is alertness of the spirit. This can only be achieved through spiritual movement and exertion. It is because of this that Jesus Christ cautioned His listeners not to be like the Five Virgins in the parable, who did not keep their lanterns filled with oil in readiness for the Bridegroom.

All the parables given to man by Jesus Christ were meant to be understood in the spiritual sense. Just like the five foolish virgins did not prepare themselves for the coming of the bridegroom by keeping their lanterns filled with oil, so will it be now when spiritual lukewarmness will keep many from recognizing the Son of Man. They will not recognize Him because they have not prepared their spirits for such recognition, and the Law of Attraction of Homogenous Species, working in the Law of Reciprocal Action, will make such recognition possible only for those who strive towards the Light, who strive to know Its Will.

But the signs are here for all to see, and the Judgment, which commences with His coming, is already underway.

We stand today in the Judgment brought about through the increased Light-pressure that now penetrates the World of Matter. At this time the cycles of all past events are hastening to a close because the World of Matter is receiving a stream of Light so strong that it has never been witnessed in matter since its creation. Guiding this Light-Ray down is the Radiant Star, which is also known as the Star of Bethlehem, and which makes its way down to this part of Creation from Primordial Creation. This Star comes also to complete a cycle which was opened with the coming of Jesus Christ.

It is filled with spiritual substance and has a sucking effect on all that is in the World of Matter. Its effect is able to pull the earth and its inhabitants up to the course that they should be on at this time in the course of their development. Everything that is not able to withstand the pressure of the Light, because it is not in line with the Laws of Creation, will be crushed. While everything that strives to abide by the Laws of Creation will be strengthened by its Ray.

With the streaming in of new powers with increased strength the animistic beings who fashion the forms of man's intuitive perceptions, thoughts, words and deeds, are quickly developing to fruition all that has yet to manifest for men. All the forms which are still in the process of development are now being forced to ripen and be harvested by their originators. This includes everything in the World of Matter that is along its course of development.

Every seed sowed by man, which has yet to be redeemed, will now ripen with a speed that has never been experienced in the World of Matter before, so that man can taste of the fruits of his labour and, through this, be judged.

All that he has allowed to remain dormant within him must now manifest in deed, and all that he has neglected to develop he must now quickly develop or be crushed by it. The earth is being encircled by the Ray of the Star, which is a Ray of Divine Love, and which is surrounding and closing in on all the evil forms and the darkness within, bringing about an intense pressure that forces everything to manifest so that in becoming deed it can be recognized for what it is and be destroyed.

For man there is nowhere to hide or run to. He must now quickly sever his ties from those forms which are base and which must now be destroyed, or go down the path of disintegration together with them.

This includes those things that have been developing for centuries or longer. Everything must now develop to fruition. All base and good volition must now show itself in the deed. There is nothing that can remain hidden under this increased Light-pressure because it forces everything out. In its quickening effect it causes everything to go through the process of development much faster than hitherto. Everything will be dragged before the Light and will, through itself, be judged.

At this time also, many shall know the Truth and all that is false will become easily recognizable. With tremendous frequency, cycles will close for individual human spirits, bringing to the fore many a thing which they thought they had done away with. This will also include cycles opened in past lives.

The frequency of the cycle-closures will force men to act, one way or another, upwards towards the Light or downwards towards destruction, together with the material forms towards which they directed all their volition.

Men will now be put in conditions and situations where they will have to reap all that they once placed in Creation as forms. How they fare will depend on how much knowledge of the Laws of Creation they have acquired through experiencing before the Sword of the Light strikes them. And It will strike individual human spirits at times that are specific for them. All around the signs show themselves for those who are willing to see. The prophesies about this time are being fulfilled through men and their actions. The activity of the Laws of Creation are intensifying and are bringing together homogenous species so that they may present their true colours to all.

All those things, which have up till now only existed in thoughts, shall be forced to manifest in deed so that they may be seen for what they are and be destroyed. And all those who contributed to their development will also have to share the fruits of such activities. How this fruit impacts them in accordance with the Law of Reciprocal Action will depend on their nature at the time of the reaping and also the nature of the seed sown.

All of this is happening because the earth is now receiving undimmed Light-Power following the incarnation of a Spark of the Light here on earth. In Him worked Imanuel, the Prince of the Light, Who also works in Parsifal, through Whose Radiation the entire Creation came about.

Imanuel works in Parsifal as God works in Imanuel. An unbreakable bond of radiation, which goes all the way up to the Godhead, connects them. This line of connection was extended to the earth, as the furthest point in Creation which can still be saved, in the person of Abd-ru-shin, Who gave us the Work: In the Light of Truth – the Grail Message.

As King of the Grail Castle, which houses the Holy Grail at the Summit of Creation, Parsifal is responsible for the transmission of the Power of God for the entire Creation. He, as the Holy Spirit of God, uncovers the Holy Grail, at specific times, for the release of life-sustaining power throughout Creation, and as such is the starting point of all happenings in Creation.

Those open for it can experience the uncovering of the Holy Grail, which is known as the Outpouring of the Holy Spirit, around the period of Pentecost every year. It is so called because the Holy Spirit pours out Power from God to the entire Creation during the period of this happening in the Grail Castle.

He is the Alpha and Omega since He is the starting point of all the Power which streams through Creation, and He will be the only One remaining should the Creation for whatever reason cease to exist.

Imanuel, the Holy Will of God, works in Parsifal. Parsifal is the anchorage of the Divine Will at the boundary of the Divine Realm with the Primordial Creation and is One with Imanuel and One with God. It is through this Will that all of Creation came about, as an expression of the Volition of God; "Let There Be Light." It is because of this that the planes of Primordial Creation, and all the later copies of this Creation, form seven basic divisions, corresponding with the seven letters in Imanuel.

He is the Volition of God Which took on form to allow for the Light of God to spread beyond Its previous boundary, at the point of the Divine Realm which is furthest from the Light.

Working also in Parsifal, He prevents the withdrawal of the Radiation of the Light from Creation. He is the Power of God at the summit of Creation. From this Power comes movement which is able to generate heat and bring about the Radiation that courses throughout Creation, having brought about this Creation. For the salvation of deserving human spirits, a corresponding degree of this Power was extended down to earth and anchored in Abd-ru-shin.

Through His presence here on earth, and through His activities in battling the Darkness, He brought about the kind of Radiation that is only possible for One from the Light. This Radiation is a result of His Divine core which bears undimmed Light-Power that is able to radiate and energize all existing radiation pathways here in the World of Matter, causing everything to become animated and to quickly develop towards its end.

Being a Part of the Holy Spirit, a Part of the Light, He brings to this part of Creation the Volition that there be Light. This Volition was able to take on form in all the spheres of matter above and including the gross material plane and exert Its influence on all that exists.

Through Him the earth received a connection with the Light so that streams of Light could flow for the rapid development of all happenings and the commencement of the Judgement. Those who are willing to sever their ties to the Darkness can make use of this rapidity in the development of cycles to ascend. Those who wish to remain ignorant will also quickly receive their sentence in the outworking of the effect of the Light-pressure existing in the World of Gross Matter today.

There will be a separation of what is light from what is dark in the process. Only that which can bear the pressure of the Light through being able to swing in harmony with the Will of God will be lifted up. All else will be destroyed in order to make way for the harmonious development of the World of Gross Matter and the human spirits who wish for ascent.

It was to bring this Light-Power to earth that caused the Envoy of God to incarnate on earth. He is the Son of Man spoken of by Jesus Christ the Son of God. The designation Son of Man is due to the fact that He stands at the boundary between the Divine and the Spiritual, forming the bridge through Whom the Power of God gets to His Creation. In this way He is closer to the species of the Spiritual, where the Paradise of the developing human spirits is, because He has to be cloaked in Primordial Spiritual substance, albeit a cloak of the greatest brilliance and perfection, in order to maintain the connection between the Divine and Creation, as there cannot be any gaps in the working out of the Will of God.

He, however, remains connected with the Godhead, Who works in Him. The term Son of Man merely indicates His connection with Creation which issued from His Radiation. He is the out-born Son of God because in His activities He remains separated from the Godhead, unlike the Son of God Jesus Christ Who returned and became One again with the Father after His departure from earth. He is the Holy Spirit, Part of the Holy Trinity, Which Itself is an expression of the different activities of God.

He had to go through a long period of preparation in order to be able to know the faults and weaknesses of men through personal experiences. Only after that could He pave the way for lost mankind, as a shining Light, out of the entanglements in which they had bound themselves.

Because He had to personally battle the Darkness, and suffered immensely through its minions on earth, He was able to show mankind the way out of the darkness. As the only One strong enough for this, since He came from a higher Origin, He bound Lucifer for a time and took possession of the Holy Spear, the Divine Knowledge, with which he was able to entice men to sin against the Light and disobey the Laws of Creation. Coming from the Light and bearing a Spark of the Light within Him, He could battle Lucifer and rectify the distortions which arose out of his wrong principle.

In the process of this rectification all that is wrong and all that has wrongly developed will have to be destroyed.

With His coming also comes the closure of a cycle in the development of the human spirits on earth, and the beginning of a new epoch for mankind. So now all the cycles opened in the past, through the activities of men, must come to a close, as the beginning is connected with the end. Men will now receive the just reward for their actions in strict accordance with the Will of God.

As promised by the Son of God Jesus Christ, the Son of Man has given to mankind the knowledge of Creation, with which man can get to know and recognize the Laws operating in Creation and abide by them. Only full knowledge of Creation can now save those who are willing to do the necessary work, because man must now attain conviction if he is to be saved. He is at the point in his development when he should have become convinced about the Will of God. Only this can allow him to consciously make the right decisions. And only the promised World Teacher could bring this to mankind.

Since men did not heed the callings and warnings of the prophets of the past, and have lost the opportunities given to them to change their attitudes and sow good seeds, they must now reap what they have sown.

The only thing that men can do now is to experience consciously the Laws of Creation as the reciprocal actions bring to them the results of their past deeds. With this knowledge they can lighten the impact of the blows that are yet to hit them. For nothing can be wiped clean from their plates until they have recognized the wrong in their past actions and closed the cycles of their deeds.

Only then can the ties to the base forms and to the dark realms be severed, through being lived off in the experiencing of the consequences of nourishing such forms. Then they can rise through, becoming lighter and freer, and can attain to higher knowledge, which will help them mature through further experiencing.

In no other way can man mature but by experiencing. Man only makes his condition worse when he postpones what he must do in order to mature and to return to the Spiritual Realm. The longer he puts it off, the harder the reciprocal actions would have to hit him because they would have to impact him in much coarser forms, since he would have fallen deeper and would require a stronger stimulus for an awakening.

It is in accordance with the Laws of Creation that the longer one delays the necessary awakening of his spirit, and continues in the hitherto harmful ways of living, the more wrong seeds he sows. Because every delay, every postponement is a decision that takes on form. This form will develop, like a seed develops into a fruit-bearing plant, and react back on him in a corresponding manner at the time of harvest.

The increased pressure of the Light that is being experienced during this period causes all cycles to close faster than hitherto. This means that men would start to experience the consequences of their actions much more quickly than hitherto. They are also able to mature quickly under this pressure because the light forms produced by man will also develop quickly to yield corresponding fruit and bring him knowledge.

Man needs knowledge of the Laws of Creation in order to mature, and he needs to mature in order to be able to recognize the Laws of Creation in his experiences. This is because he is always experiencing new things in the moments of every hour. His ability to recognize the working of the Laws of Creation depends on how much of this he has been able to recognize prior to any given moment.

He must then stay alert because in this time he receives many more opportunities to experience the working of the Laws of Creation than has been the case hitherto, since many more cycles will now be closing for him every hour.

He will become able to understand the saying: "A thousand years on earth are like one day in the spiritual." This is because he will become able to experience much more in a day than was the case in the past. The increased Light-pressure causes many more cycles to close within a given period of time than hitherto. So he will now experience what might have taken many years to experience within a very short while.

Already the experiences of millions of years in the development of man are now packed within the childhood period of his present earth life. Similarly all other cycles, which previously would have taken thousands of years to experience, can now be experienced in a few months. This is brought about by the increased Light-pressure currently in the World of Gross Matter.

For the same reason the experiences of a thousand years on earth can be experienced in a day in the Spiritual Realm, because the pressure of the Light is much higher in those Luminous spheres than they are here in gross material earth. Those in higher spheres are lighter and more permeable to Light radiations and so they are able to absorb more of these radiations and experience more in a given period of time.

The increased activity of the spirit of one who takes advantage of the increased Light-pressure on earth today, will bring about a maturation of the spirit which will cause it to become more permeable to the Ray of Light, giving him the opportunity to experience faster through increased mobility.

It is the same with water molecules, which become more mobile when they receive increased energy, which causes them to become more mobile and to expand and rise in the form of steam or vapour. The human spirit is able to experience more due to its increased activity and mobility, and is able to attain a higher knowledge of the working of the Laws of

Creation in a considerably short time under this increased pressure of the Light.

This is also love from the Almighty God because man gets the opportunity to redeem many a guilt and to mature spiritually as he recognizes the working of the Laws of Creation in the cycle-closures. Since he is able to experience a lot in a very short while, he is able to change his nature in a very short span of time, so that he may yet have the opportunity to develop those spiritual abilities which he has up till now neglected to develop.

Just like the individual human spirit will be gripped by the effect of the increased Light-pressure, so will it happen with masses and nations and the various peoples of the earth. In accordance with the Law of Attraction of Homogenous Species, men will be brought together with those with whom they will experience similar fates. The exchange between men will disclose their true natures and men will experience through one another what they have nourished in their thoughts.

The pressure of the Darkness will be greatly felt by mankind during this time because the dark forms which have been nourished by men for ages must now develop to fruition, very quickly, and will torment all those who have not voluntarily severed ties to them through the necessary inward changes.

The knowledge brought down from the Light will help any man who earnestly seeks to change inwardly and sever ties to all base forms. In the most perfect way it guides the human spirit through the path that leads it out of the present confusion and entanglements. It brings the Truth to mankind in an undistorted form and clarifies all the misconceptions that have developed through the Fall of Man.

But man must prepare himself for the reception of the Word in the Grail Message, for only on the right soil can it bring about deliverance from the Darkness. It will remain sealed to all who seek with the intellect and in a superficial manner.

Only spiritual exertion and a good volition can prepare the spirit of man for the right receptivity towards the Truth in the Grail Message, and give to him what the Creator intended for him in the Living Word.

Man will have to discard his misconceptions about the Coming of the

Son of Man, of the promised Spirit of Truth, and understand that He brings with Him Power from the Light, which will bring about the destruction of everything that is not in line with the Will of God, and the strengthening of only that which swings in harmony with this Will.

He must prepare himself through personal effort and spiritual exertion for the reception of the necessary help in the Word in this time of the Final Judgment.

THE IMPLICATIONS OF THE TIME

Today the Ray of the Light is encircling the earth, and mankind with all that they still have attached to them will have to experience within this enclosure the fruits of their labours as they quickly ripen for them.

There is no escaping this and there is no postponing what must come in the coming days for each individual human spirit. It makes no difference whether one wants to accept this or not, for the Will of God must be fulfilled regardless of the opinions of men.

His Will lies in the working of the Laws of Creation and this brings to man what he deserves in accordance with the nature of his spirit.

What is left for man to do is to face what lies in the weaving of his carpet of fate, either ignorant of the Laws of Creation or more knowledgeable of them, so that he can make the best of the opportunities which shall present themselves with the coming series of events.

The purifying Ray of the Light must now destroy all that has not adjusted itself to the Laws of Creation. This must happen in order to usher in the new period, which has been referred to as the Millennium, during which the establishment of the Kingdom of God on earth shall take place.

This period will be a time of peace and of the fulfillment of the Will of God here on earth, during which those who make it through the purification will be schooled in the ways of God. Those who wish to resurrect from the World of Matter will be able to consciously experience the working of the Laws of Creation under the reign of the Holy Spirit, Whose Radiation will be felt more strongly than ever before on earth at that time.

For this to happen, all the darkness on earth and surrounding the earth today must be annihilated, so that they may no longer hinder the progress of the maturation of those human spirits who wish to make the fulfillment of the Will of God their sole volition.

So this is the time for the "either-or" for man. Either he wants to make it through this period of the purification and become part of those who must live in strict accordance with the Will of the Light, during which he will be trained in all that he has not yet been able to experience on his own for millions of years, or he wants to continue in his hitherto ignorant state of being, and become a part of what has to be destroyed in the purification process, as a hindering object in the machinery of this Creation.

So far man has never known how he is to act in this Creation. He has never been able to understand the reason for his being here on earth and what he is supposed to do with his time while here.

He has sunken to the state of just going through life on earth as if in a maze while subscribing to the opinions of others, as long as he does not have to exert himself too much. To him life has become the struggle to live as comfortably as he can and to push thoughts of personal responsibility as far away from himself as he possibly can.

Where he attempts to consider things more seriously he cannot get past the earthly way of viewing everything, because he has never yet been able to escape the grip of his self-enslavement to his intellect, which is bound to the World of Gross Matter.

All his efforts *come to naught* because he does not see the big picture, which alone will allow him to make the right decisions. Living in this confused and dark state he has formed the wrong conceptions about everything, and he makes his every decision based on these wrong conceptions. He does not see his connection to the rest of Creation where most of the living in Creation takes place.

He passes on these wrong conceptions in his thoughts, words, and actions, and they spread all over the earth and the surrounding ethereal environment.

In the process he binds himself to countless other souls without knowing it, and he sinks further down into the world of darkness that keeps him bound and comfortable and makes him not want to wake up.

His conceit and his narrow-mindedness grow, because he is devoid of true knowledge and of light. He attracts to himself the conditions which keep him in darkness because in the process of making his hourly decisions he expresses the volition to be kept in the dark. The reciprocal actions of his thoughts and his actions bring him the fruit of darkness, because the seeds that he sows while in the dark are of the same species as the darkness he receives.

His conceit and narrow-mindedness do not to allow him to receive of the right kind of guidance, and so they cause him to attract only that which is homogenous in nature. So he continues in his blindness to sow those seeds which calmly develop without his knowing it, and which react back on him when he does not expect it.

His desperation grows, together with his distrust for everything, because the wrong conceptions that he has formed lead him to disappointments and despair. He cannot find true peace or happiness through his calculated and intellectual ways of thinking. All this while he continues to contribute to the development of centers of dark forms that continue to molest others and to keep him chained to the World of Darkness.

So far removed from the Light, he continues to form totally wrong and misleading conceptions of what this life is supposed to be about. This becomes his reality and he acts accordingly, all the while serving the Darkness, which has control over his over-developed intellect.

His walled-in spirit slumbers on, and time and again he fails to heed the call of the helpers sent by the Light. They appear bothersome to him because they do not agree with his conception of the world, because they disturb his quiet slide downwards into the abyss of his destruction, during which he is able to indulge his growing selfish desires. He stops resisting the temptations and yields to their urgings, because he finds it easier to acquiesce to the Darkness rather than to fight for the Light with a steadfast good volition.

His fear grows, because now he cannot see himself living without all that he has attached himself to through his wrong way of thinking. His lack of inner strength makes it impossible for him to break away from them. His spiritual ignorance keeps him from seeing why he must, that is, if he is not to suffer spiritual death through the disintegration of all that make him personal.

His lack of understanding never leaves him satisfied, and makes him worry more about the future, keeps him afraid and lacking the confidence to break away from underneath the wrong conceptions that keep him in the dark and devoid of true knowledge.

He becomes more rigid, because nothing else makes sense to him. His wrong conceptions form an invisible wall around him and keep him on those rigid tracks which lead to certain definite and false earthly goals, causing him to pass by the helps which are available to him on his way. He fails to develop spiritually because he has not taken the time to recognize and know the Laws of Creation, which alone can allow him to see clearly.

Spiritually indolent and dying, he is not able to develop any confidence, because only through recognition of the Laws of Creation can one trust in the Will of God. Only through trust in His Will can man gain confidence in God and in his own activities and abilities here on earth. But he needs to have this confidence or he will be easily swayed by the false opinions and ideas spread around by ignorant men on earth.

He will continue to succumb to the enticements dangled in front of his weary eyes, because he would not have developed any confidence regarding the Truth and how one must live here on earth. He will continue to think of material and superficial things as of greater importance than that which really matters—his spiritual development.

So he continues to repeat old mistakes and to affirm for himself a worse fate. He does not realise that he keeps himself in despair. That the Laws of Creation, whose working he is ignorant of, continue to drive the development of all that he places in Creation with his thoughts, words and actions. He does not see how he is an effective tool of the Darkness in this, and that he is one of those who work against the Light here on earth.

He is used by the Darkness to do its bidding because he lacks true conviction. All that he thinks he knows are the products of his wrong conceptions and those of others who think like him, and there are countless others. He lacks the conviction to resist the flow of the tide that now threatens to sweep him along into perdition, into the abyss. He lives in fear of thinking for himself, of being individual. He lives in fear of his fellow man.

His lack of conviction is due to his lack of confidence, because he can never get himself to stay on the right course without losing confidence in himself and in God. He is not able to develop confidence in God because he has no trust in Him. He has no trust in the Creator because he has not known the Will of God. Without knowledge of the Laws of Creation, which he can only attain through experiencing his environment with a steadfast good volition, he will continue to view the happenings around him as arbitrary. He will continue to fall victim to the enticements of those who claim to be able to deliver him from his misery, solely for their own gain.

These "false prophets," who prey on the weaknesses of men, because they themselves do not know why we are here on earth, and because their perceptive horizon is limited to only what is earthly, are able to catch men by the thousands using material wealth and the promise of a life of bliss as bait. But they only catch those who lack true knowledge of and confidence in the Laws of Creation, and there are many on earth today.

For this reason the development of the earth has been mainly one-sided and dark. Men have fallen for the bait and have fallen hard. Their goals are mostly the same and they destroy each other while reaching for these false goals. They strive towards them at all costs because they think of nothing else. In the process they sow only seeds of darkness because they tread on dark paths.

This one-sidedness which man suffers from today is a result of his one-sided development of his intellect, while abandoning the development of the spirit, his true self. He is like a puppet at the end of a string, controlled by the Darkness through his intellect. The Tempter's lure worked on him all too well. For all these are outgrowths of the wrong principle of temptation introduced by Lucifer. He alone is the personification of the Antichrist who fights against the Light with the help of the slaves of the intellect on earth.

This one-sidedness causes man to look at things only superficially, seeing only what is on the surface, just like he sees only the final ramifications of the happenings in Creation, that is, only that which the intellect is able to scrutinize. He does not bother to look beyond the surface in any matter because he lacks the ability to do so. He has buried this ability, which lies only in the spirit, under the blown-up intellect. For only the active spirit is able to make sense of anything beyond the superficial here on earth.

As a result of this, his goals are also superficial and so are his words and his actions; the reasons for his actions stem from superficiality and not from conviction of the spirit. Living in this way, even with a good volition, he has no way of knowing whether his actions are in line with the Will of the Light or not, because this knowledge can only be communicated to the active spirit through experiencing.

And if one is not certain that his actions are in line with the Will of the Light then he lacks conviction. And since only true conviction in the Will of the Light can lead man to the Light today, he serves the Darkness and does its will.

It is because of this that envy rises within him since he can never become convinced of his true abilities and of his rightful field of activity. He lives for the approval of his fellow men and strives outwardly to please them. He is not centred. He continually reaches for the unattainable and constantly imagines that the other man is in a better condition than he is. He cannot attain satisfaction, because the urge to develop to self-consciousness never leaves him. As he travels along the wrong path it never leaves him in peace.

His false admiration for others is borne of envy, and often of hatred, because he lacks confidence in his own standing, and fears that the other person will take away his glory. His idea of success on earth is distorted and so he strives for it through the wrong means.

He does not want his lack of confidence to be discovered. So he puts up a false front and even more desperately rejects any help from above. His false assumptions about other people and his distrust cause him to neglect the necessary help which we all need to survive. His fear of being ridiculed by others causes him to hold on more rigidly to his old and false conceptions. His focus on others causes him to make his decisions based on what he assumes they might think of him, clearly showing that he lives for the approval of his fellow man and lacks the necessary confidence and conviction to be individual in all his actions.

As a result, his envy, hatred, and distrust are also directed towards his fellow men, bringing about an increase in the strength of the Darkness here in the World of Gross Matter.

It is like this that mankind have developed over a very long time as they continue to nourish those forms that make it impossible for help to get to them. Even a great number of those who claim to believe in the various teachings brought by the prophets and Called ones of the past, and also by the Son of God Himself, only interpret the teachings in ways that make sense to them in their narrow-minded ways of thinking.

They try to understand these teachings using their intellects instead of experiencing with their spirits, through which alone they can attain the right understanding of the help from the Light. The teachings do not make the right impressions on their spirits because they do not allow them to penetrate that far. They only want to accept them in the forms that allow them to continue in their indolent ways, without spiritual exertion, so that they can continue to live a life of ease, while at the same time deluding themselves that they serve God. They lack true conviction regarding the knowledge of the Laws of Creation because in their rigid ways of thinking they bypass the opportunities that reveal the Will of God to them.

They try to comfort themselves and please their fellow men by outwardly performing the rituals mandated by the various groups to which they belong, while at the same time, resisting any help which may bring them to a better understanding of the Laws of Creation and of the Will of God. But with all the varieties of outward performances, their inner nature remains the same and can be recognized by those who earnestly strive to understand and know the Laws of Creation.

They suffer from the same narrow-mindedness and rigidity that the non-believers bear within them, often even to a far worse degree. They try to cover up their lack of understanding with gestures and outward behaviours that suggest knowledge, while they hide behind age-old rigid doctrines, which cannot be reconciled with the Truth.

They satisfy themselves with the thought that the fulfillment of the demands of the church, temple or other gathering places automatically grants them a place in Paradise. But they only serve their churches and their temples and not God if they do not know the Laws of Creation and act accordingly all the time. They continually bind themselves to millions of souls, which they lead astray with their baseless doctrines, and to whom they shall have to remain bound until each one of them comes to recognition of the Truth.

At the root of all of this is the striving for earthly power and influence. Today, mankind is chained together by numerous threads connected to the base forms that allow for the reign of the Darkness, for it is through these base forms that man remains connected to the Darkness. The false goals which they strive for keeps them only focused on this gross material part of Creation, because the intellect, through which the driving influences are being spread, cannot raise its gaze beyond what is earthly. It is naturally impossible for it to do so because it is a product of the earthly physical body.

While striving for these false goals, which are enticingly held before him, man neglects all warnings and ignores all calls for a change in his attitude. The signs of decay that he witnesses everyday around him do not seem to penetrate through to him any longer. He is not able to reflect deeply on the frequency of the events occurring all around the world today. He likes to think that these things have all happened before in the past, but he does not allow himself to reflect on the degrees to which the happenings reach today and their higher-than-ever-before frequency.

He has become so coarse and dense that he no longer senses of the danger into which he is quickly sliding. He has become so coarse that it will require very strong blows of fate to wake him from his spiritual slumber, if indeed it has not become too late for him to make the necessary changes within himself before he is struck by the Sword of the Light in this time. His nature at the time the powerful Ray of the Light hits him will determine the direction in which he will quickly develop towards—upwards or downwards.

His narrow-minded focus on what is earthly keeps him from reflecting seriously upon his actions, because in his superficiality he is devoid of *deep inner feelings*. He must get to his earthly goal at all costs, no matter how many Laws of the Creator he transgresses in the process. In fact, this narrow-minded view of his has caused him to even question the existence of a Creator. He lets go of all that he has been able to acquire in the form of self-respect. He values the enticements of the Darkness too greatly to care. He lets himself go and tries to snuff out any semblance of shame left in him.

He regards shame as something primitive, something that stands in the way of progress. Showing clearly how far removed he is from knowing the Will of God. In fact, he refuses to acknowledge this Will or obey It because he has surrounded himself with forms of envy, conceit, greed, narrow-mindedness, spiritual indolence, lustful sensuality and others, and they now define the way that he exercises his power of free decision. In his interactions with his fellow man he molests them with these dark forms. He digs a deep grave for himself in the process. He has trapped himself in a dark world and can no longer extricate himself without help from the Light.

One of the outgrowths of the principle of "letting oneself go," which itself is an outgrowth of the principle of temptation, and which many people have chosen to adopt so that they can more easily indulge in their selfish desires, is the rapid spread of images of sordid sensuality throughout the globe.

Having pushed shame to the background men now seek to explore all sorts of gross sensuality, without regard to the harm that this is sure to cause. The thoughts which take on form in the process of these activities, where people indulge openly in all forms of sexual situations, be it in the form of conversations or in films or other forms of entertainment and public displays, are able to molest many others, some of whom may be trying to walk a straight path despite the depravity existent on earth today.

The thought-forms generated are able to poison the thoughts of many and cause them to falter in their efforts and to slide downwards towards disintegration, along with all that is ugly today, and which must be destroyed.

This result of the exaggeration of the sexual instinct through the over-cultivation of the intellect, which keeps men from realizing their true worth and which degrades them to a level lower than that of animals, who still obey the Laws in Creation, has turned into one of the most potent traps used by the Darkness for the souls of men. Through suggestive talk and provocative images man is lured towards continually thinking dark thoughts and feeding the dark forms that keep him chained to the world of darkness.

The thoughts of men are clouded and darkened in the process, and with the one-sided development of the intellect, which produces the thoughts, they cannot receive of any pure radiations from outside of the earthly environment.

They chain themselves to this earth because it is only in this plane that they can enjoy those things which they have directed their volition towards. In the reciprocal action they shall remain tied to the base centers of Creation because they have sown the seeds of wanting to occupy themselves with such activities as keep them tied to such centers.

Their spirits have been stifled and they can no longer hear and obey their intuitive perceptions. In addition, this sordid sensuality, and all that goes with it, has been tied to the economy of many a nation, so that it appears like a natural part of the life of the people of a nation, something to be proud of, something that indicates progress. But progress in which direction?

Here, she who is supposed to be the Priestess of Purity, and who is supposed to lead by drawing pure radiations from the Light down to earth, for the natural development of mankind, has fallen the deepest, because she has a higher responsibility in Creation. Woman has allowed herself to be trampled underfoot and cheapened in every base way possible.

So much so that the mere appearance of the "modern" woman of today automatically bears the seed of sin, because she dresses herself in a manner that suggests an intention to seduce. She reveals parts of her body that have no real reason to be exposed, rather than for the purpose of enticing men to think thoughts that cannot be healthy or uplifting. She now does this consciously, and almost as though it is the natural way to be.

And she is not alone because she is encouraged by the depraved man, who urges her on with his debasing looks and his animal-like calls, in order that he may satisfy his own base urges, thus keeping the dark cycle of a quick descent going.

The one thing that would have prevented all of this, shame, has been pushed aside and designated as being of the old, as being primitive and not in accord with progress. But shame was given to the human spirit developing on earth for the purpose of recognizing limits beyond which he could not go without losing the treasures of his spirit to the Darkness. It is the counter-poise of wayward behaviour, given to man for his own support in his development on earth. It is like a protective cloak, which shields him from falling in times of temptation. He has thrown it away in the time when he needs it the most.

By adopting the principle of "letting oneself go," that is, by overstepping all natural boundaries for the sake of indulging their selfish desires, many people succumbed wholly to the enticements of the Darkness. They thereby stripped themselves of all the helps given to them for their protection from destruction. They took the bait offered by the Darkness and proceeded to serve it with all their beings.

Today however these forms which have been nurtured by men over millennia, and which have developed to tremendous proportions, must yield fruit for all their originators. Under the pressure of the Light, Whose Ray is closing in around the earth, everything must develop to fruition so that its cycle can be quickly completed and all that is not able to bear this Light-pressure can be destroyed.

As long as man still clings to the old which must now be destroyed, he can expect to be destroyed along with it. The Son of God has already said that "everything must become new" in this time. This means that everything is wrong, has developed wrongly. Only knowledge of the Truth can help those who wish for it to extricate themselves from the doomed "old."

They must do this quickly or else they themselves are equally doomed. There is no more time for warnings. All that man has placed in Creation is already making its way back to him. Everything that has been placed in Creation since the beginning of his period of development and which has yet to close its cycle, must now present itself to man so that the cycle may be completed and the old done away with.

As it shows its barrenness at this time of harvest, man will see the emptiness of the promises of the darkness, whose fruits are now ripening.

All cycles of all happenings are now closing for the Final Judgment.

It is because of this that the Truth must also come out in this period. Man now has available to him the last pieces of the puzzle necessary for his spiritual development. Also, the truth of all the helps that have been sent to man must be presented in this time because it is a part of what has taken place in the course of his development. The beginning must be connected with the end in this process. For the natural Laws of Creation, which in this World of Matter brings about development in cycles, will it so.

The end must be connected with the beginning, because only then can any cycle be completed, and for this reason man once again gets the opportunity, for the final time, to receive the Truth in an unblemished form. I call out to the *true seeker* of Truth and I point him to the Source of Truth, so that he may use this opportunity to sever his ties to those forms which have to be destroyed now.

He has the opportunity to voluntarily sever his ties with all that is wrong and base. For many people this will not be an easy thing to do. But the Light-pressure acting in the Sphere of Gross Matter today is enforcing a separation of the old from the new. In its activity it waits for no man. With sharp clean thrusts it delivers death blows to all that must go now.

Any delay or postponement of the necessary separation will increase the pain associated with a tearing away of the old from the new. Men will experience this tearing away through physical, emotional, and psychic pain. This pain will only increase in severity the longer it takes for the necessary separation to occur within the individual human spirit.

In this matter there is no consideration for the opinions or wishes of men. Each person shall be treated as an individual regardless of how he has come to be connected to the base forms which must be destroyed today. For ignorance is no excuse in the matter, because the condition of being ignorant is in the first place the fruit of the seed of neglect of spiritual duties in the past.

Spiritual exertion and maintenance of a good volition and an earnest striving for the Light is a seed that will yield the fruit of spiritual knowledge. The opposite will lead to ignorance because the fruits will have to be of the same species as the seed.

In this time when all cycles have to close it is the duty of man to become vigilant so that he does not miss the last opportunities for gaining recognition of the Laws of Creation as the cycles of his past deeds close before his eyes.

Today men are mostly driven by the base forms to which they remain connected. The forms of vanity, envy, greed, conceit, spiritual ignorance, fear, distrust, gross sensuality which men display in the course of their everyday activities, whether at work or in their leisure, are some of the ones marked for destruction today. Man must now change the way he makes his decisions if he wishes to sever his ties to these forms in time to avoid being sucked down with them towards destruction.

He *must* now reconsider the reason for his every action, small or big, if he wishes to align his volition with the Laws of Creation and save himself.

He must now decide differently if he wishes to avoid spiritual death. He must now become aware of the order of Creation so that he can better recognize the working of the Laws of Creation and act accordingly in his decision making. In this way he will be able to sever his ties to the burden of base forms, which keeps him held down to the regions that have to be destroyed in this time.

If he succeeds in this he will become able to rise higher because of his spiritual maturity and corresponding increase in lightness of his soul. He will no longer be blinded by the Darkness and he will free up his spirit and come out from underneath the canopy of wrong conceptions, which have caused him to think and act wrongly in the past.

He must do all the work himself, however, because the goal is spiritual maturity, which can only be attained through spiritual exertion. In this no human spirit can do the work for another, for life is inseparable from movement. He will also be able to see more clearly and avoid the deceptive traps of the Darkness into which he has fallen so many times in the past. See that you are awake during this period of a final judgment of all that exists.

EARTHWOMAN

Womanhood in all of the spheres of Creation, from the Summit of Creation to the World of Gross Matter, forms the link between the species to which it belongs and the next higher sphere from which the species split off in the process of taking on form.

As such, she acts as a bridge for the Light-radiations which flow down from the Source of Life to all of Creation. These streams of Light-radiations are needed for the development of the species because they transmit to them the Power of God, delivered to Creation through the Holy Spirit. It is she who first receives it before it becomes available to the rest of the species.

This is possible because she retains a part of the higher species which her species separates from in the process of taking on form. Upon the formation of the coarser masculine part of the species, further down in the order of Creation, the feminine part is left standing closer to the higher spheres because of this closer connection.

Being the finer part of the species, and being of a lighter nature in accordance with her activities, she remains more closely connected to the higher species from which she is meant to draw spiritual currents for the Light-willed activity of the species. In accordance with the Law of Attraction of Homogenous Species, she stands closer to the higher spheres because she retains a part of the nature of the higher species in order to effect a transition from that species to the one of which she is a part-species.

Through this connection she is able to transmit Light-radiations to the coarser part for the harmonious development of the species. As I mentioned in the chapter "The great Creation," the higher species is always able to penetrate and influence the lower one because of the finer nature of the higher one relative to the nature of the lower one.

Just like here on earth where certain rays are able to penetrate solid substance because of the finer nature of the substance of the rays. In this way the womanhood of the spheres in Creation is able to draw Light-radiation down from above and transmit this radiation to the coarser and denser part of the species which it is able to influence according to its nature.

It is the same with earthwoman. She retains a part of the Spiritual that is lacking in earthman, and is meant to serve as a bridge for the transmission of Light-radiations to the developing human spirits. For this reason she is supposed to preserve the purity of the radiations that stream towards mankind through a personal striving towards purity. To help her with this she has been endowed by the Creator with the gift of a delicate intuitive perception, which is unique to earthwoman, with which she can draw streams of Light for the development of her surroundings. She alone has this ability.

In accordance with her nature the activities of the woman are of a negative, more passive and delicate form, which is receiving and preserving in nature, while those of the man are coarser and more positive and active in nature. The activities of the woman are directed towards the reception and drawing down of Light-radiations, through her ability to passively receive, while those of man are focused on the execution of the volition of the species on the coarser material of the earth. With his coarser intuitive perceptions he is better armed to work in the coarser material of the earth.

The woman and her surroundings are able to benefit and succeed in their development only when she strives for purity in all that she does. Her entire being must conform to this volition in order to bring into her surroundings only those radiations which are pleasing to the Light. Only in this way can she maintain and develop the gift which she was given, precisely for the purpose of ennobling her surroundings and her species.

The more the volition of the species is in line with the Will of the Light the closer the species will be drawn upwards towards the Light in the course of its development. The species will sink lower in accordance with the Law of Spiritual Gravity the further away from the Will of the Light its volition becomes. It will be drawn closer to the Darkness through the Law of Attraction of Homogenous Species, which works hand in hand with the Law of Gravity.

Working at their posts and side by side the split-species, which make up the species of the human spirits developing on earth, are able to achieve the necessary balance that is required for their lawful development upwards towards the Light.

The coarser and denser nature of earthman makes him suitable for the coarser activities on earth and in the World of Matter, while the more delicate nature of the woman allows her to function properly in that field which she is gifted for. When both part-species are focused on their tasks, using the abilities which they were endowed with by the Creator to the best of their abilities, then they will raise their species towards the Light because they will achieve the necessary balance required in the fulfillment of the Will of God in Creation. Here, as always, I mean the spiritual and physical tasks of man and woman, with the spiritual leading and preceding that of the physical.

The Living Cross of Truth, Which radiates from within the Holy Spirit, through Whose Radiation Creation came about, shows this necessary balance in the positive and negative activities of the creatures in Creation in its four equal arms. The vertical arm represents positive activity and the horizontal arm represents negative activity. Working equally together both negative and positive activities in Creation maintain the balance in Creation. This equality in the two types of activity is seen in the equal lengths of the two arms of the Cross of Truth.

The Holy Spirit is the starting point of the Radiation that formed the entire Creation, and as such is Himself the Cross of Creation. And since the Holy Spirit is the Divine Will of the Creator, from Whom the Divine Laws of Creation emanate, every creature which strives to obey the Will of God must heed the necessity for the maintenance of balance in the activities of its species.

While at her post the woman is meant to be the Priestess of Purity. When she faithfully strives for purity she guarantees that the species gets a constant supply of the necessary spiritual currents, which are undimmed and uplifting for all of mankind.

She is meant to be the Guardian of the Flame of Holy Longing for the Light, and she is supposed to transmit this longing to mankind so that the works formed by man, in his coarser activities, would be pleasing to the Creator and would be in his glory. The radiations drawn down by the true woman should lead to the formation of a world that is a coarser replica of the first Creation, where the Primordial Spiritual Beings reside, and where all the radiations that support the rest of Creation emanate from.

The finer nature of her intuitive perceptions allows her to draw these fine radiations from above. It is her responsibility to do this because she has been endowed with the ability to do it. She received this ability following the decision by her to participate in the development of the World of Matter in the capacity of a woman, by occupying herself with the more delicate and negative (passively receiving) activities associated with being a woman here in the world matter.

Upon making this one-time resolution she was allowed to incarnate in the body of a woman here on earth, after taking on corresponding female cloaks in the spheres of matter which precede the earth in the course of her descent from the Spiritual Realm as a spiritual seed-germ. All the cloaks which formed around her in the course of her descent to earth also correspond to the nature of her chosen field of activity. Through them a link is to be maintained for the transmission of Light-radiations to the developing human spirits on earth.

Her role in the World of Matter or on earth is not limited to that of motherhood or childbearing since this is only associated with the physical flesh, which itself is only a tool of the developing spirit, as a means for the entrance of souls into earth for the purpose of their own spiritual development.

The high honour of motherhood is not the highest goal of the woman on earth because it originates in the Animistic Realm, which is below the Spiritual origin of man. This is just one of her abilities which also gives her added responsibilities should she choose to be a mother. She alone can act as a bridge for the incarnation of a soul from the Ethereal World which may seek the opportunity to come to earth for the further maturation of its spirit.

The highest goal of the woman must then be a spiritual one, because she is of the spirit. To be of value in Creation the human spirit must strive for a spiritual goal as nothing else will suffice to lead him to the right kind of development.

When the woman makes her goal the attainment of spiritual maturity, then she will also, in the process of her earnest striving towards the Light, carry out the task of being a mother in the best way possible. She will bring to this task the seriousness and knowledge that can only lead to the best outcome for the soul of her child and herself.

The conception of motherhood as the highest honour of earthwoman is a by-product of Lucifer's Principle of Temptation, which causes the developing human spirit to focus his attention one-sidedly on gross material issues, forgetting the higher spiritual goals and pursuits.

Because motherhood itself is a noble task when it remains pure, and because man became unable to understand the reason for his existence in the World of Matter and on earth, mankind was led to develop a distorted view regarding the issue of motherhood. It was elevated to a position where it did not belong. It took the place of drawing Light-radiations for the development of the human spirits on earth, as the highest goal of the woman.

Due to the distorted view of mankind regarding motherhood, many women become dejected when they find that they are not able to bear children. They feel incomplete, empty and unfulfilled, because they have placed the concept of motherhood above their true tasks as spiritual beings. They become distracted from this task and often never fulfill in it.

Also, many of those women who are able to have children, and who indeed do have children, often do not realise that they have a higher calling than motherhood, even though motherhood may fall within their responsibilities when they choose to have children. They often feel accomplished, as though they have done all that they came to do on earth, without realizing that the scope of their task is much wider than the gross material, to which alone motherhood belongs. Like most of mankind they neglect the spiritual responsibilities which they bear within them.

Without the necessary guidance from above man's distortion of the conception of motherhood dealt a great blow to mankind in the reciprocal effects of the happening. Mankind became increasingly separated from the Light because the woman was regarded as just having value as a mother. She was not enlightened to her higher and main role in the development of the species. The general attitude towards the woman also reflected this ignorance. Inevitably the entire human race developing on earth had to suffer from this neglect of duty.

It is because woman alone is able to form the bridge along which the radiations can penetrate to the species that she is also responsible for the attraction of souls which wish to incarnate on earth in order to develop further. Man does not have the ability to form this bridge, just like he lacks the delicate intuitive perception of the woman, which allows her more easily to draw Light-radiations from above. With this gift woman is able to lift up her entire surroundings through the maintenance of a good and honest volition. She is able to draw Light-radiations which are able to penetrate the ethereal environment of her surroundings and influence the development of her species. And this she can do quietly without having to coarsen herself and lose the very ability which she needs to develop.

This ability of woman, however, also makes her more easily susceptible to base or dark vibrations when she lets her guard down. She more easily can pick up dark radiations from the ethereal environment of the earth and pass these on to her surroundings because of her delicate intuitive capacity. This delicacy of intuitive perception makes her the more sensitive part of the species of the developing human spirits on earth.

As the more sensitive part she is also the psychically stronger part, because her strength lies in the capacity to draw radiations from the Light, and because all that exists came into being through the Power of the Light. She is psychically stronger than man. Man and woman are required to work with equal strength here on earth, with the man focused on the coarser substance of matter and the woman on drawing the necessary Light-radiations from above for the development of the species. They are meant to work as equals but differently.

The man is best equipped for the denser and coarser activities while the lighter and more delicate and sensitive activities are reserved for the woman. In this lies her true strength, but not in coarse activity. In this way she acts as a window through which influences of various kinds get to the developing human spirits on earth. However, through this window dark vibrations can also flow to the species.

This is only possible when woman allows it to happen through the wanton disregard of her finer intuitive perceptions. With this she is able to tell apart the different kinds of vibrations, good or evil, and would need to forcibly ignore the warnings of her intuitive perceptions to be able to fall prey to the forces of the Darkness.

Since she retains the free will to choose, she can be responsible for the transmission of dark vibrations or of light radiations into her surroundings, depending on her volition. The nature of the woman determines the kind of radiations she passes to her surroundings.

It is because of this that Lucifer targeted her with his wrong Principle of Temptation to which she succumbed, and, in falling, essentially cut off the link to the streams of Light desperately needed by mankind for their development.

Lucifer targeted the link to the Light-radiations because he knew of the immense importance of this link. He knew that without this link functioning in the right way that mankind would be lost. They would have to focus all of their attention on only what is earthly, because they would be cut off from the happenings in the higher spheres. They would be devoid of Light-radiations and so would live in darkness, in ignorance.

Woman, being of a more sensitive nature and with a finer and lighter intuitive ability, is able to penetrate the coarser intuitive perceptions of man and influence him through her actions. She is able to transmit radiations to man. The nature of the radiations that she attracts to herself determines the kind that she transmits towards man. She cannot remove this ability from herself nor can she shirk the responsibility that is attached to it.

She can only change the kind of radiations which she attracts to herself and passes on by changing her own nature. Therein lies her immense responsibility, the knowledge of which should force her to strive towards purity in all that she does.

She realized in the beginning stages of the development of mankind on earth the effects of her charms on man, and she exploited it, causing man to respond by doing those things which would get her attention. In this way she gave him the forbidden fruit, the fruit of directing the power of God in Creation towards activities that work against the development of the spirit, which he accepted and ate of.

His response to her charms, through the over-dependence on his intellect, in order to fulfill the desires of the woman and keep her to himself, is akin to the acceptance and the eating of the forbidden fruit illustrated in the Scriptures. His focus turned more towards the acquisition of material wealth and influence and further away from the obedience of the Will of God in Creation.

This marked the beginning of the scheming nature of men. Woman used her effects on man to indulge her selfish desires, man used his physical strength and his coarser intuitive capacity to indulge in the acquisition of wealth and power in a bid to draw her closer to himself and keep her for himself. This was the response to the lure of Lucifer who introduced the Principle of Temptation instead of the principle of Divine Love, which only leads upwards towards the Light.

The more noble intuitive sensing of the man to protect the woman from the dark currents of the coarse world turned into a craving for wealth in order to please her and keep her comfortable and physically protect her, since he is physically stronger. The effect of the more delicate intuitive capacity of the woman on man presented itself in the ugly form of seductive charm, thereby producing the opposite effect of what was intended by the Light when she was endowed with that great ability. Both parts of the species focused their attention on each other rather than on the Light and the fulfillment of Its Will.

The turn towards materialistic ends, with the awakening of the intellect and its over-development, led to the nurturing of mainly base and earthly volitions. Woman's attention was turned to material issues only. In this way she no longer focused on drawing Light-radiations to earth for the development of the species. She drew the dark radiations from the ethereal environment of the earth which corresponded to her nature and the nature of the thinking of mankind on earth.

Having lost the bridge across which the Light-streams were to reach mankind undimmed, all activities of earthmen were turned mainly towards what is earthly and material. Greed, envy, vanity, spiritual indolence, sordid sensuality, all arose with the Fall of Man, as mankind's conceptions about life on earth became more and more distorted.

The forms that he generated and also attracted to himself through his base activities, which include his thinking and his speech, weighed man down and caused him to sink in accordance with the Law of Spiritual Gravity. His view of life became greatly narrowed because he had sunken to lower depths and so could only overlook a very limited space. This grew worse the more he relied solely on his intellect while making his moment-by-moment decisions. And with the one-sided growth of the intellect, Light-radiations were kept out and repelled by the emanations which resulted from the worship of the intellect.

The Light-radiations became of an alien species to mankind because only what the intellect could accept as right did they consider to be worth doing.

So increasingly the earth got darker and sunk deeper through the fall of mankind. There was no longer any anchorage for the Light-radiations on earth because the bridge through which they were to travel had been cut off. Only dark vibrations made their way across to mankind through the woman because they were of the same nature as she was. It could not have been any other way since homogenous species must attract one another.

Woman, who was to be the Priestess of Purity, had forgotten her duty, and man had fallen along with her. But he did not have to. He welcomed the attention he received from her because it flattered his selfish desires. Her fall allowed him to remain complacent and to exert himself even less to attain spiritual maturity.

He liked the fact that she had fallen because he could then exploit her in order to satisfy his base urges and desires. He only needed to stay firm in his obedience to the Will of the Creator and the woman would have lost the incentive to seduce. He did not have to acquiesce to her enticements, but he too had succumbed to the will of the Darkness and started to rely more on the earthbound intellect. All the while no one was guarding the posts, and over time the necessary balance in the activities of men and women was lost.

The only will that was being obeyed was that of the Darkness. Obedience of this volition does not require the maintenance of the flow of Light-radiations through the woman who remains at her post, rather it requires that the woman be distracted, and that she focus her attention on everything else but the transmission of undimmed Light-radiations down to earth for the harmonious development of her surroundings towards the Light.

So the Darkness won because it was able to cut off the necessary Light-radiations from the earth by luring the woman to recognize her charms on man and use it for selfish purposes. It hit at the most sensitive and the stronger part of the human species developing on earth, and thus at the more vital part, at earthwoman.

Today she displays the effects of the amplification of this influence with indifference and a certain glee at being able to live without apparent responsibilities. She has long since forgotten her role in life and even openly entices man to sin. In all their actions most women entice men to sin. In their thoughts and their actions they lead all of mankind towards the commission of sin against the spirit.

Their actions fuel the generation of base and ugly forms which populate the ethereal surroundings of man, and which give man further impetus to think and act in ways that only harm the spirit. Man's volition towards these base forms and activities only serve to tie his spirit down and prevent its ascent, because he strengthens his ties to them as he nourishes them through his actions.

Woman had to suffer under the brutalized man because she was not in her rightful position, and the cycle of this neglect had to close in suffering and despair. Today she feels this pain and the suffering that goes with it, but she does not know the root of the problem. She blames man for being so brutal and uncaring, but she forgets that she is not in her rightful place and must receive just recompense for her neglect in accordance with the working of the Laws. She does not see her part in the failure of this mankind.

In thinking that she is only useful as a wife or a mother, because she could no longer perceive the spiritual currents from above the gross material world of the earth, she placed herself in the position where she had to be under the control of the physically stronger man and his desires. She did not develop her abilities and mature spiritually. She continued to draw to her surroundings only those radiations which bring about disharmony, pain and suffering. The coarser man executed the volition inherent in the dark vibrations which she attracted to earth.

She became widely regarded as the weaker sex, because mankind was no longer aware of the other regions of Creation, which lie beyond the perceptive scope of the intellect, to which latter they had subjugated themselves. All they could see were the physical surroundings of the World of Gross Matter where the man appeared stronger, more significant and of more value, just like man today looks upon the intellect with regard to his spirit. He considers the intellect to be his guide and his master but does not realise that by doing so he neglects that which actually should lead and which alone has the capacity to be alive. It is similar to the way man is considered today with respect to the woman, except that both parts have spirits, but the woman should lead through striving towards the Light.

But her present condition is simply a reciprocal action of her neglect of her main duties. She is actually psychically stronger than man and only needs to will aright and faithfully act in the sense of the Laws of Creation, and then she would be able to lift herself out from underneath the dirt that she has immersed herself in, raising her surroundings up with her.

Then man, whom she always has an influence over, will also regard her with the right degree of respect. Today she only receives the fruit of the volition which she has so far expressed through her thinking, her words and her deeds.

She directed her volition towards the man and what is earthly, instead of focusing her gaze upward toward the Light, and so she received as reward the control of the man, who was devoid of guidance from the Light, and who could act in no other way but in a manner that showed depravity and gross behaviour. She also attracted to herself the false and rigid concepts under which she could only be viewed as a wife and mother. These became her ultimate goals because her gaze was not directed upwards but was focused on the material. This was a trap set by

Lucifer through the control of the intellect. She fell for this trap and dragged mankind down with her.

Her neglect helped in the creation of the conceptions that led to the conditions which kept her from developing her spiritual abilities. Her focus on what is material and earthly kept her from recognizing her true gifts and her abilities, and thus from developing them.

Soon it came to be that women could no longer envision life without being married to a man, because that had become a great goal for earthwoman. Her surroundings had developed over time in such a way as to value even a sham marriage over living life as a noble spinster. She became pressured to attach herself to the man because it seemed as though she could not attain her material goals or gain material security without the help of the physically stronger man.

The more materialistic the world became the more she was forced towards the man, whether she wanted it or not. But she helped bring about this condition where the material assumes a position of great importance and has the upper hand. She could no longer survive in society without being subjugated by man. Out of fear of being ostracized by society, her parents and other interfering relatives, and also in order to gain the securities inherent in living as a married woman in the wrongly developed world, women rushed into marriage with men they did not even care for, or whom they hardly even knew.

They are not able to attain recognition of the Laws of Creation and thus of the Will of God before they start their own families, and so they take over with them the same wrong conceptions which they adopted as they grew up. Through wrong education they pass these on to their daughters and sons who are thus hindered in their own spiritual development and who, in turn, pass on the wrong traditions to their own offspring.

In many parts of the world women have been treated like merchandise and traded openly between parents and future husbands. In the households of their husbands these women are not in a better position to develop spiritually and to unfold their abilities for their ascent and for the good of mankind. They have to deal with the issues that present themselves following such marriages, which seem more like mere business contracts, in complete ignorance of what is required of the human spirit and of woman.

They spend most of their time in despair and sorrow. They brood over what they missed out on in life and how they do not feel free really to express themselves. They often feel that other women, who in many cases would be acting in very loose and careless ways, are getting more out of life than they are, because they lack the true conception of what life on earth should be about. So they never get to the point where they are truly happy; they never feel like their environments suit them. They always feel that they deserve more or better, but never get to the point of recognizing what has led them to their conditions. They waste their entire earthly existence because they do not gain spiritually during their entire lifetimes.

Other women get married because tradition prescribes it or even demands it in quite subtle ways. They lack the right kind of conviction in their actions that can only come from true knowledge. They are prevented from attaining this knowledge through the wrong kind of upbringing and exposure to wrong and misleading conceptions about what life on earth should be about. Through the wrong kind of literature and forms of entertainment these wrong conceptions are spread throughout the earth.

At best some of these women immerse themselves in the duties of raising their children and being good wives to their husbands. However, they still do not recognize their higher duties of drawing Light-radiations down to earth. They become too engrossed in material issues and become lost in them. They do not fulfill their duty in Creation.

In many cultures, if the women are not married at a certain age then they are deemed worthless because of the concern that potential suitors would think that there is something wrong with them. As if this is the reason for the existence of womanhood in Creation. This fear causes their parents, especially their mothers, whose anxiety is often born of negative personal experiences, to marry them off before they even get to know what this life on earth is about, before they have had the chance to experience and mature spiritually.

They end up going into the rigid system of wrongly established unions, with their husbands and their husbands' families, where they are often forced to live up to strange, abnormal and unhealthy expectations, only to pass on these unhealthy habits to their own children, to the detriment of all of mankind. They help to foster the misconceptions and the wrong habits of this mankind because they are not able to reconnect with the Light, without Whose radiations mankind would not even exist.

The situation has come to this point because the earth has been immersed in darkness for quite a long time now. Everything was bound to develop wrongly and into very ugly and rigid forms, including the relationship between men and women.

This wrong development was also bound to bring about suffering and despair for all concerned, for even the man who brutalizes his wife cannot find peace in his actions, he is often a very angry person who lives in despair.

Unions between men and women which do not originate on the basis of a mutual spiritual attraction between uniting parties who are striving towards noble goals, are bound to yield fruits of suffering, despair and disharmony. It gives evidence of an intellectual scheme to bring the two together, rather than a spiritual attraction between two people who, while individually striving for spiritual development, offer love to one another for the attainment of this goal. To ask for anything else will be to ask for imperfection in the Laws of Creation.

One reaps what one sows. Where a union is formed based only on intellectual scheming and not through a process of mutual attraction in the process of striving for spiritual growth, then the fruit of such a union, if they remain together, will have to bring about pain and suffering, or at least a certain emptiness, as a sign of the diseased nature of such fruit. It will show its barrenness with regards to what it has to offer the human spirits involved in the union and their surroundings. The fruit must be of the same kind as the seed.

Since the human spirit can only grow when supplied with spiritual nourishment, the only beneficial union will be that which brings about the opportunity for the development and absorption of uplifting spiritual impressions and experiences.

Those people who come together to form a union, for instance, in the case of marriage between a man and a woman, and who individually strive towards the Light, will offer to each other just that which they need to complement their individual abilities and develop more wholly towards the Light. They will aid the ascent of each other as they individually strive towards the Light. It is because they individually strive towards the Light that they will be attracted to each other, since only like can attract like. And since their volition is one that is light, only harmony will exist between them. Their works will then bring peace and joy to their surroundings as they take on form in the Ethereal World.

The fruit of such a union will be a harmonious spiritual and physical development. They will live in constant state of exchange of love in the process of developing spiritually. The love which they will sow in their activities will take on form and also influence a wider circle in their surroundings.

Here the love which they will exchange is the true love that seeks to lead the recipient of this love to the knowledge of the Laws of Creation for his ascent and his resurrection from the World of Matter, not the caricature of love that men practice today, which is based on a material way of thinking, and which seeks at best only to make life as comfortable for the other as possible, leniently letting him have his way in every matter, even if it is harmful for him.

This false notion of love does not recognize the need for spiritual and physical movement, as a necessity for ascent towards the Luminous Heights above through the maturation of the spirit, which can only occur through personal experiencing by the one concerned. Ignorance of why we are here on earth causes people to think that the goal of the human spirit is to avoid all pain and all suffering at all costs in order to live as comfortable an earth-life as possible.

They do not realise that no two individuals are alike and that men would have to go through various kinds of experiences in the course of reaping the fruits of their past deeds, through which alone they can atone for them and come to recognition of the Laws of Creation working in the happenings of this Creation. This misconception will also have to be dispelled in this time. The true kind of love will have to become known to mankind if they are to survive the great purification in the Judgment.

If individual men and women strive towards the Light in their activities they will do nothing but give genuine love to one another. If they decide to form unions, such will be as a result of an attraction between two part-species coming together for a noble spiritual goal. Only peace and harmony will reign therein because they will complement each other with their abilities as they strive upwards towards the Light. They will strive towards the attainment of balance as they develop themselves.

But the woman does not need to form a union with a man through marriage or any kind of acquaintance in order to transmit Light-radiations and ennoble all activities. She just has to personally strive for purity and her intuitive works will pervade the ethereal surrounding of the World of Matter and help uplift everything of a homogenous nature.

To whom much is given much is expected in return. This is a common saying that also rings true in the case of earthwoman, who has squandered the great gifts given to her by the Creator through His Will. She must become the Priestess of Purity if she is to enjoy peace and harmony, for no one else has the ability to draw the necessary Light-radiations down to earth for the right and harmonious development of mankind. The Laws cannot be overturned, and they state that the woman's position is that of the bridge across which streams of Light are to flow to mankind. This will always be so because it is the Will of God, Which is perfect.

In the midst of her suffering mankind fell further away from the Light as they turned more towards the worship of the intellect as an idol. The Will of God was not obeyed and mankind lived in darkness.

So, naturally, the woman got darker herself and, in accordance with her darker nature, drew to earth darker souls, which incarnated on earth with the passage of time. Such souls as she attracted were still supposed to be maturing in much lower and darker spheres, where they could only come to the right recognition through living in the kind of gruesome environment that they helped form in accordance with their volition while they were on earth and also afterwards.

There they could not harm anyone or incur more guilt because all the souls in their surroundings were of the same nature and could only grow to feel disgust for the state of their surroundings by suffering through the consequences of what they helped form. This feeling of disgust could help effect a change in their inner attitude and lead to their developing the wish to leave such surroundings.

Only when this wish has been genuinely expressed would they get help from above such dark spheres as a reciprocal action. But then they would have already gone through the necessary maturation that will qualify them for existence in lighter or more luminous surroundings. They will not be prematurely attracted to such lighter spheres as is the case when the darker nature of earthmen forms a bridge for such souls to incarnate onto the earth, because human spirits of varying degrees of lightness and darkness are able to coexist here, thus creating the opportunity for them to commit more sin against those of a lighter nature, and to entangle themselves further in dark threads, thereby falling deeper than they previously did and dragging a good portion of mankind down with them.

Today most of the souls on earth do not belong here on earth because they only came to earth as a result of the lowering of a bridge for their incarnation through the darkened nature of mankind. Leading in this is earthwoman because she is responsible for the type of souls attracted.

As I mentioned earlier, she has the immense responsibility to determine the kind of soul that is attracted to her for incarnation on earth. In accordance with her nature, light or dark, she attracts the soul of a homogenous nature during the process of incarnation, around the middle of pregnancy.

This also has formed part of the suffering which she has had to go through as a result of her neglect. She has drawn to herself those souls which have caused her much grief and sorrow through their actions. The more seriously women take these responsibilities of theirs the happier they will be.

The lighter the woman becomes, as she strives to develop inner purity, the lighter the souls she attracts will also be. This is in accordance with the Law of Attraction of Homogenous Species. So single-handedly she is able, through this ability of hers, to determine the nature of her descendants, who in turn can bring blessing to their surroundings.

She is able to spread light in so many ways if she only chooses to. In many ways woman holds the key to joy or suffering for the developing human spirits. She only needs to adjust herself to a certain kind of radiation and she will transmit that kind of radiation to her environment, either ennobling it or poisoning it.

In more recent times earthwoman has gone through some changes, but not for the better.

In her efforts to get herself out from underneath the pressure of the brutalized man, and to secure for herself material wealth so that she would not have to rely on man, and also so that she could show that she is able to do so contrary to the false image of a "weaker sex", she delved further into the coarser activities that had been mostly engaged in by man.

She also could find no other way to exert herself since she had since fallen from the high position of Priestess of Purity who is to draw Light-radiations to earth, and consequently lost all connections to the Light in that regard. She could see no other way to channel her energy. She had become blind to her true nature and goal.

Over many years traditions had formed around what various peoples of the earth intuitively sensed to be right with regard to feminine activity and masculine activity. But following the increasing and deepening fall of man, men have forgotten why these traditions even began. The difference between men and women was reduced to only the physically visible differences, and these, in the opinions of many women and some men, were not enough to prevent the woman from participating in the coarser activities of the man.

Women saw no reason why only the men could participate in those coarse activities which led them away from their homes, and which seemed to them to be more exciting than taking care of the home and maintaining an atmosphere of peace and harmony through light activities.

They considered the traditions which precluded women from certain activities as primitive and archaic, mainly because mankind has lost the ability to sense intuitively and to act on their intuitive perceptions. They no longer can say why it is wrong and detrimental to the development of the human spirits on earth for women to engage in certain activities. But this is because they have never really known the role of the woman, nor why the traditions existed.

Even those who intuitively sense that there should be a difference between the activities of men and women can no longer explain why it is unhealthy, spiritually and physically, for women to engage in coarse activities, which had been dominated by men for centuries.

The ignorance of the true role of man and woman in Creation led to the assumption that the exclusion of women from certain activities was only due to a deliberate persecution of women, or an adherence to meaningless and primitive traditions.

But even if this is the case with some men, or even with many men, initially, at a time when mankind still vibrated somewhat in the rhythm of the Laws of Creation, the roles that men and women played in different communities were dependent on the degree of coarseness or fineness of such roles. The more delicate activities were reserved for the women, while the men tackled the coarser ones, in accordance with the their physical and spiritual natures.

The intuitive sensing of men at that time had not become as dull as it is today and in response to their intuitive perceptions they naturally kept the activities separate. These activities then became tradition, the observance of which became more rigid and lacking in understanding with the passage of time and as man sank lower towards the Darkness.

Without pure intuitive perceptions to guide them men have forgotten the reasons for the separation between the activities of men and women. In their superficial way of viewing things many see no reason for the separation. They feel that woman should engage in any kind of activity which she desires as long as she is physically able to do it.

Many who think like this also fall into the group of people who want to appear "progressive", because they subscribe to the notion that the separation of masculine and feminine activities is something that belongs to the old and so has no place in this "modern" time. Even when something within them tells them that there is something wrong in the forceful blending of the activities of both parts of the species, they try to ignore it for fear that they would be branded as primitive, old fashioned or not "politically correct."

They would rather please their fellow men than listen to the urgings of their intuitive perceptions, which express the will of the spirit and which alone can guide them towards the Light if they pay constant attention to it and act according to its urgings. They do not know that in the execution of the Will of God the opinions of men are not considered.

Men and women must play different roles while developing here on earth if there is to be balance in this part of Creation. It is no mistake that the Creator made men and women. It is in accordance with His Will as It is expressed in this part of Creation that the two part-species perform different functions which work together to bring about the necessary harmony that leads to the Light.

All other life-forms observe the Laws of Creation except mankind, who were supposed to be the crown of the World of Matter and should lead through serving the Light in their activities. It is because of the necessity for different activities by men and women that they appear different also on the outside, in the forms of their physical bodies.

Their physical forms are only the result of their spiritual natures, further indicating the need for man to heed these differences and boundaries in all that he does. Man has only paid attention to the physical and not the spiritual in his investigations. It is because of this that he has not recognized the significance of the delicate intuitive capacity of the woman and the need to keep it pure and light. In the same way as he relies too much on his intellect, he focuses too much attention on the physical manifestations in Creation. The ethereal and spiritual workings elude him.

By acting and thinking accordingly, a very long time ago, woman was able to maintain her ability to perceive those fine radiations which mankind so desperately need, and for which task she has been gifted by the Creator.

Using this gift, in a tending and preserving way, she is able to quietly maintain the flow of the Light-streams for all of mankind, so that the man who engages in the coarser substance of this world is not lost in it, but is able to find strength in the radiations passed on by the woman.

Her role is not in public life, for there she is not able to carry out her duties as the Priestess of Purity. She will become caught up in the coarse activity of public life and this will coarsen her delicate intuitive perceptive capacity, making it impossible for her to transmit undimmed Light-radiations for the development and upliftment of her surroundings. She will lose this ability through lack of use, because she would not be able to keep it in step with the rhythm of the Laws of Creation.

This is because a Law that governs everything in Creation, the Law of Motion, strengthens those species which are able to maintain the right kind of motion, but crushes those which are not able to adjust themselves correctly and move in harmony with the Laws of Creation. It is motion that brought about the formation of Creation. The three Laws of Creation already discussed in this book work to maintain the necessary motion in Creation. They animate Creation. Where this motion ceases there stagnation and retrogression ensue, leading to disintegration and death.

So earthwoman must develop her abilities through spiritual exertion if she is not to be cast aside as useless in this Creation. She cannot do this, however, in the coarse field of activity of the man. She only coarsens herself in the process and this is tantamount to a complete neglect of duty. The reciprocal action of this will be devastating.

In the home she is able to exert such an influence as can refresh her surroundings with Light-radiations through her Light-willed actions. There she can develop her abilities to the fullest, and also be in the position to rejuvenate the coarser man, who needs the Light-radiations which she alone is able to transmit, if he is to develop spiritually in the right manner and be useful fruit in Creation. He needs this connection to the Light-radiations in order not to become one-sided and lost in worldly issues as he engages the material world in his coarser activities.

Therefore man must honour woman and her role in Creation. He must recognize this role for what it is and treat her accordingly. She will be forced to readjust herself to her rightful position when this happens. She does not have to be married or to be in the same region as the man whom she is able to help with her finer intuitive perceptions, because the forms of the intuitive perceptions are not as bound to space and time as the physical forms which we can see with our physical eyes.

The effects of her activities can be felt on the opposite side of the earth from where she may be living. Indeed it can be felt throughout the entire World of Matter. All that is required is that there be someone who is homogenous in nature to her, and who might be in a position to receive the help that comes to him through her activities. This person is then able to act on this volition, which she has helped modify in the process of its development and made accessible to him.

In order to achieve this woman must recognize her true role in Creation. She must look beyond the physical in her search for her true mission in life. It is only when she makes the striving for spiritual maturity her goal that she will also act accordingly in her physical activities, and be naturally attracted to those activities which are suited for her and which will not interfere with her ability to fulfill her spiritual duty. For there really is no separation between her spiritual and physical abilities, since one is the natural result of the other. Her physical activities are only the gross material manifestations of what has already taken on form spiritually.

When she has resolved to focus her attention on the highest point, on striving towards the Light in order to develop spiritually, her material surroundings will also develop in a manner that will facilitate the observance of the Laws of Creation, because she will get the fruit of the seed which she plants through spiritual exertion.

But women today want to engage in all kinds of activities because, having lost all connections with the Light, they feel the need to show that they are more than wives and child-bearers and can also engage in all the masculine activities as well. In trying to escape from under this image she has decided to go out there in the coarse world with the man. She does not see how this is not liberation but enchainment to matter, and a further stifling of her delicate intuitive capacity.

She does not realise the necessity for the boundaries instituted by the Laws of Creation and expressed not only in the intuitive perceptions of men and women but also in the physical forms that they bear on earth. The woman can only work effectively when she is at her post and maintaining the fineness of her delicate intuitive perception for the benefit of all mankind.

When she tries to become more intellectual through participating in coarse activities of various all kinds, she nourishes the development of the coarser side of her and this side becomes predominant and shows itself in everything that she does. Consequently she will always bring about disharmony wherever she goes. Her surroundings suffer because the necessary connection to the streams of Light-radiations is missing. Dark vibrations become prominent and influence the activities of many.

When she is not at her post and is standing side by side with man in course activity, an imbalance is generated. She loses her ability to intuitively perceive those finer radiations which are too fine for man to perceive. She pushes her gift of a delicate intuitive perception to the background and causes it to wither off due to lack of use.

This is because she becomes coarser and of a different nature from the delicate intuitive perceptions. She cuts off her connections to all those spheres to which she alone could attain in her intuitive perception and plunges all of mankind downwards towards the Darkness. She destroys the bridge to the Light and to the possibility of joy and harmony. She introduces into the environment distorted forms which only lead to disharmony and chaos. These forms disrupt through their nature the necessary balance in the development of the human spirits on earth.

It is because of this distortion through engagement in the wrong kinds of activities that a large number of feminine souls are now incarnating in masculine bodies, in accordance with the weaving of their threads of fate. Such weaving corresponds to their volition to engage in the coarser activities on earth, so the threads are knotted in a manner according to law that corresponds with this volition. In this matter the activities include their intuitive perceptions, thoughts, words and actions, because they all fall under the term "activity."

Having woven for themselves those threads which lead towards coarse activity, they now have to live in coarser physical bodies like those of men, even though they can never really become men. They remain who they are within such masculine bodies, which appear more feminine than those that harbour male souls, they remain feminine souls which have forced into being the stifling of their delicate intuitive perceptions and focused their volition on what is coarse and dense. They bear distorted souls as long as they have not made efforts to channel their volition in the right direction so as to ascend upwards and develop their buried spiritual abilities.

As I have already mentioned in the chapter "The development of the human spirit on earth", such souls will have to come to recognition of the fact concerning their condition and adjust their attitudes in such a way that they fulfill the tasks for which they were originally gifted by the Creator. Only this can bring about the fulfillment of the Laws of God. Only this can bring about salvation for such souls. Women must focus on their tasks while here on earth and engage in the right kind of activity or they will lose their Light-willed gifts through lack of use.

Another sign of the coarsening of the woman presents itself in the increasing difficulty with which intellectual and "progressive" women conceive and give birth to healthy babies today. Because of the coarsening of the woman, which adversely affects her ability to form a bridge for the incarnation of souls into earth, many women, who otherwise possess all the organs necessary in order to become pregnant and give birth, are becoming less able to become pregnant. And when they do become pregnant they often lose the pregnancy around the time incarnation should occur, or even later during the course of the pregnancy, due to the incoming spirit's inability to maintain itself in the developing body in the womb.

The bridge necessary for the transition of the soul into the earth plane is not in good condition in such cases, and this is as a result of the nature of the woman. She has lost the ability to form a bridge for the incoming soul.

Some of those who are able to deliver their babies experience many complications with the births, or give birth to babies which require significant medical attention in order just to survive. In such cases they will also attract to themselves just those souls which require such conditions in order to go through the necessary experiences on earth which are in accordance with their volition. In all such cases however the deviation from the natural way of living by the woman is the chief cause for the attraction of such conditions.

Woman is always the reflection of her ethereal surroundings because she is the one who is most sensitive to their effects. She is therefore the window into the ethereal world and presents to mankind the ugliness of the world that we create with our thoughts and our actions. But we usually do not see these forms until they manifest physically through the deeds of those who bear within them a volition that is of the same nature as such ethereal forms, and one that is strong enough to express it in deed.

The ability of women to perceive the fine radiations in her surroundings, due to her delicate intuitive perception, makes her able to respond most readily to the dark vibrations surrounding the earth today. It is because of this that the present woman, who likes to call herself "modern", presents a very ugly picture of what the ethereal surroundings of the earth look like. They are filled with the expressions of the base and ugly volition of today's mankind.

These base vibrations from the forms nourished by men through their thinking, speaking and actions, first take hold of the woman due to her nature, and show themselves in their true nature through her. For this reason one need only observe the woman of today and he would get a good idea of how far this mankind have sunken, and how much work still needs to be done by those who are still able to muster all their strength for the necessary shedding of the old.

When women start to act differently and when men start to view them in the right manner and with the right kind of understanding, then this will also be reflected in the behaviour and attitudes of women, because they will draw to themselves different kinds of forms from what has so far prevailed. This change will also first manifest in the woman before it is able to take hold here on earth.

The time has already come when the necessary changes must commence through those who do not wish to be swept away as useless in Creation by the Power of the Light, which now penetrates this part of Creation more intensely than has ever been the case since the creation of the World of Matter. This change waits for no one, and happens automatically through the working of the Laws of Creation. Everything must now swing with these Laws or be crushed by them in the course of their natural working.

In this increasingly materialistic world, issues of the spirit do not even come into play in the decisions of many people. But it is precisely spiritual knowledge that can save mankind today.

It is to gain spiritual knowledge through the experiencing of the working of the Laws of Creation that we came down to earth.

Having lost our way we now focus on material gains and superficial issues. It is now more important to the woman of today what kind of career she has than how much she is striving towards spiritual purity. She is too busy seeking this or that praise for this or that achievement, without a thought as to the real reason why she exists. She lives for the recognition of man instead of for the expression of the glory of God.

She has become a slave of fashion, desiring attires that reveal her body to the glares of people of various natures, not realizing what she attracts to herself in the form of thought-forms, which bind to her ethereally and weigh her down. They tie her to countless souls which she is able to affect without ever meeting directly. She has no idea of the harm she does to herself and her surroundings, because she has no idea of the nature of the working of the Laws, which put into form all that she expresses using her abilities and the power that lies in Creation for use by all creatures.

She intentionally entices men to imagine all kinds of base things and to think base thoughts, because she feels empowered through this. She does not realise that she would have to remain connected to all the souls that she leads astray, until every single one of them has come to recognition of the Truth, or at least gets the opportunity to do so.

She is now a slave of her vanity, and continually nourishes the forms which she attracts to herself through her careless way of thinking. She does not realise that in her thoughts she has the ability to influence her surroundings one way or another. She imagines that she can think whatever she wants and escape the repercussions, simply because they cannot be seen physically. But they unfailingly manifest in the conditions that she attracts to herself in the future. She weaves her carpet of fate in her thoughts and actions, strictly according to her volition!

From the moment many a woman wakes up in the morning to the time she retires to bed at night, she has in mind the effects of her physical body on men and she thinks of ways of presenting herself in a way that will be most enticing. Feminine clothing today is now known by its scantiness, by its deliberate design for the capture of lustful looks.

The direction of the fashion industry today is towards the enticement to think and imagine all kinds of sexual situations and images, which take on form, and which go on to molest many a person, most of whom might not be on their guard, and who often succumb to the influences of the thought-forms, as they find it more difficult to receive pure intuitively perceptions and to resist the temptation to indulge in such thoughts.

In this it does not matter how innocently people try to explain the state of the attires that women clothe themselves with today, it does not matter how they might try to disguise the true intent of the wearer, the result remains the same, that the wearers of such clothing are not being prudent enough in their consideration of the effect they have on their surroundings, on the kinds of thoughts that they engender in men to the detriment of many a soul. Their vanity holds a position of higher priority than the attainment of spiritual purity!

It does not matter for what reason such an attire is being worn, the main objective of the woman must be to draw Light-radiations down to earth. It is only the perversion of mankind that has allowed it to become acceptable that women engage in such activities as make them feel that they have to dress in as little clothing as possible.

Take for instance women and sports. How can sports help in the ennobling of the surroundings of the women? How does it help her channel her volition towards the Light, which is her primary goal in life, for which she must bestir herself continually in order to fulfill? It is only after she has left her true vocation, and strayed into other harmful and useless activities, that she runs into those situations where she feels she has to expose herself to the glares of everyone around.

Through engaging in the wrong kinds of activities she has attracted to herself the wrong kinds of attributes. Many women and young girls today are becoming more aggressive than ever before. Men today do not know what to make of this condition, or what the cause of it is. It is directly connected with the coarsening of the woman. It is just one of the numerous manifestations of it. It points to the fact that the woman is forcibly changing her nature. The physical manifestations of this gross distortion is just the natural effect of those forms which have already manifested in the planes where our thoughts and intuitive perceptions take on form.

With the physical manifestations of these base forms mankind will also be able to see the evil which they have perpetrated through careless and loose behaviour. Now they have to face the beast they have created in their intuitive perceptions, thoughts and words. They have to now see it manifest in deeds through the woman. Maybe now the shock of it can cause some people to reflect more deeply than they have hitherto. The superficial way of looking at things today is the reason why men cannot see the danger in the current attitude of women.

When investigated quite objectively she dresses the way she does because she wants to be admired or looked at, because she has completely pushed aside her sense of shame, which was given to her in abundance just so that she would not fall in the manner that she has. Today, she does all that she can to rid herself of the last vestige of shame, and as if that is not enough, she even tries to encourage other women to do the same, because she does not want to be the only one and feels more confident when she lies in the pits with fellow lost souls. The Ray of the Light will be blinding as it strikes such souls. They will be overcome by its effects without being at all prepared for it.

The mere presence of many a woman today no longer inspires thoughts of the Light, as it should where she draws from the Light in purity, but engenders base thoughts that not only cling to her but also influence other people to think in the same manner. Thus the work of the Darkness has been made all too easy through the woman. She channels the dark vibrations to her surroundings through her nature.

She, who is meant to be the window through which the Light-radiations stream towards man, has given herself over to the Darkness so that she now draws base vibrations from the dark centers in the beyond to all of mankind. She allows herself to be used by the Darkness as bait for the souls of men, to be used to sell to mankind anything and everything, as long as her material quests and her vanity are satisfied. She serves the Darkness with her entire being.

She schemes and calculates her actions in ways that will further some selfish agenda, without thought for what is willed by God in the matter. Only that which she desires does she like to see developed. She detests everything that requires that she exert herself to act in purity, and she will attack in blind rage anyone who dares to point this out to her. She will like to remove him from her path towards the attainment of her selfish goals and she will use any means at her disposal for this purpose. At all costs she strives for the fulfillment of her selfish desires.

She does all of this while hiding behind the veil of the conception of being a member of the "weaker sex", while also at the same time fighting it. This way the blame and the focus of all investigation into the evil and decadence suffered in the world today falls mostly on the coarser man. She should know within herself that she is not weak and that she is able to accomplish much using her abilities, that she is more capable of influencing her environment than man is, but she is not prepared to make her work that of serving the Light. She only uses her powers for selfish goals.

But she will have to come to a reckoning in this time. She has been endowed with a great ability and so she will have to account for what she has done with it in the time when the cycle has to close for her in the Judgment. Now the truth of all matters must be revealed. Nothing can hide in the dark any more. Everything must come to light and be revealed in its true nature. The Light-pressure on earth today forces everything to quickly bear fruit, ripen and become exposed for what it really is.

This is literally happening and can be seen by anyone who wishes to open his eyes and look around him earnestly and objectively. He will see the cycles closing for all kinds of happenings. He will see the results of the decisions of people and of nations. He will see the truth unfold before his eyes in his experiences if he only strives earnestly to *see*.

The saying is true that to whom much is given much is expected. I will like to call out to the woman who earnestly seeks the Truth, and remind her that she has been given much, and let her know that much is now demanded of her. In this the Laws will be exact in what they will expect from woman today.

She has fallen the deepest because she should stand half a step higher than man in the order of Creation. She will rise to a higher position, one which is closer in the order of Creation to the Light, if she makes the right effort to dig herself out from under the entanglements and the burden of base forms where she has placed herself through her actions during the course of several thousands of years. For this she will have to employ all the strength which she can muster.

She cannot hide behind the tricks and the coquetry with which she has sought to deceive and scheme her way through life on earth when it comes time for her to be unmasked in this time. Soon all who care to seek it in earnestness will know the truth. She had better pull herself together, because soon men will also know the truth about what she has been given and what she has done with it. They will know what she really should be like in Creation, because these men would have found what this life is supposed to be about and would immediately recognize all that is false.

Then they will turn away from her and they will no longer be deceived for they shall know the truth of it all. It is time for women to cease the superficial attitude towards everything and realise what it is that they must do in this time to get back to that standing which they should already have attained at this time, but which they have failed woefully to reach. For mankind is lost without genuine womanhood.

FAMILY

The family is one of the many institutions of this mankind that are held to some degree in high esteem, and considered to be of importance in the development of mankind. But here, as well as in all other aspects of life on earth, wrong conceptions have led to distortions in the way families are formed and what their roles should be in the development of the human spirit on earth.

The mission of man on earth is to develop towards spiritual maturity through experiencing the working of the Laws of Creation, which express the Will of the Creator. He is able to know the Will of the Creator and abide by It when he rightly understands and obeys His Laws as they manifest in Creation.

Since the Laws of Creation are the forces that drive the happenings in Creation and bring about the conditions which he must live through, and through which he is able to experience their working, as they deliver to him the fruits of the seeds that he sowed in the past and which he is always sowing every moment, he comes to know the Will of God through recognizing the activities of these Laws.

That is his primary goal in this life. He is on his way to success when he makes his volition the striving for the knowledge of the Will of God through the recognition of the Laws of Creation in his experiences.

He learns how to direct the power of God coursing through Creation in a direction that will not go against the working of these Laws, and in the process, puts into Creation forms which are in line with these Laws and which will be raised high towards the Light by the activity of these Laws.

He becomes a fruit in Creation that is worth keeping at the time of harvest, rather than one which is decayed or overripe and which must be cast out because it only serves to poison the healthy and good fruits because it cannot remain fresh.

In the formation of the good and healthy works of man on earth, the positive and negative (passively receiving) activities of man and woman are required. With these two activities complementing each other the world is developed in a balanced way, and in a way that is in line with the Laws of Creation.

The split in the activities into positive and negative had to occur as the Light Radiation of God drew further away from the Source of this Radiation, causing the two kinds of activities to become more separate, and to no longer work in equal strength within the creatures that took on form outside of the immediate vicinity of the Creator, which is known as the Divine Realm.

So in Creation these activities are split into positive and negative types, and there are also corresponding beings or creatures of Creation which carry out these activities for the harmonious further development of Creation.

I have already mentioned that the case is the same here on earth with earthmen and earthwomen. The activities of the two complement one another to yield beneficial fruit, which leads to the lawful development of mankind and their surroundings on earth and in the World of Matter.

The men and women whose works, that is, whose intuitive perceptions, thoughts, words and actions complement each other need not even know one another. They could live on opposite ends of the earth, but their works could become attracted to each other through their homogeneity, and with the right kind of volition they could yield good fruits through their various actions.

All that is necessary is that men and women abide by the Laws of Creation and their works will find light centers where they will be attracted to, and where they will aid in the harmonious development of the world around us.

Any kind of one-sidedness on the part of either the men or the women, will lead to a distortion that will lead to disharmony, which will be against the Laws of Creation, hence against the Will of God. Man will not achieve his purpose in the World of Matter or in Creation because he would not have achieved that balance in his activities, which he must if he is to be successful in recognizing and abiding by the Laws of Creation through which balance in the entire Creation is maintained.

At the present there is a clear one-sidedness in existence in the activities of man, which is due to his over-dependence on his intellect, which should only be used as a tool of the spirit, which latter should lead in a cooperative and balanced activity with the intellect.

This last point will be useful in understanding the importance of the right formation of the family unit by this mankind.

In the course of development during a lifetime on earth, a man and a woman may come together for the purpose of forming a union, which will have the goal of striving for the spiritual growth of both parties of the union, as they complement each other's abilities.

Naturally this union will only bear the right kind of fruit, in terms of what it is able to contribute to the spiritual development of mankind, if the attraction of the two parties into the union is based on spiritual homogeneity and the yearning to aid in the spiritual development of each other.

In this there could be several ideal partners for a particular person, who will be able to form a complement with him of her. There is not just one person for each person but there could be several. One only needs to be patient and vigilant, and if he maintains the right kind of volition he will be led to that ideal person with whom he can enter into an earthly partnership for the mutual goal of spiritual growth.

As split-species they will be able to combine their efforts in the formation of works that will be beneficial for them and for all of mankind. The activities of one would be able to draw out and enable the development of a part of the other that has remained dormant through lack of use. In this way the two who enter into such a union are able to fully develop themselves in ways that they might not have been able to in one lifetime, had they not formed this union.

But this union, which is referred to as marriage, has been so trivialized by man that it lacks all semblance of the seriousness that it should engender in those who enter into it.

It has become a purely material affair entered into for many varied earthly reasons, which have nothing to do with the spiritual development or growth of those who enter into it. And only those unions, in marriage or in other circumstances, which are entered into for the right reasons, and which lead to the spiritual growths of the individual human spirits involved, can claim to be made in heaven. Because they lead up to heaven and the works that they produce are able to reach up to the Luminous Heights in Creation.

The materialistic way of thinking of the present mankind, which has caused them to focus only on that which is earthly and material, has so darkened and debased the institution of marriage that almost all the time it is entered into without those partaking of it being aware of its true significance.

So very often men enter into it for the wrong reasons and with false expectations. They inevitably encounter disappointments of various degrees, become bitter, and pass on this injurious and poisonous burden on their offspring in the forms of wrong conceptions and wrong education, who then, mainly out of ignorance, repeat the same mistakes of their predecessors.

When a man and a woman enter into such a union fully aware of its significance, while abiding by the Laws of Creation in their individual activities, they are also able to bring into their midst one or more souls through the process of incarnation, or through the process of adoption.

Having knowledge of the Laws of Creation, they will be aware of the fact that the incoming soul will have to be trained aright in the recognition of the Laws of Creation, so that when he attains the right age of maturity he will have been given the right foundation for the building up of a spiritual life that is pleasing to his Creator, and which will bring him happiness and joy.

Through their efforts on themselves, the partners in this union will be able to attract into their midst, a soul that will bring harmony into their company, rather than discord. They will also realise that there is no question of ownership of this individual soul, but merely an opportunity to give love where it is needed, through the right kind of upbringing, for the right development of this soul during the earth-life in question.

In caring for him, in trying to give to him that training which he will need if he is to be able to be productive in life at the time when he will have to be on his own, they will also gain tremendously. This is because in giving one receives. In their attempts to give this soul the right kind of upbringing, they will have to exert themselves spiritually. In return they will be able to receive the joy of aiding the development of a human spirit who has been given the chance to further develop himself on earth. They also gain from the knowledge and enlightenment that they will receive in the process of giving this child the right kind of upbringing. Only then can the child truly be a blessing for its parents.

For this reason they will have to be ready to deliver the right kind of training and aid before seeking an opportunity for procreation. They will have to be sure that they are ready to care for the incoming soul in the right way, according to the Laws of Creation, before they allow for the opportunity for this soul to incarnate into their midst. This is because if they seek the opportunity for procreation and create an opportunity for the soul to incarnate, they will be bound to whatever wrong teachings they pass on to the growing child, knowingly or not.

They will not be freed from this bind until its spirit has been able to come to recognition of the truth, and severed itself from the tie to the product of the wrong teaching delivered to it by its parents while on earth. This could take many lifetimes or a very long period of time in the regions beyond the earthly physical plane, where the soul of the offspring might have to sink after physical death as a result of the wrong teachings from its parents.

The parents thus implicated will have to follow this offspring to whatever level or plane in such regions until the thread that connects them to the soul of this offspring has been severed though recognition.

Where, however, the parents-to-be are striving towards the Light, and consciously allow for the opportunity for a soul to incarnate in their midst, or to come into their midst through the process of adoption, so that they can take care of it until it is able to take care of itself, then they are able to receive blessings through their efforts at trying to prepare this alien soul for life on earth and for spiritual growth.

Just like a teacher has to do research if he is to be good at his work of educating young minds, so does a parent have to exert himself in the process of raising a child, if he wishes to raise the child in a manner that is pleasing to God. Here it makes no difference whether or not the child comes to the parents through incarnation following procreation, or if the child is adopted. The important factor is that the motive for the admittance of this soul be for the opportunity to give it the right training for spiritual ascent.

That is the only way that can be acceptable in accordance with the Laws of Creation, since we are here to recognize the Laws of Creation. If we do not have as our volition the striving towards recognition and obedience of these Laws, then we are not on the right path, that is if our goal is the recognition and obedience of the Will of the Creator in Creation.

If that is the goal then one must raise one's offspring in a manner that creates the right foundation for the recognition of the Laws of Creation. When this is achieved then the child has a good prospect of developing into valuable fruit in Creation, being able to use the right foundation provided by his parents to develop his spiritual abilities, and aid in the spread of light in the various regions of the World of Matter.

Without the right kind of foundation, that is, one that is formed on the basis of the Laws of Creation, the years of childhood of the offspring will not be formed rightly. During this period in the life of man on earth he is not fully spiritually active yet. He is still mostly walled in spiritually by the animistic covering of his soul, which must form the transition to his spiritual core, just like the Animistic Realm forms the transition to the Spiritual Realm when ascending from the World of Matter into the Spiritual Realm.

During this period he must be allowed to develop as a child and should be introduced to the activities of the animistic beings who do the weaving in Creation. This will be the right kind of education which he would need for the right development of his spirit, since this kind of education will correspond to the predominant radiation of his soul, which is animistic in nature.

It will be wrong to already introduce him to adult situations or allow him to take part in adult conversations, because it will interfere with the necessary formative period of childhood where he should not be burdened with adult issues. This will also allow for the normal development of his brain, instead of emphasizing the development of the frontal brain and the intellect through unnecessary one-sided education.

The point at which the spirit is able to break through from out of this protective shield occurs at the point of maturation to early manhood or womanhood. During this time the spirit of the youth is able to engage the world and at the same time can also be influenced by the world around him.

The reciprocal actions of his past deeds are able to impact him more fully at this time, and he influences his surroundings in the manner in which he responds to the conditions created by the weaving of his threads of fate. In the chapter "The development of the human spirit on earth", I mentioned how during this period in his life on earth man makes contact with the neutral power that courses through Creation, and through the attainment of generative power is able to generate forms which reach into the different spheres of matter in their activities, and impact the spheres of the World of Matter in accordance with the natures of the forms.

Through the same process he can also be influenced by the world around him. If he is not wise to the nature of the working of the Laws of Creation, if he had not received the right kind of foundation in the period of his childhood, then his conceptions about life will be distorted and this will affect the way he will respond to the conditions that he will find himself in as an adult.

These conditions will appear before him in order to present him with the opportunity to sever ties to old forms which he placed in Creation and which have ripened for harvest. They could also serve to strengthen him in his spiritual development, based on his volition and what he has drawn to himself in accordance with it.

Either way he only gains when he responds to the conditions in accordance with the Laws of Creation. He is burdened through ties to more base forms when he responds wrongly due to misconceptions and spiritual ignorance.

His spiritual gain is enjoyed by his surroundings because it takes on form in his intuitive perceptions, and brings joy and help to those deserving of it as they carry out their own activities and in accordance with their own spiritual natures. Through his visible deeds he will also contribute to the development of his environment.

But his neglect and his failure causes harm to his surroundings because the forms that they engender, which will act in accordance with their nature and contribute to the development of other similar forms, will lead to a further withdrawal from the Light, and bring about more suffering and despair, and a further enchainment of the spirit to the world of darkness.

Through a one-sided way of thinking and of viewing the world he will attach himself, through his volition, too firmly to matter to be able to escape in time from what is material before its necessary disintegration.

So the right kind of upbringing leads to the formation of the right concepts, which is necessary for the right recognition of the Laws of Creation, and which helps him avoid becoming lost in the darkness of this world. At the same time this rightly trained one will aid in the liberation of his fellow men from the tentacles of the darkness through his ability to make the right decisions, which will show in his works.

Through him more light will penetrate to some people whom he might cross paths with one way or another. He is also able to pass on his knowledge of the working of the Laws of Creation to his offspring if he decides to form his own family later in life. In this process the earth will become a lighter place because only souls of a homogenous nature will be attracted to these enlightened human spirits, because like can only attract like.

The dark souls in the lower regions of the World of Matter, which are not yet ready to incarnate into this earth because they have yet to go through more experiences and mature inwardly, would no longer be given the opportunity for premature incarnations on earth.

As I mentioned in the previous chapter, through premature incarnations onto earth these souls not only hinder the progress of those who wish to strive towards the Light here on earth, but their own development is tremendously slowed down. They are set back many years, even thousands of years, because they will still have to redeem all the guilt that they place in the world through their wrong actions while on earth.

This is because they receive the opportunity to incur fresh burdens, whose cycles will still have to close for them, and which in the meantime will drag them even further down than would have been the case if they had not received the opportunity to incarnate at the time they did.

In the lower regions where they exist together with others of a similar nature, they can do no harm, because they give to others exactly what they receive from them. And through their mutual adverse treatments of one another they are able to develop disgust for themselves, and possibly the desire to leave such regions.

Only when they have got to this stage does despair arise within them, which could eventually lead to the formation of fervent prayers for help to leave such regions. By this time they would have developed so much disgust for themselves and their environment that they would not want to consciously bring about the conditions that will send them back to such regions.

They would have genuinely changed inwardly and become different from such environments. It is this change that brings about the opportunity to leave such planes, because in accordance with the Law of Spiritual Gravity they would have become lighter than those in such regions.

It is different however for those who get the opportunity to incarnate on earth from such regions because of the depravity of mankind on earth. Through their base attitudes men have reached out for those souls who have not yet matured enough spiritually to incarnate onto earth. This is in accordance with the Law of Attraction of Homogenous Species. Through their base attitudes men have lowered the bridge for these souls to incarnate on earth, and this has led to disastrous effects for all concerned.

Consequently most of the souls on earth today do not belong here but should still be maturing in regions below the earth-plane.

In order to rectify this man has to change his attitude, because it is his base attitude that made it possible for a link to be formed between the earth and such regions as harbour such dark souls.

This link is now being cut by the Power of the Light on earth through

His Holy Will. Automatically those creatures and forms which cannot stand the pressure of the Light as it encircles the earth and its surroundings, will be swept away as disturbing elements from this part of Creation to those regions where they rightly belong and where they will have to undergo disintegration with over-ripe and decaying matter.

For this reason he who wishes not to crushed by this power must make a change for the better through striving with all his strength to vibrate harmoniously in the swinging of the Laws of Creation.

A change in his attitude for the better will also affect the way he regards the subject of family. He will realise the seriousness inherent in the responsibilities of parents, who are the heads of the family. He will learn to honour the concept of father and mother according to the Fourth Commandment of God, which He gave to man through Moses, but which has been misinterpreted and misunderstood by men.

The fruits that emerge from families, in terms of the works formed by the offspring of men, are able to affect societies one way or another. They can be good when those who give the early training provide the right opportunity for the development of what is good through proper training in accordance with the Laws of Creation.

They can only do this when they themselves have sought the Truth and made Its knowledge their own. This can only happen however when human spirits on earth first of all make it their volition to strive for recognition of the Laws which operate in Creation, the knowledge and obedience of which alone can lead them upwards towards the Light and to higher knowledge.

Today children are burdened with so much that is unnecessary and actually damaging to their spiritual development.

The teachings imparted to them by their parents point to a lack of understanding of the Laws of Creation. Only the pursuit of worldly issues is emphasized in the upbringing of many an offspring, if at all the parents take the time to be involved in the raising of their children.

The lack of understanding of what life is about shows itself in the directions to which parents today push their children. Through their own personal behaviours they pass on their own misconceptions about life to their children without caring that they could be wrong.

They do not try to understand those things which they still have questions about before passing them on to their children. In this way the children end up repeating the same mistakes made by them even though the outward forms of these may differ.

The cycle is repeated with each generation so that the earth is dragged down further into the world of darkness, which slowly but surely swallows up those who appear helplessly trapped in it, like men trapped in several miles of quicksand in the darkness of night.

In many ways the actions and beliefs of parents form traps for their offspring, which make it difficult for them to fully develop their abilities here on earth. Due to their own wrong conceptions they have expectations which they wish to see fulfilled in their children.

All their actions are then focused on the fulfillment of these false expectations. The binding effect of these expectations then causes the offspring to feel trapped and imprisoned because they do not wish to disappoint their parents. In the process they fail to recognize their own abilities, because they have their eyes fixed on the goals manufactured for them by their narrow-minded and selfish parents.

In many cases the actions of the parents may spring from the volition to prevent their children from the suffering and the pain evident in life on earth today, but they forget that certain experiences may be necessary for the spirits of their children, who are really individual human spirits who must walk their own paths in life.

They actually hinder their spiritual developments by placing restrictions on their abilities through the enforcements of certain rigid traditional beliefs, the reason for existence of which they cannot sensibly explain. Through this wrong and hindering ethereal bonds are formed between the parents and the children, which only bring about grief and disappointments, not to mention increased spiritual ignorance and lack of self-confidence.

The end result is that the offspring never get the chance to know what life on earth should really be about. They develop wrong conceptions about family and about life in general, and they transfer these wrong conceptions to their own offspring through the wrong kind of upbringing.

Here also the seed is sown for the development of those base desires in minds of young girls and boys, which lead them towards the wrong goals and towards spiritual death in the course of living out their earth lives.

Many of those who attempt to raise their children differently from the way they themselves were raised still lack the knowledge of the Laws of Creation, because they never were able to recognize them and become knowing ones in this Creation. What is passed on to their children, in the forms of teachings and ideologies, will be the embodiments of their own versions of spiritual ignorance.

With knowledge of the working of the Laws of Creation parents will be able to place the right kind of restrictions on their children so that they do not stray onto wrong paths and into bad habits while growing up. This knowledge will also let the parents know when to let go of their children so that, as young adults, they can begin to find their own paths in this world.

They will realise that their offspring have to follow their own paths towards their own salvation. In the same way as the apple tree must let go of and dispel its ripened apple fruits, so that the process of development of the species can continue and in order to avoid standstill and retrogression, so also must parents let go of their offspring when it is time for them to walk their own paths and develop naturally through experiencing. They are able to do this when they have realized through the right recognition why we are here on earth.

The continual focus on only what is earthly and material further removes most men from the knowledge of the workings of the Laws of Creation, and they continually leave this earth-plane unprepared for life in the Ethereal World.

None of what they find important and worth spending time on while on earth will aid them in their wanderings through the various spheres of matter, which they will be drawn to in accordance with the density of their souls.

While on earth they focus their time and attention on only what is material and earthly so that their volition becomes directed only towards matter. The invisible threads which connect them to the homogenous worlds of their intuitive perceptions and thoughts continue to attach to them those forms which are basically only base in nature, and which cause them to develop a propensity for only what is earthly and base.

These connections remain with the soul, however, unlike the transient material acquisitions and concerns, which keep people occupied while they are here on earth. And it is these connections that determine how deeply one who leaves his earthly physical body must yet sink in order to live through all that he has caused to take on form in the regions beyond the earthly physical plane. The weights of the forms which become attached to the soul cause it to become denser and heavier, and to sink to those regions that are homogenous and therefore of equal weight.

Also, parents, out of false love, try to provide for their children everything they imagine would make life as comfortable and as free of stress as possible, instead of letting their offspring exert themselves for the things that they may need in life. Through such exertions the human spirits concerned are able to mature inwardly, and are able to find more value in the little things in life.

They will not trivialize issues as often because they would have had to go through experiences which would have caused them to become more familiar with certain matters of importance on earth. Through personal experiencing they would have learned to become more compassionate, having been in situations which are similar to what their fellow men may be going through. They will become more broad-minded and understanding.

But when parents try to make life as comfortable for their children as possible, probably because they themselves had to suffer to survive or to earn a living, or simply because it symbolizes success to them, they rob their children of the opportunities for the necessary spiritual exertions that go with personal decision-making in the process of dealing with various obstacles in their lives. The natural development of the spirit is hampered in the process.

If man concentrates on providing for his offspring the necessary foundation during his period of childhood, then he should rest assured that this right training will be useful for the spirit of this child when it comes time to walk his own paths in this life. The clinging nature of this mankind to their mature offspring causes stagnation in the necessary flow of spiritual currents through this part of Creation. Movement is a Law in Creation and is demanded of all creatures in Creation that wish to align themselves with the Will of God.

Without movement everything comes to a standstill. This is true with water and with other elements and molecules that have been observed in the various fields of activity of this mankind. It cannot then be, and is not different in the case of the human spirit.

The necessary struggle in life, which helps in keeping the spirit alert and awake, is taken away from the child who grows up believing that he has the right to the wealth or property of his parents. This is wrong because it goes against the Law of Reciprocal Action.

The offspring believes that he is entitled to his parents' wealth without him having to do anything in return for this wealth. The necessary giving and taking is lacking. It is different where the offspring does work which requires payment from the parents. But it is one-sided where he receives without giving anything in return and believes that he is entitled to the property of his parents. This goes against the necessary giving and receiving which characterizes healthy movement in Creation. It leads to the development of indolent spirits.

It is different where the parents decide to give the child a gift that is not linked to any predetermined obligation.

During the early period of the offspring's life he gives his parents respect while they give him protection. And in the process of giving him the necessary education, spiritual and earthly, they also gain and mature spiritually. Wherever this balance is missing there also will be the seed of a disease that will show itself sooner or later.

And when he refuses to let his mature offspring walk his own path, by clinging to him and imposing his own wishes on him, he stands in the way of the development of the spiritual abilities of this offspring. This will be the same as killing the opportunity for the development of said abilities. He will be as guilty as one who physically murders a person because in both cases the essential spiritual maturity of the individual is prevented. It will be a transgression of the Fifth Commandment of God, which states that man *shall not kill*.

Through man's subjugation to his intellect, which only can and is meant to focus on what is material and earthly, he has formed distorted concepts of what life on earth should be about. He no longer knows of the spirit because the intellect cannot perceive from above the sphere of what is Gross Material. So everything is seen by him in a one-sided manner and is also developed one-sidedly.

That is why the concept of love that man knows of, and which he tries to practice, is that which only deals with what is material. It does not consider what will be right for the spirit, the core of man, without which the physical body cannot be animated.

Being devoid of the necessary knowledge about the spirit man does not give it what it needs to develop rightly. But when he genuinely begins to strive for recognition of the Laws of Creation, and as he severs the connections to base forms which keep him chained to matter, he will also come to know what the spirit needs, and he will act accordingly.

His conceptions about the family and what it entails will also change. And from the family formed by enlightened ones human spirits who will only bring peace, harmony and joy will emerge.

SUPERFICIALITY

Following the formation of the first Creation, the Primordial Creation, the rest of Creation developed in accordance with the densities of the corresponding species which formed the different planes or gradations of Creation. The resulting increase in density corresponds with the distance of the species that took on form from the Source of Life, Almighty God.

In the process of this development three major species became evident in Creation.

The first and the highest part, because of its closeness to the Source of the Creative Power of God, is the Primordial Spiritual Part. The second part, which developed much further away from the Light and so is denser in consistency, is the Spiritual Part.

The densest and lowest part of Creation, and as such the part that is least permeated by Light-radiations and which is consequently the most sluggish in its movement, is the World of Matter. This lowest species of Creation is mainly a covering for the species of Creation which have to develop in it, and does not have any life of its own. Hence it must be animated by the spiritual or animistic species in order for it to be set aglow and be mobile.

The Animistic Realm forms a transition to this lowest part of Creation from the higher and lighter spiritual part. The animistic species permeates the species of matter and causes it to become mobile, generate heat, unite through the attraction of homogenous species and take on form. The spiritual beings are able to develop in the World of Matter and carry out their activities in it through the transition provided by the animistic beings.

Through the activities of the animistic beings the volition of the human spirit in the World of Matter is given a form, which corresponds to the nature of the particular volition. So the animistic beings form the intuitive perceptions of man.

These intuitive perceptions are the expressions of his spirit. Through them the spirit sends its volition out into Creation, to uplift or degrade its surroundings. It is also through the intuitive perceptions that the spirit is able to receive guidance from above, because it is the intuitive perception that forms the channel to the spirit. This intuitive perception is also known as the inner voice.

And since the animistic beings work strictly in the Will of the Light, they weave for man exactly what he puts into Creation through his every thought, word or deed. They also make certain that he gets the finished product of the forms, which they care for, good or evil, to the point of fruition and ripening, when they inevitably have to be harvested by their originator. This is in accordance with the Law in Creation that all happenings in Creation must return to their respective origins in the completion of their cycles.

Within the World of Matter are two major parts, the Ethereal World and the World of Gross Matter. The World of Gross Matter is the part that is directly connected to what is earthly and is the densest part of Creation. It separated from the Ethereal part of the World of Matter in the process of sinking further downwards, in order to take on form at a further distance from the Light due to the difference in species of both parts. This Ethereal part, which had to form before the Gross Material part, because it remained behind as the coarser gross material part severed itself and descended downwards in order to form itself, is of a finer consistency and hence its substance is more mobile and more permeable to Light. Due to this finer consistency, it is able to permeate the denser substance of the earth and exert an influence on it.

The gross material part of Creation is the point of the final and last ramifications of all the happenings in the World of Matter and in the entire Creation. Here the happenings that take place in the higher parts of Creation occur at a slower rate, due to the density and coarseness of the substance of the gross material species. The same Laws operate throughout the entire Creation, but they only manifest in forms which correspond to the density of the particular species, to their nature, which also brings about their density.

So despite the difference in species the gross material part of the World of Matter is one with the ethereal part of it. No gap exists between the two parts. Whatever affects one also affects the other. They, however, do not blend as they must remain different species and thus alien to each other.

It is in this coarse world that the human spirits developing on earth are able to mature the fastest, because they are faced with a coarseness that forces them to exert their spirits in order to overcome obstacles. It provides the best soil for the awakening of the spirit. It is because of this that the earth-life of the human spirit is a very important span in his long period of development in the entire World of Matter.

The higher one rises in the World of Matter the looser and more mobile the substance of the species becomes. Thus the more permeable to Light the species is and the more animated it is. This increased animation also means that one is able to experience more in a given span of time than is possible in the planes of the lower, denser and less mobile species.

The perceptive scope is also wider the higher one rises upwards towards the Light. This is because the increase in height, and thus the closeness to the Light, allows one to *see* more through being able to experience more in a given span of time. He is able to absorb more experiences through the looseness and the increased mobility of the finer substance of the higher planes. To get to this point however, the developing human spirit must first exert himself in the lower spheres where he is able to gain the right kind of knowledge through spiritual maturity attained in the process of experiencing the working of the Laws of Creation.

I have already touched upon this before in earlier chapters, but I wish to repeat it here for the sake of a better understanding of the topic of this chapter.

Man on earth wears within him the cloaks from the planes which he had to traverse on his way down to earth from the Spiritual Realm as a seed-germ of the spirit. So he is able to receive currents from the planes of the Ethereal World while he is still on earth in his physical body. He alone bears all the species of the World of Matter, of Subsequent Creation, within him.

While in this physical body, he is also able to determine the nature of the development of the finer cloaks, which he wears within. This he does through the nature of the volition of his spirit; because it is only the spirit which is alive within man, and which is able to absorb the power of God in Creation for the purpose of his development. The volition of his spirit depends on the purity of its intuitive perception. The purer the intuitive perception the higher it is able to reach and the higher the spirit is able to draw from in the planes of Creation.

The physical body keeps him anchored on earth and in the World of Gross Matter because he always sinks or rises to that level to which the densest cloak that he is wearing belongs. When he leaves his physical body, following physical death on earth, he is drawn to that plane which is homogenous to the densest cloak that he wears within. This is in accordance with the Law of Gravity. He fashions his inner self in accordance with the nature of his volition.

Through his connections with the other spheres in the World of Matter he is able to receive the currents of power that course through the entire World of Matter, and also from the Spiritual Realm. The stronger his connections to the higher spheres in the World of Matter the more he is able to receive guidance through them.

Through a steady and upward development he is then able to finally perceive from the Spiritual Realm. And from there he can draw spiritual power in the form of knowledge, which allows him to see more clearly the Laws of Creation and to obey them. He enjoys the reciprocal effects of his ability to *see* in Creation, and obey its Laws, in the way that his conditions are formed here on earth. In this I do not mean his material conditions alone but his overall state of being, both psychic and physical. He will suffer less from ignorance and will more consciously enjoy his life and be happy.

He was given the intellect for the purpose of dealing with the issues of this earth during the course of his experiencing here. The perspective of the intellect is restricted to only what is earthly because it is gross material in nature, as a product of a part of the physical body, and cannot rise above its own nature.

As I have already mentioned in an earlier chapter, he was supposed to use the intellect to put into deed the will of his spirit. Also, through the intellect he was to receive earthly impressions, which were to be used by the spirit for its development and maturity. With the active spirit leading the intellect he was to effectively spread Light-radiations down here in the World of Gross Matter. He was to cooperate in the execution of the Will of the Light, Which is that "there be Light." He was to transmit light in this Creation through his activities.

In the process of his development on earth, which is a short span of time in comparison to the period that he has to spend in the entire World of Matter for the purpose of his maturation, man was to draw spiritual currents from above and transform these into deeds.

Only thus could he understand the workings of the Laws of Creation. He is able to plant a seed through his actions, which include his thoughts and words, and he is able to experience the result of it. Through this he was to recognize the Laws of Creation. The spiritual currents from above were to guide him in the development of the world around him in a manner that accords with the Laws of Creation. But he had to pay attention to his intuitive perception and obey it in order to receive these currents of power.

He was given the opportunity to recognize the logic in the Laws of Creation, which are the same as the Laws of Nature. With more recognition and obedience of these Laws was to come more knowledge, higher knowledge, through the absorption of more spiritual currents from above. In this he was to recognize the cycle of giving and receiving. He would have become able to draw spiritual currents from the higher and lighter spheres of the World of Matter, and finally also from the Spiritual Realm, if he continually exerted himself to recognize the Laws of Creation in his personal intuitive experiences.

This ability to draw from higher, lighter spheres would have been reflected in his actions, and there would have been a spreading of light down here on earth through such actions. This is because he would not have been able to receive of these currents of power without first abiding by the recognized Laws of Creation, and abiding by the Laws of Creation leads to the spreading of light.

His efforts would have led to the maturity of his spirit so that he would have become more knowledgeable about Creation and its Laws, and able to oversee a much wider region in the world around him than he is able to today. He would have had the answers to all the questions that plague mankind today, and would not have had to experience so much suffering and grief as he has had to, not to mention commit so many errors.

Man's insistence on focusing his attention and his volition on mostly material and earthly issues, through relying mainly on his intellect for guidance, rather than allowing his intuitive perception to lead in the process of making his decisions, cut him off from the streams of Light from above and directly led to his fall.

His fall occurred because man became concerned only with the issues of the physical, material world. He did not allow himself to intuitively experience the world around him in a way that will enlighten and strengthen him spiritually. Rather he paid attention mainly to earthly issues and the enjoyment of earthly pleasures.

The sole motive for his actions soon became the acquisition of earthly wealth and fulfillment of selfish desires. The few people who still tried to preserve some sense of purity in their thoughts were forced to think more and more in solely material ways, because of the increasing pressure of the surrounding darkness.

To fulfill his earthly desires man relied more and more on his intellect, and channeled to it the power that was supposed to go towards the development of his spirit. He raised his intellect to a position of higher status and pushed his intuitive perception to the background. His focus on mainly material or earthly issues resulted in this. But since the spirit is the only part of man that is living, the only part which can make contact with the spiritual currents flowing through Creation for his development, he essentially cut himself off from this power.

So man effectively placed himself in the dark. He surrendered his power of decision to the Darkness since the Darkness, using the intellect as its tool, was able to cause man to divert power to the intellect and allow the latter to rule over the stifled spirit.

The intellect now rules over the spirit because the will of the intellect is the one that man takes the most seriously today in the process of making his decisions. He no longer listens to his intuitive perception, which he often confuses with feeling. But since the intellect is devoid of real knowledge and is restricted to space and time, it cannot lead the human spirit upwards. It cannot make connection with the power that is able to pull the spirit upwards in the course of its necessary experiencing.

Rather it leads man downwards because its focus and its abilities lie only within the spectrum of what is earthly. He is not able to recognize the Laws of Creation in his experiences due to the fact that his focus is primarily on the pursuit of earthly desires.

Man's focus on matter instead of on spiritual development and growth has caused him to become more superficial in his actions and his experiencing. He is no longer able to look beneath the surface in any issue in order to understand the actual root of it. Similarly he is not able to understand the starting points of the reactions that shape his conditions here on earth and in which he must live.

His inability to recognize the Laws of Creation, through deeper reflections about the occurrences around him, has caused him to remain ignorant of the effects of his decisions. Consequently he expresses his will through his actions without prudence, and without consideration for the Will of the Light. And yet he is in existence only because of the Power of the Light. His conditions are shaped in exactly the same way as he wills them through his use of the power of the Light in Creation.

His ignorance, which quickly and steadily grew into the worst kind of conceit, has caused him to remain in the dark regarding the true nature of Creation, leading him to believe that the happenings around him are arbitrary, and that he can impose his will on his surroundings with impunity. He is not able to see how his use of the power of the Light brings about the conditions that he has live through. Every single one of them!

He always imagines that things work differently from how they actually do, in accordance with the simple Laws of Creation. And so he continues to make his decisions in accordance with his imagination, his wrong concepts.

This inability to see the logic in the working of the Laws of Creation has caused him to exert his spirit even less, because in his narrow-mindedness and one-sided way of thinking, he has concerned himself with the enjoyment of only one earth-life, believing that the world he sees is all that exists. He seeks today to rush through life in order to taste of all its pleasures. But he does not make use of the opportunity to prepare his spirit for life after he has left this life on earth.

A great number of those who believe in some type of life after death lack a true and logical conception of how this happens to be. They lack true knowledge of the order of Creation and the workings of the Laws in it. And so they lack conviction, without which they cannot stand firm here on earth. Eventually they fall to the Darkness at the times when only conviction about the truth can help them.

Only knowledge of the working of the Laws of Creation, achieved through experiencing and abiding by these Laws, can lead man to conviction. When he has attained conviction he will no longer be easily swayed by the vibrations of the Darkness spread through men. Without conviction he will remain in ignorance and will act accordingly in the course of experiencing the reciprocal actions of his past decisions, which come in the form of his hourly and daily conditions.

Today man lacks conviction. He sows poison through his actions because, being ignorant about the way the Laws of God work in Creation, he is not able to act accordingly. He is not able to abide by these Laws and hence obey the Will of God.

But he must obey the Will of God if he is to receive the good fruits that inevitably arise as a natural consequence. That he has constantly experienced pain and suffering is testament to the fact that he has not yet known the Will of God and has not abided by It. He has not even bothered to know God's Will because he has been focused on doing only his own will, on satisfying his own selfish desires.

However, during the long period of time that he has been given so far for the maturation of his spirit on earth, and in the other spheres of matter, the Laws of God have kept on weaving for him the carpet of his fate. So as long as he has thought, spoken and acted in a superficial manner, without consideration for the effects of his actions on his surroundings in accordance with the Laws of Creation, he has also woven for himself a dark carpet of fate. He remains connected to all the forms which he has caused to materialize through his actions. Their cycles will all have to now close and bring him the corresponding fruits.

He has had the power to determine through his past decisions the way the fruits of his labours will have to taste today, bitter or sweet.

Their taste will get even worse as time goes on if in the course of making his decisions he does not consider the Will of the Light, because the fruit will always be homogenous to the seed. One cannot sow corn and expect to reap rice. Any action taken by man without consideration for the Will of God will yield for him corresponding fruit; one that leads away from the knowledge of this Will. As the Son of God has already taught us, "What a man sows, that shall he reap."

If in his decision making process he is motivated by selfish desires or purely earthly goals, then he shall reap the condition of being kept in the dark, of being ignorant of the Will of the Light, because through his decision he expresses his volition for only what is earthly. He chooses to be ignorant of the Will of the Light, because knowledge of the Will of the Light only comes through a striving towards knowledge of the Laws of Creation. Knowledge of the Laws of Creation can only be attained when one makes striving towards knowledge of the Laws of Creation his volition and the motivation behind all his actions.

Hence he will not want to partake of any activity without considering first whether or not it is in line with the Will of the Light. Because any activity that is not in line with the Will of the Light will move him further away from the knowledge of the Will of the Light, which is reserved only for those who earnestly seek the Truth and act accordingly.

This will occur automatically in accordance with the self-acting Law of Creation, which states that similar species must attract each other. Those, who in the process of making decisions act superficially and do not bestir themselves to act in accordance with the Will of the Light, shall be kept from the knowledge of the Will of the Light. They do not deserve it because their expressed volition calls for the reciprocal action of superficiality.

Superficiality however can never lead to the knowledge of the Will of the Light because the latter requires spiritual activity, which is incompatible with superficiality. It requires deep inner reflections and not actions motivated by habit or tradition.

If one is spiritually active then he will always be careful about what he says and does. He will not play in his thoughts thinking that they are hidden from any scrutiny. But he will at all times have the fulfillment of the Laws of the Creator in mind. He will understand that to obey them means to honour his God. It means to obey His Will. And through his actions, through his thoughts, words and deeds, he will only do that which will uplift instead of harm his fellow man.

But to harm one's fellow man also includes contributing to the growth of the Darkness around him. It is just on this point that those who act superficially lack understanding, because they do not see the effects of their words or their thoughts. In fact they do not even truly know the effects of their physical deeds. They only see the effects as far as the physical senses can let them. But this is not enough since their inability to perceive the happenings beyond the scope of the intellect precludes them from truly knowing what is good for the spiritual development of their fellow man. They will always act wrongly when they act without knowledge of the Laws of Creation because only this knowledge can lead to uplifting activity!

All else leads to the transmission of evil because it lacks the right kind of guidance that can only come through knowledge of the Laws of Creation. This is true even if they think that they act rightly. It is only the traditions and customs that have arisen as a result of mankind's long-term rule by the Darkness, through the intellect which they crowned master, that have caused many to think that they act correctly when they actually do not. And over time these traditions have even developed more one-sidedly as they cater mainly to the earthly wishes of man.

Distortions have arisen through the spread of these falsehoods regarding the Truth so that nothing is as it should be today. The difference between the Truth and what men try to represent It with today is like night and day. They are complete opposites. These traditions lead the human spirit astray because they do not lead man to the understanding of the Laws of Creation, which alone can still save him from spiritual destruction, spiritual death.

But mankind continue to spread these false traditions through their actions, while at the same time refusing to listen to anything new that might differ from what they themselves, in their indolence, have accepted to be true, and which might shed some light on issues about life that cause them to despair and which hinder their ascent.

This however is only the fruit of a long period of sowing seeds of superficiality. The result as it can be experienced today is the existence of rigid doctrines to which may people subscribe. They have become rigid because they no longer indicate to man what they originally were created for. They have now become habitual behaviour, carried out just so that one can appear on the surface to be polite or pious in the presence of his fellow man.

Often some of these traditions, which man adheres to today, are carried out grudgingly, just so that it can be quickly completed and man can get back to his real wishes of fulfilling his own desires. They are not done to please the Creator, because those who carry them out are not even convinced that they do the Will of the Creator. They merely wish to satisfy themselves or other men, so that they can rest assured that they have done their duty towards their God as prescribed by tradition.

But man gains nothing when he lacks true conviction. His action is always superficial when he acts without conviction. It shows that he is merely putting on a show for the benefit of his conceit, his peace of mind and his love of ease.

His lack of understanding, which always goes with a lack of conviction, should already show that he could be wrong in what he thinks about the Will of God. The fact that he continues in his usual habits points to his spiritual indolence and his unwillingness to really know and obey the Will of God. If he really wants to know His Will he will never settle for habitual rituals and ways of behaving. He will want to know why he is doing whatever he is doing, and how it is connected to his ability to know and obey the Will of God.

He is actually indolent in spirit or else he will investigate everything he is told and not just accept it to be the truth. He will strive for conviction so that he can be sure that he is pleasing his God.

Where such conviction is lacking, there has been no real knowledge of the Laws of Creation, which express the Will of God. And without this knowledge there cannot be any upbuilding activity by any man. Behind conviction lies a driving force that enables man to always fulfill. It gives him the strength to surmount the doubts and the fears that plague man today and which lead him to non-fulfillment. So man needs conviction because every non-fulfillment is an act that will revenge itself on the perpetrator in the reciprocal action of the deed.

This condition, which he exists in, and which keeps him from *seeing* in God's Creation, from being able to know, is the fruit of the superficiality which he has been sowing for sometime now. He now reaps superficiality, a lack of a deeper understanding; hence he knows nothing, but runs around with others like one in a herd.

One way in which he has been able to effectively spread this superficiality in Creation is through the word.

The ability to form words was given to man as a gift from God so that he can communicate in an upbuilding manner in His Creation. Only through the right use of the word can there be ascent of the human spirits involved.

At the point when they left the Spiritual Realm, the goal of the spirit-germs was to mature through experiencing in the World of Matter so that they may return as conscious human spirits who are able to serve the Lord.

Man today needs to attain consciousness of spirit in the process of his experiencing so that he may resurrect from matter before its disintegration. His sole goal, if he is to be successful, is to know the Laws of Creation. This knowledge, however, only comes through personal experiencing of the working of these Laws. So it benefits him when he is aided in this process.

The only way that man can be aided in his efforts at understanding the Laws of Creation is through being shown the right paths to follow.

But man has to walk a path that is solely his own in order to close the cycles that he opened in his past and gain recognition of the Laws of Creation in the process.

These cycles, which must close for him, take him through various kinds of experiences, involving other human spirits who are also on earth for the same purpose as he. This means that if all those people with whom he may make contact in the process of his experiencing were to guide him aright and not mislead him in any way, he stands a good chance of gaining this valuable knowledge and ascending.

If, however, they all misled him through their actions or their speech then he might have a more difficult time in recognizing the truth, if he ever does at all.

In order for him to be helped in the best way by those whom he comes into contact with, they all would have to speak only those words that are helpful for this particular human spirit's development and ascent. It then follows that if a human spirit wants to be useful in Creation and stop sowing seeds of superficiality, and if he really wants to help his neighbor, he must make the necessary effort to use the word correctly. This way he is sure not to harm anyone through the wrong use of the word, since he is usually in contact with others in the course of his daily experiences.

He will also not speak unnecessarily because anything unnecessary will automatically also be harmful, because it will not be necessary for the spiritual development of the listener or listeners. All unnecessary talk is born of evil. Somewhere behind the unnecessary speech is an evil or wrong motive. Somewhere will lie conceit, envy, narrow-mindedness, fear, spiritual indolence or lack of confidence.

If the true intention of a speaker is to ennoble his surroundings then his every speech will lead upwards. There will not be an unnecessary word spoken. He would have become so convinced of the need to speak thus that he will not have a problem in restricting his speech to only that which is important for the ascent of those around him and of himself as well. He will do this no matter what those around him think of him or how they may regard his approach to life.

This person will then be in a position to really love his neighbour because he will only be interested in giving to him that which will help him upwards towards the Light.

But to know what will benefit your neighbour requires that you know the Will of the Light yourself. One cannot assume that one is helping his neighbour just because he thinks that his actions are right. In this matter the opinions of men do not matter. The Will of God is what It is. It does not vary from people to people or from country to country. Therefore one must be sure that he does not assume wrongly when it comes to the issue of obeying the Will of God.

He can only gain the necessary confidence in this matter when he makes his life's effort that of recognizing and abiding by the Laws of Creation. Then no one will be able to deceive him through superficial behaviour. He will always be able to act rightly because he will have the conviction which is living and which was gained through the personal experiencing of the Laws of Creation.

In order to avoid spreading superficiality through the word the willing man will have to strive for the knowledge of the Laws of Creation, and then make sure that in his speech and actions he does not go against them.

To begin with he can start by making his speech as simple as possible. He must keep it as simple as possible because simplicity is akin to clarity and purity. He must be truthful in his utterances. For instance, he may not say he knows something when in actual fact he may have only heard about it or read something about it.

To "know" something means to have experienced everything about it so that one can describe every aspect of it without erring in any way. Today people use the word "know" so superficially that it no longer makes the right impact on the spirits of those who hear it.

Yet many people talk about so many things which they really do not know about, but which they may only have heard of or just seen. This means that the greater part of mankind today spreads falsehoods and acts irresponsibly while speaking.

Many people contribute to superficiality because they do not talk in order to help the hearer ascend but to nourish the forms of conceit or narrow-mindedness attached to them. These nourished forms continue to develop and gain in strength as they contribute to the growth of the influence of the Darkness on earth and in the entire World of Matter.

Others talk about people whom they may have never met before but whom they may claim to know. In such conversations things could be said of the one talked about which could cause an impression to be formed in the mind of the hearer. Such a person who is the subject of the conversation might have his reputation ruined through this. And the whole affair need not even have taken place if the talker just admitted that he really did not know the one whom he talked about.

Damaging another person's reputation is akin to stealing from him, stealing his name, the respect that he enjoys in the eyes of others. One who does this transgresses against the Commandment of God that says that man *shall not steal*, since this Commandment is not restricted only to material possessions but must include spiritual ones, as well. There is most likely no man alive today who, in course of his long development on earth, has not contributed to this crime.

Often it is just the craving to impress another, or to present oneself as knowledgeable, or in a light that is pleasing to one's fellow man, that is at the root of such behaviour. But it is not for the benefit of the hearer's spiritual development. It is a sin to talk unnecessarily because it usually promotes evil. It usually leads to the nourishing of such forms as emanate from the Darkness. It goes against the Law of just giving and receiving.

In the observance of the Law of Reciprocal Action one would only give where it is necessary and he will give only what is necessary. Here of course "necessity" concerns the needs of the spirit for its development. If one cannot give what is necessary for spiritual development then it is best that he keep silent. Because it will always be better not to say anything than to say something that is wrong and so is misleading or false. The reciprocal action of this will bring about corresponding fruit at the closure of the cycle.

Where one does not seek to mislead another with his speech he would respond only to serious questions or matters, and as simply as possible. In his efforts he will strive to answer only yes or no because he will not have the motivation to try to dress up his response for the benefit of his vanity. In so doing he will be heeding the admonition from the Son of God, as written in the Scriptures, that says: "Let your communication be yea or nay; for whatsoever is more than these cometh of evil!"

When one resolves to only speak when it is necessary, and when he can be true to his intuitive perception and use the right expression for his thoughts, then he will also be able to recognize the extent to which this gift of speech has been dragged down to a meaningless pastime, used for the spread of evil through thoughtless chatter.

He will recognize this because he will be in a better position to observe others in this regard. Only when he strives to rise out of the habit will he really notice it in his surroundings. Then he will also be able to recognize the underlying factor that causes people to talk more than they should.

He will be able to imagine the nature of the ethereal environment of this mankind where the thought-forms thus generated must be teeming and contributing to the weaving of the fates of men. This will cause him to be more cautious with his words. He will see how they affect the thoughts and the actions of men, and how superficial talk has contributed to superficial thoughts and actions.

In his actions, also, he will avoid superficiality, because he will not want to spread superficial behaviour through them. He will engage in only those activities that are beneficial, and so, necessary for the development of the spirit. Only then can he serve as a useful fruit in Creation, one which does not poison but helps keep Creation fresh.

He will also start to perceive more than just the superficial from his environment, because he would have risen above the plane of superficiality, where he previously sowed superficiality and received superficiality.

It is the tendency to focus only on the surface in every issue that has caused man to lust after physical gratifications of all kinds. Be it the lust for food, for wealth and power, or the lust for physical contact between men and women and the gratification of all sorts of sensual desires in all the different ways that it manifests today. The focus on only the physical through the one-sided development of the brain, and the associated stifling of the spirit, has led to this.

The new spiritual man will recognize in all that he sees and hears things that benefit his spiritual development, because he would no longer hear or see them in the same way as he previously did, and because he will be able to see deeper than just the surface in every matter. Then he will be on his way to becoming knowing in this Creation, and will also strive to enlighten those who approach him in his daily activities about this happening through his careful choice and use of words.

In his striving he will discover those spiritual abilities which he had never allowed to flower due to their suppression by him. This process will also lead him to the knowledge of his purpose in life, as he gravitates to that field of activity that best matches his developing spiritual abilities.

All envy and conceit will be gone from him because he will realise that Creation is vast and provides room for innumerable other creatures with their own special abilities, and that everyone of the creatures in Creation, including man, gets just that which he needs in order to develop himself.

The woman would also have to take the lead in this matter because man would naturally follow when she no longer gives him reason to strive towards superficiality. He would follow her lead because of the influence which she naturally has on him. In this matter she has fallen deepest because she had the most to lose, because she naturally should stand higher than man in the order of Creation. She was given more than any other creature in Subsequent Creation. But today she is closely associated with lose talk and gossip.

For this reason, she will have to struggle with all her might to become womanly once again, and return to the position where she can draw Light-radiations down to earth for the harmonious development of all mankind. She would have to stop being a slave of fashion and vanity and rise to her high goal of being the Priestess of Purity. Then mankind will develop upwards to the Light in joy, peace and happiness, as they spread light around the World of Gross Matter and also the entire World of Matter.

MYSTERY AND MIRACLES

It is false and misleading to say that the Way of the Creator in His Creation is mysterious. Those who speak thus do not know the Way of the Creator as He shows It to us in His Creation.

Through His Creation He speaks to us and He shows us His Will.

Understanding His Will means knowing His Way. And His Will is expressed in the Laws of Creation, the Laws of Nature through which all happenings come about. He wants us to know His Will and that is why He allowed us to come down to this part of Creation for the purpose of our maturation through the experiencing of the working of His Laws in Creation.

Understanding these Laws and abiding by them leads us to the point in our maturation where we are able to consciously serve Him in Paradise, our origin in the Spiritual Realm.

We can only serve Him when we know His Will, and so it must be possible for us to know His Will if it is at all possible for us to ever serve Him.

What shall always remain a mystery to the human spirit are the happenings beyond the perceptive scope of the human spirit. So that the human spirit, even at its highest point of purity, cannot consciously know of the happenings in the spheres which lie higher up than its origin in the Spiritual Realm.

But man does not need to know this. He only needs to know as much as his species is allowed to know in accordance with the Law of Creation which states that one cannot go beyond one's origin in any matter. We may receive spiritual pictures from the higher spheres of Creation through the Grace of the Creator, and only for our necessary development, but we can never really know, that is, fully and consciously experience the happenings which occur higher than our spiritual origin. The difference in the species would not allow for such a close interaction. It does not accord with the Law of Attraction of Homogenous Species.

It is only the conceit of man that makes him want to know more than he needs to know. He thus expresses his unwillingness to exert himself and patiently absorb what he really needs in his daily experiences. He sees himself as too important to bother with the little things and already wants to know of the bigger and even the impossible things. He does not see that the little things are what build up to and lead up to the bigger things, just like the experiences of the moment influence the conditions of the future.

His spiritual indolence allows him to believe that the Way of God is mysterious, so that he continues in his usual manner to transgress the Laws of Creation in his every action, as if he could offer the excuse that he did not know the Will of God when the time comes for him to reap what he has sown.

It is a formulation of the Darkness, meant to keep the spirit asleep and ignorant. The Creator wants the creatures in His Creation to become *seeing* in Creation. Only then can they fulfill His Will, that is, serve Him.

The assertion that the Way of God in Creation is mysterious only affirms the ignorance of the speaker, or his inability to have as yet known this Way. Nevertheless, it leads to spiritual death because it encourages indolence in spirit.

The fact that some happenings have taken place on earth, which those who witnessed them could not explain, because they were not mature enough in spirit at the time, does not prove right the statement that the Way of God is mysterious. Rather it plainly shows that those who witnessed the happenings but could not explain them were ignorant of the process by which the happenings took place.

Every happening in Creation takes place through the activities of the Laws of Creation, which I have often talked about in this book. There is nothing that is beyond the scope of these Laws because it is through their working that the entire Creation came into being. They penetrate the entire Creation, from the Summit of Creation down to the densest part, fulfilling the Will of the Creator.

They carry the Power of the Creator through the different spheres of Creation.

Due to the differences in the substances of Creation, they bring about different forms in the different parts of Creation, i.e., they manifest differently. However, they bring about these different forms while expressing the Will of the Light in Creation. The expression of the Will of the Light, the one Law which governs the entire Creation, causes them to manifest differently in the different substances or gradations of Creation, which resulted from the slackening and consequent cooling off of the Radiation of the Light. They issue from the same Law, the Will of God.

The speed at which they bring about happenings in the different parts of Creation depends on the closeness of that part of Creation to the Source of Life, Almighty God.

The closer the particular sphere is to the Source of Life, the Source of the Power borne by these Laws, the faster the happening, the faster their activity. This is because the pressure of the Light is higher in the regions closer to the Light.

It is also because of this phenomenon that the presence of the Son of God on earth was accompanied by many happenings that occurred at rates which men were not familiar with and which they termed miracles. Unfortunately the limited understanding of those around at the time, and those who passed on the narrations of the events at that time, caused errors to creep into the accounts of the happenings.

Thus exaggerations were made in some cases and others were not correctly accounted for.

But the accounts that did not result from exaggerations and were related as closely to the actual happenings as possible were all in accordance with the Will of the Light. Everything that the Son of God did while He was on earth was in line with the Will of the Light. He could not have acted in opposition to It!

For example, the raising of Lazarus from physical death took place quite naturally and in accordance with the natural Laws of Creation. The condition of his physical body had not deteriorated or changed to the point that the act of recalling him to his body was impossible. Also, the silver cord, which links the soul to the body, was still intact. Fully aware of this and knowing that it was the Will of the Creator that he be recalled, the Son of God called Lazarus back into his physical body.

Lazarus' soul had to be obey the Divine Will expressed through the command given by Jesus, the Son of God, Who Himself was directly connected with the Light while on earth.

The fact that those who witnessed the event had never experienced such an act is understandable since they did not know of the Divine Power with Which Jesus Christ operated. But it does not change the fact that the Laws were fulfilled in that case. The opinions of men, and their amazement at something that was new to them notwithstanding.

This was also the case with so many other happenings, which have been termed miracles. The natural process is still observed but the speed with which the cycles are closed in the process of the happenings is faster. The faster speed in this case is the result of the closeness of the inner nature of the One carrying out the act to the Source of the Power of God.

The higher a person stands spiritually the closer he is to this Power and the more he is able to experience in a given span of time. Being able to experience a lot in a given span of time also allows one to accomplish a lot in given space of time. But in every happening in the World of Matter the various cycles connected to it have to close. It is the rapid closure of all these cycles, bringing about a result that would not have occurred otherwise, that creates the phenomena described as miracles.

Therefore miracles are not arbitrary as some would like to believe, but they occur in strict accordance with the Laws of Creation, which govern all happenings.

Others, who might want to spread the wrong interpretations of the actions of Jesus Christ, or the circumstances surrounding His coming and His life on earth, might do so in order to remain indolent in spirit. They do not want to allow themselves to accept that such happenings could be explained through the understanding of the Laws of Creation, because it will cause them to exert themselves for the purpose of achieving this understanding.

Many of them also stand to lose influence over those who believe in the doctrines that they spread in their churches and groups, and cannot bring themselves to admit that there really could be explanations to happenings which they have termed too mysterious to explain. In their conceit they fear the loss of influence and power, which they wield over the adherents of their false doctrines.

They want it to remain mysterious and in the dark so that their teachings of the reasons for the coming of the Son of God may stand unchallenged. If some happenings could be termed mysterious and unexplainable, and if this is accepted as the truth by the adherents of their teachings, then they would not have to logically explain the contradictions surrounding their teachings about the reason for the coming of the Son of God. They could just continue to say, with feigned humility, that the Ways of God are too mysterious to understand; or that "God works in mysterious ways."

Many of these people believe that God sent His Son to come down to this earth, which had sunken into darkness due to man's sins, for the sake of sacrificing Him for the sins which men themselves committed, so that man can be freed from these sins without atoning for them personally, since the Son of God would have taken them all upon Himself.

There is no place in Creation where this can pass as lawful! It only flatters man's conceit and keeps him thinking that he is more valuable than he actually is in Creation. It keeps him from realizing the vastness of Creation and his near-insignificance in the scheme of things. It prevents him from mustering up all the strength within him to strive for the recognition of the Will of God and abide by It.

If some things remain unexplained and in the realm of mystery, then people can remain spiritually asleep while believing that they only need to believe in Jesus Christ as their saviour and all their sins will be forgiven them without they themselves doing anything in the form of atonement. It fosters spiritual indolence where spiritual movement is required. It is the work of the Darkness spread by men. And it has spread so easily because of the fall of man and the associated love of ease and comfort.

In the first place the Son of God came because of the sins of man and He suffered and died as a result of these sins, but His mission was to show mankind the path that leads to the Light, to their salvation. That was His true Mission.

His Sacrifice of Love, which ended in His dying on the cross, was the act of His coming into this dark world, with all its potential dangers, to bring to the fallen and sinking mankind a connection with the Light through His Word and His actions, in fact His whole Being, so that those who strive for salvation could be delivered through them.

He accepted before hand the dangers that might befall Him on this Mission into the dark world of this mankind. He sealed His Mission on the cross when He did not go back on what He had said in the face of all the torture. Had He done that, had He retreated in the face of danger, not much would have been thought of Him afterwards, and His Message of Truth would have been forgotten in a very short while.

That He did not shun death, as He maintained His position, showed those who witnessed the whole affair, and those who heard about it later on, that He was not just some person with some ideas seeking recognition for Himself, but that He spoke with true conviction. He was so convinced about the Truth which He brought to mankind that He did not back away from It even in the face of torture and death. Such conviction could have only come from knowledge. Knowledge of the Laws of Creation and hence of the Will of God.

The fact that He perceived and spoke of His death before it happened does not mean that He wanted it so from the beginning. No! He came to give man the Word Which He bore within Him as a part of Him! He was the Word Incarnate on earth and through His Being man was to *see* the Truth!

However, the Will of God allows for man to have free will, and in exercising their free will mankind rejected the Truth Which the Son of God had brought. This rejection was expressed in the form of the hostility against Him from those who at the time saw him as one who posed a threat to their established way of life. They feared the loss of influence and power which the absorption of the Truth would yield. Their intuitive perceptions, thoughts and actions could be understood by Christ for what they really meant and He could already sense of the end result of their scheming.

Just like I have already said that one who is closer to the Light is able to experience faster and more than others the happenings in Creation, so could Jesus Christ already see the resultant effect of the volition of those against Him. The working out of this volition from intuitive perception to thought and to deed could only take place in accordance with the Will of God. Anyone who then knows the Laws of Creation and how they work will be able to see how such volition must manifest if those involved do not change their attitudes at the last moment.

The Son of God saw what was about to manifest in deed and He made this known to His disciples. He also let them know that He would return to His Father after His physical death.

But this is in accordance with the Laws of Creation, the Will of God. For nothing else could manifest but a fruit of the same nature as the seed. So it was the Will of God that the decisions made by men must manifest in deed. This must be so whether this volition of men is good or bad, because it is through such a manifestation that the cycle of the happening can close and the reciprocal action of the act can return to those who perpetrated it. So the act of crucifying the Son of God was the manifestation of the volition of men, who wanted to remain in the dark and devoid of Light! Consequently, men must reap the fruits of that act, for the Truth that was brought was for them, for their salvation!

It does not mean that Jesus Christ came into the midst of men so that by killing Him they would cast their burden upon Him. Only the Darkness could have come up with such an illogical explanation for what happened to Him!

But in facing His death with the conviction of One Who came from the Light He defeated the Darkness, which tried to defile Him through willing men.

Also, His declaration that He will return to His Father after His physical death only expressed the truth in accordance with the Law of Attraction of Homogenous Species. He came from the Light and must return to the Light having left His physical body, which anchored Him down here in the World of Gross Matter during the period when His physical body was still in good condition.

Just like all that is spiritual must return to the Spiritual Realm, either fully conscious and able to serve the Creator, or as a seed-germ resulting from the disintegration of his so-far acquired personality together with matter, the Divine core of Christ had to return to God the Father from Whom It was severed, and unite closely with Him. There He is King of the Divine Realm because He remains personal, having been severed from God the Father for the purpose of bringing Emergency Help to mankind.

His declaration that He will return to the Father did not mean that His physical body would rise up to the Divine Realm with Him. Such a thing is impossible, because being of a gross material nature no physical body can rise beyond the gross material sphere. In addition, without the spiritual or Divine core to animate the physical body, it remains lifeless and unable to do anything.

The assertion that Christ rose physically from the dead after He had been crucified has been spread because His body had been moved from the tomb in which it lay, and also because He appeared to His Disciples afterwards.

But this does not mean that the Laws of Creation were transgressed and that the physical body of Jesus Christ rose from the dead. It only expresses the narrow-mindedness of those who make the assertions and their ignorance of the working of the Laws of Creation.

When He appeared to His disciples they saw His ethereal body, which He wore beneath His physical body, just like all men bear within them, and which remains as part of the soul after it leaves the physical body following physical death. They saw this body with their ethereal eyes because only like can recognize like. This also explains why some of them did not recognize Him immediately. The fact that men have not understood this happening until this time only shows the limited scope of the perception of this mankind and how much we are devoid of true knowledge.

If this were not the case then it would not have been readily accepted as true that the Son of God appeared to His disciples in His physical body after this body had been destroyed in the crucifixion. Those who had knowledge would have also known that it was also possible that the ethereal body of Christ was what His disciples saw. They would have known of this possibility and would not have allowed themselves to be

SAMPSON IRUOHA

restricted only to the possibility offered by those who are intellectually inclined, and thus limited in understanding.

This only shows that mankind have been restricted to the perceptive sphere of the intellect which is not able to account for such happenings as involve ethereal or spiritual substances.

Hence the assumption was made that the missing body of Christ, coupled with His appearance to His disciples, meant that He had risen physically from the dead. No other possibility was offered and so the distortion was spread far and wide.

Some who spread this distortion think that they exalt the Creator through it but their assertions actually serve to debase Him and oppose His Laws. When men try to look at the actions of Christ with the right understanding of the Laws of Creation they will discover a greatness which exceeds all that they previously imagined.

It is this knowledge that He came to impart to mankind. But men themselves will have to strive for the attainment of this knowledge with the help of the teachings which He brought. Another person cannot relieve any man of the burden of his guilt.

Man himself must experience the working of the Laws of Creation as they bring to him the fruits of his past labours. In the closure of each cycle, when he has to harvest a ripened fruit, which happens every moment, he is given the opportunity to recognize the nature of the action which he carried out in the past, and which now brings him the fruit.

He has the opportunity to recognize the nature of the seed through experiencing the fruit which it brought forth for him. In this way he learns of the strictness of the Law that "what a man sows that shall he reap."

With a steadfast good volition, he is able to sever his ties to the forms generated as a result of his past actions. He is then liberated from that burden and can rise higher or proceed to the next liberating experience.

It is to help man with the recognition of the Laws of Creation, by showing him how to rightly think, speak and act, that the Son of God came into the darkened World of Gross Matter.

So despite His great Sacrifice of Love, and especially because of this sacrifice, all men who have not availed themselves of the right understanding of the teachings of Jesus Christ, and who as a result go on sowing evil seeds, will now be struck by the Sword of the Light in this time of a final reckoning. It will be the fruit of the seed that they sowed in the rejection of the Truth that He brought to mankind.

When men come to see the simplicity that lies in the teachings of Christ and in the working of the Laws of Creation, they will also be able to unravel for themselves the truth hidden behind the veil of mystery.

They would also understand that Jesus Christ, the Son of God, came into this part of Creation, into the flesh or the physical body, through the normal lawful process of incarnation. This involved a normal process of procreation, which led to the incarnation of the Son of God into the growing body of the baby in the womb of His earthly mother. This was then followed by a normal birth.

There was no need for it to have occurred any differently with Jesus Christ. The Laws of Creation had to be fulfilled even in this case. Especially in this case!

The notion of an immaculate conception has to do with the spiritual motivation of those who came together and provided the opportunity for procreation, leading to the incarnation of Jesus Christ into the developing physical body.

It is the kind of conception that is different from the ones predominant today, where the thoughts of those involved are of such a nature that they cannot be considered pure or immaculate.

The concept of virginity as it was used in the prophecy about the birth of Jesus Christ is also different from that which prevails today. It refers to the virginal state of the reproductive organs of the earthly mother of Jesus. He was to be the first child from her womb according to the prophecy.

The true meaning of the prophecy did not imply that something as unnatural and impossible as birth without physical procreation was to take place. Such a thing, again, would not be in accordance with the Laws of Creation, which are the same as the Laws of Nature.

The only way possible to materialize in the flesh is by the incarnation of a soul into a growing body that is the result of some process of physical procreation. And procreation at that time involved physical intercourse between a man and a woman.

Also the notion that the earthly mother of Christ was also at the same time the mother of the Creator, or even the Queen of Heaven, only shows the limited understanding of the Laws of Creation by mankind.

Mary helped in the formation of the physical cloak which the Son of God was to use while on earth. There absolutely had to be a woman who would act as a bridge for the incarnation of the Son of God on earth. This is the same with all incarnations into earth.

She was however prepared for her mission over a very long period of time, even before her incarnation in that lifetime when she was the earthly mother of Jesus Christ. She had to be so prepared in order to be able to carry out the high mission of being the earthly mother of the Son of God when He came to earth. But she was not at the same time made superhuman or more than spiritual. Her species remained the same, as it is impossible for a species of Creation to change into another species.

The Queen of Heaven has never been on earth and only Her radiated picture has been seen by those so fortunate.

Soon men would be able to see the greatness in the simplicity of the Laws of Creation, and they would no longer wish to infer that the Creator is imperfect through their assertions that He went against His own Laws in order to bring help to this near-insignificant mankind.

NARROW-MINDEDNESS

The one-sided cultivation of the intellect by man had multifarious effects, all leading him downwards and into the abyss.

One of the many outgrowths of this one-sidedness is the inability for man to have a broad view on any issue. Just like he has chained himself to gross matter through his self-enslavement to his intellect, thereby making it impossible for the necessary spiritual currents to penetrate to his spirit, and thus for him to perceive from beyond the sphere of gross matter, he is also unable to see beyond his immediate homogenous environment here on earth.

With his fall man became more conceited since he could no longer perceive the vastness of the Creation around him and imagined himself to be the center of everything. The wrong concepts, which he adopted through his one-sided way of looking at things turned into rigid traditions, which he firmly adhered to.

The more firmly he adhered to these wrongly formed concepts the more he resisted any help from the Light, from without the narrow confines of his restriction. With all his attention focused on fulfilling his earthly desires he remained firmly attached to those concepts that allowed him to nourish his desires. In the process, however, he fostered all the wrong attributes and fueled their development and growth.

He interrupted the flow of spiritual currents, which were to bring fresh powers into the World of Gross Matter through the upright actions of men, and take back up to the spiritual part of Creation the currents resulting from the good volition of men. Because in adhering so strongly to his rigid ideas he neglected the important things in life, the things that have to do with the development of his spirit.

Since most of mankind became caught in this stagnation, homogenous groups formed or came together in different ways for the sole purpose of striving for earthly power and influence. But because the flow of spiritual currents had been interrupted, these homogenous groups only sowed poisonous seeds in all their activities.

They sowed seeds of envy, jealousy, distrust, fear, conceit, spiritual indolence, sordid sensuality and greed. Their primary goal was material wealth and comforts, so they sowed more poisonous seeds to attain them and also to maintain possession of them. Their every decision was based on the hope for the attainment of this base goal.

For this reason the groups remained isolated, not understanding one another, and keeping the knowledge of one from the other. There was no spread of love, the highest power available to men for their salvation. Hence there was no spread of the knowledge of the Laws of Creation, because every discovery made by men was exploited for the sole purpose of making money and gaining material influence.

The welfare of the human spirit was always pushed to the background. And the conceit of men did not allow them to be simple in their speech and their actions. Soon the atmosphere became like that of the Tower of Babel, which was allegorically relayed in the Scriptures, where the smooth and harmonious interactions between men became obstructed by distrust and envy. Hence only violent conflicts resulted where there should have been a radiation of love between the different groups through their individual helpful activities.

So the purpose of being on earth was never realized. The gate to this knowledge was shut through the isolation of the different groups from the Light and from each other. The different groups were supposed to work side by side in every respect, so that their different talents could be pooled for the betterment of all mankind. So that with the flowering and the blossoming of spiritual men, like a flowerbed of different-coloured flowers, the surrounding earth could develop into the longed-for Kingdom of God on earth.

In their envy and greed they remained blind to the crystal Truth. Soon they lost all possibilities of seeing clearly on their own.

These different groups have manifested in different ways and on different levels. Through their different ways of thinking they have formed Ethereal Worlds, which influence them here on earth through the links provided by the physically invisible connecting threads. That is why one is able to identify different people who think alike in the various spheres of activity, in the different countries and amongst the various peoples of the earth.

No matter where you look you will find people who think alike and who make similar decisions because they are connected to the same forms or to the same ethereal worlds. They do not have to know one another or even see one another, but through their actions and the opinions that they express, that is, through their works, you can identify them as being similar.

Some of these differences have also manifested on earth in forms known as castes and classes, and their narrow-minded ways of thinking have been maintained through their conditions here on earth. Other forms of homogenous groups exist and are held together by the similarities in their ways of viewing the world, and their shared weaknesses with regards to their understanding and obedience of the Laws of Creation.

So in the array of all of mankind different groups exist in which men are connected through the base forms to which they remain attached. These men make similar decisions because they share similar fears. These fears exist because of how they view the world and what they fear that they stand to lose to others. The more they are connected to base forms of the Darkness, the more interested they are only in material things, and the more they will fear that they may not attain their earthly goals.

This is because one who is not so attached to the idea of acquisition of material gains, and who strives to know the Laws of Creation, will discover his spiritual abilities and how he can serve the Light with them. He will not be so worried about what he stands to lose materially because he would know that, in the perfection of the Laws of Creation, he will always get that which he really needs for his spiritual development. His material needs will be taken care of as a consequence of his right striving. Such a person will also have this in common with others of a homogenous nature, because they will be in contact with similar forms and centers in the Ethereal World.

His spiritual development will be his primary concern, because he will know that the World of Matter is permeated by a higher and lighter spiritual power. The more this spiritual power is absorbed and put into deed, the better the material surroundings of the one who uses it for good will become.

Even when he has to go through many an unfavourable period, he will know that he can only gain through it, because he can in no other way sever his connections with the forms which he caused to develop in Creation, and which have come back to him as fruit for reaping so that in living through the resultant conditions he can gain recognition of the Laws of Creation and become free from such forms and their effects.

He only becomes more knowledgeable through such experiences when he lives through them aright. With his knowledge he is able to contribute favourably to the development of his surroundings through his actions. He will also know that through his earnest striving for the Light he puts a stop to the development of new unfavourable conditions which would result from sowing evil seeds. The knowledge of the strict working of the Laws of Creation provides him with the strength and confidence to live aright through making the right decisions.

In the absence of this knowledge, mankind have developed into groups of men with shared fears. And since the Laws of Creation are responsible for every manifestation in Creation, and since they develop forms in accordance with the strengths of the core volition, these fears to which men are attached are graded in accordance with the natures of those to whom they are attached. The more one is burdened with base forms, the lower he is anchored in the ethereal world to which the base forms belong, and the more narrow-minded and fearful he is.

Man's inability to transmit light to his neighbour, through Light-willed actions, has kept him from receiving light, because it is only in giving that one receives. And so he has become even more narrow-minded, focused only on what is earthly and what satisfies his selfish desires. It is because of this that the physically visible groups, which have formed here on earth, be they groups of people of the same race, religion, country or family, or ones in the same field of activity, have become so narrow-minded that their interactions with one another are mostly born of evil, devoid of light.

The individual members who make up these groups remain connected to those centers of darkness through the base forms that are attached to them and which weigh them down. So it happens that there is very little harmony between the physical groups of various sizes and natures that exist on earth today.

These groups have developed in accordance with the volition of their individual members. And so the same attributes, which these members bear within them, can be observed in the actions of the groups. Only feelings of envy, fear, conceit, distrust and greed can be perceived in the interactions between them. Today the fear has evolved to hatred. And this can now be seen all over the earth.

Through narrow-minded individuals, narrow-minded groups have formed, each striving after earthly power and influence and ignoring the real reason for the existence of man on earth. It is because of this that there has been the oppression of so many different groups at different points during the period of the development of mankind up till this point.

Those who have access to power and influence seek to keep it at all costs and with the use of force. In their narrow-mindedness and conceit they see themselves as deserving of the power and influence, which they wield forcefully over those whom they oppress. And out of fear that they will lose this influence, they ignore all intuitive thought about what is right or wrong and act only in that way that will keep them in power. Similar to the way the intellect works in keeping away from the intellectual man all that is beneficial for the development of his spirit.

They do not mature spiritually and they chain themselves more closely to the substance of the earth. They are spiritually crippled and cannot ascend to the higher spheres of Creation since they lack the necessary knowledge about Creation.

Those who are oppressed, on the other hand, develop envious attitudes as well as feelings of hatred towards those whom they view as oppressors and who, in their opinion, keep them from enjoying as much of the "good things of life" as the latter. They soon become so consumed with hate and envy that they continue to nourish these forms in the Ethereal World and to sow seeds of evil that will have to return to them as fruits.

These people, however, do not realise that every person has at one time or another, in one lifetime or another, been in a position of influence where he has had the opportunity to help others with his earthly power, and where he has also thought like those whom he currently despises.

Man's one-sided view of things today does not permit him to look at himself critically. He only wishes to find somebody else to blame for the conditions that he finds himself in. He does not realise that the solution to his problems lies in critical and objective self-examination, for there is nothing that comes to one which one does not draw to oneself through one's volition. Much will be revealed to him when he accepts his condition as something necessary for him to experience and tries to build up towards the Light from within it with an earnest volition for what is good.

In his envious state he only contributes to the Darkness that surrounds the earth today. He accuses the Creator of being unjust.

There are also those who might consider themselves to be in the middle of the two groups of the oppressed and the oppressors described above. These people often develop a complacency that keeps them spiritually indolent because they do not feel the need to exert themselves as long they remain physically comfortable in the middle. In their narrow view of Creation they see no reason to stir things up since materially they are comfortable enough. As long as they can be seen as not being too deprived of the "essential" material possessions they do not see the need to disturb things.

Due to the wrongly developed ideas of what life should be about, men have for a long time been striving for the wrong things, and those who are able to attain these false goals often automatically become more powerful than the others. This is because power and influence have been under the control of the Darkness for ages now, and the false goals on earth have become directly tied to power and influence on earth. This now serves to fuel the striving for the wrong goals in life, because men want a part of this power and influence. It drives men further away from the Light and towards the Darkness.

In such a condition only stagnation exists where there should be spiritual movement, joyous movement in the service of God through the conscious execution of His Will in Creation. Selfishness and greed take over the souls of men and dictate their every action.

Instead of a continuous flow of spiritual currents through the World of Gross Matter, like a river bringing clean water and food to all those who thirst and hunger, there is stagnation, like isolated ponds with putrid matter, fouling up the wider material environment through the production of noxious gases.

Thus man, through his narrow-mindedness, has produced narrow-minded groups of souls, which have in turn brought about the narrow-minded entities that make up the societies of this mankind. These narrow-minded entities make up the social structures of the communities that men live in today.

But man must love his neighbour if he is to attain salvation and liberation. How then is he to love his neighbour if in his narrow-mindedness he does not even know his neighbour? Here, I do not mean knowing the name of his neighbor and his likes or dislikes, on a physical level. But the inner nature of his fellow man, which alone counts in matters of real importance to spiritual development. His physical habits will always accord with his spiritual nature. And when the spiritual nature of man is understood, his outward behaviour is also understood. And help can only be given where there is true understanding.

Everything on earth has developed wrongly due to the narrow-mindedness of man. For this reason it has become difficult or even impossible for many to understand their fellow men. Without this understanding man will not be able to transmit light to his neighbour. He will not be able to communicate the Truth to him.

But this is mostly due to the conceit of man. If he were not so conceited and vain he would not go through life so superficially, leaving the work of bringing about an environment of peace and harmony to others. He will also be able to see how he has contributed, and continues to contribute hourly and daily to the horrible state of affairs on earth today.

He will not be quick to judge another, but will try to understand what makes him act the way he does. When he has achieved this then he will look to himself for those faults that he finds in his fellow man. He will then be able to see that he also acts in the same manner, and bears within him those faults which cause him to feel disgust for his fellow man, even if the forms of these faults differ in their outward expression.

Man is always attracted to those conditions which his nature or his volition draws him to. One can also say that one attracts to oneself those things which are homogenous to that which he bears within him. You will notice this when a man gets excited about the faults of another, and when you look at him and find that he bears the same faults within him to a far greater degree. When you see how it happens that the one who gets so excited appears oblivious his own faults, then you will understand how it is with all of mankind including yourself.

When man is able to look honestly within himself for those faults that he finds in others, he would have taken the first step towards severing his ties to the forms of such faults. He would then be able to resolve to change his attitude for the good. He will see how his environment is a mirror image of his own nature and he will look for his faults in his environment, in his fellow men.

In this way he can learn about himself and discover his true spiritual abilities, because it will require that he exert himself spiritually for the purpose of severing the ties to such forms as must be destroyed in this time.

Also, he will have a better understanding of his fellow man, because in the process of identifying the faults of his neighbour within himself, he will also understand why those faults exist in the first place. He will understand this because he will know from his own experiences why he has the same faults within him and how they serve to keep him fettered.

He will understand the benefits of looking at the other side of every issue, instead of just the one that he has been accustomed to seeing due to his narrow-mindedness and habitual behaviour. He will no longer quickly jump to conclusions but will strive to become unassuming in his regard of his fellow man. Then the childlike nature, which was prescribed to mankind by the Son of God, will become a part of him, and he will become more *objective* in his assessments.

No longer will he assume that the blame lies with the other person, but he will look to himself first to see how he has drawn whatever troubles him to himself through his way of thinking and acting. He will then be on his way to conquering himself, to coming out from under the entanglements of false concepts, which keep his spirit stifled and unable to shine forth.

His actions will lead to the development and growth of those spheres or light in the Ethereal World, which will help others who may be able to draw strength from there for the execution of good deeds on earth. In the reciprocal effects of his actions he will be ethereally enveloped by light forms, which will penetrate his physical environment and shield him from the Darkness and its influences.

The urge to enlighten his fellow man will then awaken in him because he will see, upon severing the ties to the base forms and faults, that his fears and worries have been greatly reduced if not completely eliminated, because they were based on superficiality to begin with, and that his knowledge of what this life should be about has been greatly increased.

He will realise that there really is no reason for the antagonism and the spread of evil vibrations that has become an integral part of the nature of this mankind. He will see that it is because of the narrow-mindedness of men that so many gruesome crimes have been committed on this earth, usually in an attempt by some group or person to force a particular way of thinking, living or of viewing the world upon others or another.

In humility he will recognize that true conviction cannot be achieved by use of force since conviction can only come through gradual understanding. His discovery will prompt him to change his life and focus his attention on striving towards the Light. Because he will realise how much time he has already wasted and how patient the Creator has been so far with him, and how conceited and petty he has been in his thinking and his actions, and how little time he must have left to make amends for his past wrong decisions.

He will no longer be narrow-minded but will have a much broader view in Creation, which will allow him to make his every decision in such a way that it will not bring harm to another person. No longer so conceited, he will be able to humbly receive help from the Light, because it cannot come to him in any other way.

Thus his every action will become a blessing to his surroundings because he will be drawing from the fountain of spiritual power that is available to all who wish to ascend and strive accordingly. He will also not be so interested in the activities of others as he is today because his focus will be on his own spiritual ascent.

When men have become more spiritual and have made their primary goal that of striving towards the Light, then they will develop side-by-side in harmony with one another. The individual members of the various homogenous groups will be attracted to one another because of their similar spiritual talents and interests, which will be developed in the process of their individual striving towards the Light.

Men will be in those positions which they are best suited for, and they will be able to achieve much more than they could ever imagine at the time when they all were struggling for mere earthly trifles.

Their works will also be more lasting because they will be spiritually inspired and developed to their best forms. In these forms they will no longer be so short lived, but will remain beneficial for long periods of time, because at their cores will lie a far-seeing and uplifting spiritual motive, which will lead to the development of useful fruit in Creation.

RESPONSIBILITY

Man is responsible for everything that he causes to take on form in this Creation. With his every intuitive perception, thought, word or deed he generates a form in a plane in Creation of corresponding density, which corresponds to the nature of the volition behind the action, and to which he remains connected to.

This form, and the connecting thread, will act as a channel through which the radiations of homogenous species of the form will reach its originator.

Like this man shapes his fate because he decides, with his ability to form intuitive perceptions, thoughts, words and deeds, the conditions in which he must live in his future. In this lies his free will because he is free to decide how to use the creative power in Creation, which God makes available to the creature man.

When he has made the free decision, he is inevitably bound to the consequences of it. He must experience the consequence of his decision because the form thus generated must return to its originator in the completion of its cycle.

Man must reap what he sows! With this in mind the concept of responsibility should be clear to all. But there is the question of knowledge, knowledge of what is good and what is wrong or evil. For the possession of this knowledge must precede the actions of he who wishes to sow only the right kind of seed.

In the adamantine nature of the working of the Laws of Creation, ignorance of these Laws cannot serve as an excuse for neglect of duty. The just reaction must return to him, who sows the seed. His ignorance itself is the fruit of the seed of not-wanting-to-know, because every human spirit was given equal opportunity to know the Truth through the recognition of the Laws of Creation.

If in the time provided for the development of the human spirits in the World of Matter, some chose not to strive for the recognition of the Will of God, but to focus their attention mainly on material trifles, then the just fruit of such a seed must be ignorance of this Will.

It is in the striving for the recognition of the Laws of Creation, which bear the Will of God, that man is given the opportunity to recognize his responsibilities in Creation. He recognizes these through knowledge of his abilities as a human spirit, which are inseparable from his responsibilities.

His abilities allow him to use the neutral power of God in Creation to produce forms, which could either uplift or harm his fellow man. There is no middle ground in the issue. He either harms or he uplifts the creatures in his surroundings. He either uses his abilities rightly or he uses them wrongly. Therein lies his responsibility. He must know what his abilities are so that he may use them rightly, i.e., if he wishes to conform to the Laws of this Creation.

Since all life is movement and everything is in constant movement, man is always sowing seeds with his inherent abilities. At the same time however, the Laws of Creation, which bring about this continuous movement, are always weaving for him the carpet of his fate, and will always deliver to him the ripened fruits of his labours. So at some point in the period of his development he has to answer for what he has done with his abilities.

Automatically and without warning he will be faced with those conditions which he has woven into being for himself through his use of the power of the Light in Creation. And the only way that he would stand a chance of making it through such conditions, in this time of the Final Judgement, without being drawn into the process of disintegration with decaying matter, is by knowing and using rightly his God-given abilities.

For this he needs to know the Laws of Creation. Already he has wasted so much time that he would have to exert himself with all his strength to be able to have any prospects of surviving the conditions which he has woven for himself. He would have to bring himself to par with that state which he should have already attained had he used his abilities wisely in the time allotted for his development in the World of Matter.

That means that in a very short while he would have to experience a lot in order to attain the right knowledge needed for his timely resurrection from the World of Matter.

He would need to experience a lot in order to counter the wrong decisions he has made for thousands of years with right ones; because only then can he extricate himself from the mesh of base forms which keep him fettered in the lower regions of the World of Matter. It is also only through this process that he can recognize his abilities.

The process of living aright, through which alone he will be able to recognize the Laws of Creation, will simultaneously lead him to recognition of his abilities, because he would have to exert himself and develop these abilities in the process. His natural abilities, which hitherto have remained buried, will come to the fore because they would become animated through being forced into action.

Now the pressure of the Light is intensifying here on earth, and cycles of past actions are quickly closing, bringing to their perpetrators the fruits of their works. All over the earth today the effects of this happening can be felt and clearly observed. Everything is being dragged before the Light; everything is coming to light. Nothing can remain hidden which must now come out in the open. The opinions of men do not matter in this, and soon, wherever men act against the Laws of Creation, they will swiftly reap the consequences of their actions.

This is because the end of the reign of the Darkness on earth is here, and the process by which it will be destroyed is also a natural one, since it cannot be otherwise. The cycles of all happenings are closing so that only those forms which can stand the pressure of the Light may be uplifted and strengthened. Everything that is not able to withstand this pressure will be destroyed, including the personalities so far acquired by developing human spirits.

Naturally this must sound just to all clearly thinking people. In this one can see the Justice of Almighty God, Which He has tried to make known to men through His various Servants and also through His Son. Now men will have to experience it in their everyday lives, whether they want to or not.

In order to make use of this final hour to recognize his abilities and thus his responsibilities, man must now rightly experience the working of the Laws of Creation. Only then can he recognize them and know them and abide by them. For this alone can lead him to the knowledge of Creation and of the part which he must play in it if he wishes to escape destruction.

He must now know his responsibilities regarding everything. No matter the field of activity of man, his decisions affect his environment and his ascent. He cannot hide behind human laws and opinions in this regard, because these have developed one-sidedly and incorrectly. They do not lead upwards because they do not take into consideration the Will of God. They do not consider what benefits the spirit of man.

A look at the way that the justice systems set up by men around the world today function can let any serious thinker see that they do not benefit the spiritual development of man. They make use of laws which were put in place as a reaction to what man has been able to observe of his immediate surroundings in the World of Gross Matter, but they do not address the roots of the conditions which he experiences. They are full of gaps and inconsistencies. They are born of narrow-mindedness. They express plainly man's inability to see beyond his physical earthly environment and so they must inevitably lead to confusion, chaos and destruction.

What goes on in the courtrooms of most countries today cannot be called justice. In most cases the earthly courts serve as a means of delivering some kind of revenge or punishment, or of one-sidedly executing the will of some party at the expense of the dignity, name and honour of another, because the former might possess some earthly power or influence, or because of some other bias that might exist. In any case there is hardly any objectivity to speak of in these courts, and yet they are supposed to be fair and just.

Also, the goal of the proceedings is hardly ever for the purpose of availing the person being tried with the opportunity to reform himself through the recognition of his wrong-doing, but is mainly for the pleasure of those who wish to see another suffer for something that has caused them to feel pain. Consequently, when such a person who has been tried and found guilty is released from imprisonment, after he has been sentenced to a predetermined term behind bars, he is not accepted in the society as a reformed person. He is ostracized and cast off as useless. In the first place he is not even given the opportunity to go through any kind of reformation.

No serious thought is given to the issue of his reformation because it is much easier to lock him up and get along with everyday life, until he has to come out and rejoin the public. The well being of the individual is not considered, and so the consequences of the neglect, of the wrongly established laws, return to make themselves felt by all concerned.

Another reason for this neglect is that man does not know the root of the problems that plague us today, and since he lacks this knowledge he cannot help one who exhibits the symptoms of today's problems through his actions. He prefers to satisfy the public and himself by putting the errant one away so that the man-made law can be fulfilled and everyone can feel satisfied, at least for a while, that something is being done. It is just like the ostrich does when it puts its head in the sand in times of perceived danger.

Little help is provided to the person who becomes incarcerated, and he is not given a chance to mature spiritually enough so that he can safely rejoin the public as a new person who has really changed inwardly through the attainment of true knowledge. Rather a predetermined sentence is meted out to him without consideration for the time it will actually take him to become reformed and able to safely rejoin society, having grown and matured inwardly during his period of incarceration. The result is that he comes out often worse than he was when he went in, causing more pain and suffering to himself and those around him.

There cannot be any justice coming out of these courts when the laws which they abide by are merely the opinions of men and produced by the intellect. These laws will never yield anything good or lasting because they do not consider the roots of the issues for which they were implemented. They are the result of man's narrow-minded view of the world around him and so must lead to a total collapse. But this will be good for this mankind for they need to experience this total collapse of all that is false in order to be shaken awake from their spiritual slumber through its painful and disappointing effects.

Also, when men act in ways that might fulfill these narrow-minded earthly laws, but do not at the same time obey the Laws of Creation, which are the same with the Laws of Nature, they inevitably bind themselves further to the Darkness. Their focus on only that which is earthly keeps men from recognizing their true nature and hence their real responsibilities. They therefore are never prepared for the conditions in which they often find themselves, and which lead them to suffering and despair and to sow more wrong seeds.

The nature of the laws made by man clearly shows his ignorance regarding the responsibility of the human spirit developing here on earth and in the World of Matter. It is a reflection of the stupidity of this mankind, who must wake up to their responsibilities soon or perish in the reciprocal actions of their neglect.

When men begin to understand their responsibilities as human spirits developing in the World of Matter, they will also develop their surroundings accordingly, using the spiritual and physical talents which they already possess and which will finally blossom under the pressure of the Light. They will make their laws in ways that will show knowledge of the Laws of Creation. This will be reflected in the harmony that will exist between the laws made by men and the Laws of Creation, because men are creatures in Creation who must obey the Laws that govern the entire Creation or be crushed and swept aside as dangerous obstacles.

Today man makes laws based on what he feels is right. It is the volition of men that determines the nature of the laws which the nations of this mankind are governed by. But men have been wrong for a very long time about what this life is supposed to be about. They have never really allowed for the right conceptions to develop within them regarding how they should live here on earth. So their laws must also be misleading, because they are made by men who themselves cannot be called knowing ones.

It is the same when men decide to elect their leaders. They invariably elect those who would support their wishes and their views about how life should be lived here on earth. Naturally these elected leaders will promote the volition of those who elected them in accordance with the Law of Attraction of Homogenous Species and also the Law of Reciprocal Action.

Such people do not give themselves the chance to recognize their faults and what they might be doing wrong, because they elect people who would allow them to continue living in the same old ways. They stubbornly enforce their will through this and do not care about the Will of God. In their selfishness, conceit and ignorance they only want their own will to prevail.

In this way the evil in the world today is perpetuated and reinforced. Very few men are willing to make the effort to voluntarily tear themselves away from the flock of slumbering souls and strive for true knowledge, by rightly experiencing the Laws of Creation and abiding by them.

In the future leaders will arise who will lead in accordance with the Will of the Light, for no other kind of leader will be able to stand in the pressure of the Light after the purification is over. It will not be up to the opinions of men, for these have proved to be worthless.

Man must now consider everything he does carefully so as not to entangle himself further through his actions. Everything he thinks, says or does takes on form and is able to affect so many other people in ways that he cannot even imagine, because all happenings in Creation have multifarious effects in the process of working themselves out in accordance with the Laws of Creation.

It does not matter what the profession of a man is, he is inevitably linked to his works and will be judged accordingly in the working of the Laws of Creation. He cannot hide behind his profession or his assumed sense of duty when the time comes for him to reap the consequences of his actions. The fruits will be served to him at the precise moment when they are due and in the right proportion.

Today teachers, journalists, leaders and many other public figures who are in positions to disseminate information, very thoughtlessly spread wrong conceptions and falsehoods through their activities. They spread information without being convinced about what the truth is regarding what they say.

In many other fields of activity men do their work without fully considering the consequences of their actions on others or even on themselves. Be they soldiers, politicians, doctors, engineers, writers, businessmen, and so forth, men have to work in their various fields in ways that show a willingness to know and obey the Will of God, only then will they be guided by the Light in the reciprocal action of their efforts. No one else can take the blame for the actions of any individual human spirit. When men abide by the Laws of Creation all the time their works will develop more beautifully than ever before.

Today men cannot fully see the impact of their actions because they cannot look beyond the gross material sphere in any issue. They are mainly concerned with making money and attaining a position of influence and importance here on earth, or perhaps having as much fun as they can while they can.

But doing anything without concern for the repercussions of one's actions, with regards to how they agree with or diverge from the Laws of Creation, can only lead to a disastrous fate, because one needs to be alert in order to obey the Will of God in Creation. He can only obey God's Will when he aligns his actions with the Laws of Creation. He can only recognize the Laws of Creation when he remains spiritually alert in his every-moment's experiencing. Where he allows other factors besides the volition to abide by these Laws to govern his actions, then he serves the intellect, and through it the Darkness.

Today wrong conceptions and ideas make it difficult for men to listen to and obey their intuitive perceptions. This is because they have placed the intellect above the spirit, so that they respond to and only act in accordance with the will of the intellect, which the Darkness uses as its tool. Similarly the talents of man are directed towards the development of this will of the intellect to the detriment of the spirit and its surroundings in the World of Matter.

It is no different with those who delude themselves into thinking that they serve the Creator when they harm themselves and others under the guise of fighting for the Creator. These people only work against the Will of the Creator because they prevent this Will from being known by those who listen to and are influenced by them. To do the Will of God does not require acts of violence and acts that harm one's body, the tool with which man is to experience this gross material environment for his ascent.

So when he starves and mutilates his physical body, or when he harms other people through his actions, whether by causing them to develop their brains in a one-sided manner or by physically harming them in other ways, he prevents them from maintaining the necessary balance between body and spirit, which is absolutely necessary for experiencing aright the Will of God in Creation.

Such actions as cause harm to his fellow men proves that the perpetrator of the act does not know the Will of God. He has not taken the time to experience and recognize the Laws of Creation and abide by them in his actions. Otherwise he would not harm anyone through his actions. Only that which helps his fellow man ascend will come out of his every deed.

It is only spiritual ignorance, indolence and vanity that drives people to want to draw attention to themselves by committing such acts as cause harm in the name of serving the Creator. Such people who act thus burden themselves with great guilt, the weight of which will drag them down to depths that will keep them chained to the World of Matter. They act against the spirit. In their efforts they work directly against the development of the spirit, because they misrepresent the Will of God to men. The reciprocal effects of their actions will be devastating. When they have passed on from this earth into the beyond they will find that ugliness which they have created through their works waiting for them.

Now, when the Darkness will have to be destroyed, and the base forms to which man is attached have to present their fruits so that their barrenness can be seen, man shall see how he has misused the talents entrusted to him. Since the returning effects of his past actions are now due to hit him, he shall feel the suffering, pain and despair, which are the fruits of the seeds he has sown. The more firmly he remains attached to these forms the more painful his experiences will be, because he will feel more closely the effects of their destruction by the Light.

Those who are not able to sever their ties to these forms, because they have fallen too deeply to be able to see clearly during the raging storm, will have to be swept away with the base forms of the Darkness towards destruction.

Others, who wish to use this opportunity to ascend quickly, will have to start immediately to strive with all their strength towards the understanding of the Laws of Creation. In the process they will be able to sever ties to the Darkness and free up their spirits and the associated free will. Then they will no longer be bound to the will of the Darkness through enslavement to the intellect, but will only wish to obey the Will of the Light, because the spirit, which always remains pure, always wishes to ascend upwards. It is the stifling of the spirit through the actions of man that has prevented this from happening for so long.

But the person who wishes to purify himself must also remember that at this time also the Darkness will try to take many souls down with it to its destruction. At this time all the dark fruits will also ripen and the dark works will be in full bloom. He will have to remain vigilant at all times in order to resist and avoid all those things that will seek to draw him back into the old.

Once the spirit becomes free and the free will is unencumbered, man will become able to use the power of God in Creation wisely. Because he will know of the working of the Laws of Creation and he will also be aware of the dangers that lie in his misuse of this immense power, which we all have access to for our ascent and for the betterment of our surroundings. May God grant it!

www.theupbuilding.com